LANGUAGE AND LANGUAGE LEARNING

NELSON BROOKS

YALE UNIVERSITY

LANGUAGE

AND

LANGUAGE LEARNING

Theory and Practice

SECOND EDITION

HARCOURT, BRACE & WORLD

NEW YORK / CHICAGO / BURLINGAME

© 1964, 1960 BY HARCOURT, BRACE & WORLD, INC.

All rights reserved. No part of this book may be reproduced
in any form or by any mechanical means,
including mimeograph and tape recorder,
without permission in writing from the publisher.

LIBRARY OF CONGRESS CATALOG CARD NUMBER: 64-13914

PRINTED IN THE UNITED STATES OF AMERICA

CONTENTS

PREFACE TO THE SECOND EDITION	vii
FOREWORD	ix
ACKNOWLEDGMENT	xiii
1 / THEORY OF LANGUAGE	1
2 / LANGUAGE AND TALK	24
3 / MOTHER TONGUE AND SECOND LANGUAGE	35
4 / LANGUAGE LEARNING	45
5 / LANGUAGE TEACHING	60
6 / LANGUAGE AND CULTURE	82
7 / LANGUAGE AND LITERATURE	97
8 / OBJECTIVES OF THE LANGUAGE COURSE	107
9 / CONTINUITY FOR THE LEARNER	113

10 / METHODS AND MATERIALS	140
11 / PATTERN PRACTICE	152
12 / READING AND WRITING	164
13 / VOCABULARY	180
14 / THE LANGUAGE LABORATORY	189
15 / TESTS AND MEASUREMENTS	199
16 / BUILDING A PROFESSION	226
APPENDIX A HOW TO . . .	241
APPENDIX B GLOSSARY OF TERMS	261
BIBLIOGRAPHY	283
INDEX	291

PREFACE
TO THE SECOND EDITION

This book was written out of respect for language teachers and for their new responsibilities. The comfortable grammar-translation days are over. The new challenge is to teach language as communication, face-to-face communication between speakers and writer-to-reader communication in books. The new technique is to model for the student, in speech and writing, all the new behavior patterns that he is to learn. Analogy, which plays so large a part in the learning of the mother tongue, now plays a key role along with analysis in learning a second language. A constant objective is to learn to do with the new language what is done with it by those who speak it natively.

The aim of the second edition is to retain all that was valuable in the first and to deal with certain matters more extensively, especially the varied forms of pattern practice, the making of tests, and the development of all four skills toward full comprehension and expression in the language being learned. What is new reflects the gist of many talks to and with thousands of foreign-language teachers, some of them participants in half a hundred National Defense Education Act Institutes, others in attendance at conferences and meetings scattered through half the states in the Union. The horizons of language teachers have widened greatly and are continuing to do so. Certain of the sciences, especially linguistics, psychology, and cultural anthropology, as well as humanistic fields such as philosophy, philology, and literature, constantly provide us with new facts and new insights that we cannot afford to overlook in our thinking, our planning, and our performance. As in the former edition, these insights have, in so far as possible, been incorporated here. Attention has remained focused upon a single point: the classroom in school and college.

In its "Statement of Qualifications" of language teachers, the Modern Language Association has expressed official support for the learning of all the language skills. In Title VI of the National Defense Education Act, the United States government has called for new and improved methods and materials for use in the teaching of modern foreign languages, and it has already expended millions of dollars toward their development. Thus the academic world, through the Modern Language Association, and the general public, through the United States government, have put much faith in our ability, working within the limits of formal education, to instill in a whole generation of young Americans a confident control of a second language. We who have received this degree of attention, of trust, and of financial support must see to it that this faith in us is justified. It is the author's hope that this edition will contribute to a better fulfillment of our promise by helping us understand more and more clearly what we are to do and how we are to do it.

For their counsel and advice in the preparation of this new edition, I wish to express my thanks to many, many colleagues, and in particular to the following: Professor Theodore Andersson of the University of Texas, Mrs. Genevieve S. Blew of the Maryland State Department of Education, Professor Mildred Boyer of the University of Texas, and Professor George Scherer of the University of Colorado. I reserve for myself the responsibility for the faults and shortcomings that the treatment of so broad a subject in so little space inevitably entails.

N. B.

New Haven, Connecticut
January 1964

FOREWORD

Our native language is a part of our natural heritage, a personal possession no less our own than the geography of our birthplace. The native tongue is quite adequate to our needs unless we wish to travel, whether in space or in thought, beyond the frontiers of the speech community in which it is current. Then we feel its limitations sharply and find ourselves in need of another vernacular.

The study of a language that is new to us has long been a discipline in formal education. As the popular tongues of western Europe matured and Latin ceased to be spoken in community life, the language of ancient Rome assumed a place of first importance in this regard, for there were (and still are) the best of reasons for continuing the study of Latin. Yet the learning of a second language in school can never be the same as the learning of a mother tongue. This difference was not clearly understood when the study of the classics assumed a special importance in the curriculums during the Renaissance. It was not understood when the contemporary languages were accorded a place of equal honor with the classics in the nineteenth century. The study of the mother tongue, the study of a contemporary language that may take its place, and the study of a classical language are in fact three separate disciplines, and the worth of each is increased when it is valued according to its peculiar merits.

The study of language as language is relatively new. Concern for orthodoxy in prayer and ritual, for validity in logical thought, for accuracy in the establishing of texts, and for the role of communication in the behavior of groups has entailed much preoccupation with the nature and functioning of language, yet only in our own times has language been allowed to occupy the stage by itself. Seen in this new light, it turns out to be one of the principal symbolic transformations that lie at the core of life on the human scale. As such, language has its place at the table of human universals somewhere between love and money, for it is probably not so old as the first, yet surely much older than the second.

A number of neighboring disciplines have contributed to the formulation of this new insight, especially philosophy with its clarification of the logic of symbols, psychology with its studies of language learning by infants and the relation of thoughts to words, cultural anthropology with its study of language as a cultural mode, and descriptive linguistics with its scientific analysis of language as a system.

The older studies of language were seriously limited not only by a burden of other interests but also by a shortness of focus. The ancient Sanskrit grammar of Panini dealt only with Sanskrit; the Greeks studied only Greek. Even the comparative philologists of the nineteenth century concentrated their attention upon relatively few languages, all rather closely related. As a result, generalizations about language based upon observation of representative samples of the thousands that are to be found were not possible before the twentieth century.

Certain generalizations that take into account the present state of our knowledge can now be made. Language is not only universal but universally adequate to the conduct of human life; no language has been discovered that is less systematic or less fluent than any other. The earliest speech is learned as verbal play rather than as a means of satisfying physical or social needs.

The infant learns the knack of language through the reinforcement of his own behavior by those around him rather than by imitation. Everywhere the child of five is thoroughly familiar with the structure of his mother tongue. The usual response to words is to the conception of the things they stand for, not to things themselves. When language is in action, grammar performs at an unconscious level; grammar is difficult to learn consciously and if thus learned is equally difficult to forget when language is put to actual use. Despite auxiliary help from gesture, pictures, and writing, language is and remains a phenomenon of sound. Language cannot be equated with communication. These two are partners in an enterprise of great extent and importance, yet it is a mistake to consider them synonymous. Communication can take place perfectly well without language, and language, in both origin and function, goes far beyond the limits of communication. Men have much in common with animals; food, shelter, family life, mating, birth, play, combat, disease, and the will to live are as important to animals as to us. But the use of verbal symbols is exclusively human. No animal has ever learned to speak in the human sense of the word. Man and language are inseparable, and life without language is nonhuman.

The accuracy of such generalizations may be tested by considering certain basic questions and deciding whether better answers can now be given than in the past. What is language? What is its role in human life? How is it learned? How is speech related to writing and how is language related to literature? What is involved in the learning of a second language and how does this differ from the learning of the mother tongue?

The study of a subject with so many aspects—philosophical, physical, physiological, psychological, cultural, economic, academic, to mention only some of the more obvious—requires a thread of common reference that will unite such disparate particulars into a related pattern. In this instance, the thread is the learning of a second language, and, to draw the thread even a little finer, the learning of a second language in American classrooms.

There is in our country today a widely held view that the

learning of a contemporary language must no longer be only in terms of books, translations, grammar exercises, and word lists—with reference made to English at every point. What should be learned instead is a use of the new language as its native speakers use it, so that we may communicate directly with them as well as study their civilization and their literature. Such learning involves the ear and the tongue as well as the eye and the hand, and it involves meanings that are valid in the new country. At the beginning it is largely centered in those areas of language with which the native speaker is thoroughly familiar before he goes to school: the sounds of the language, the proper forms and the right order of words, and a small but effective vocabulary for communication about everyday life.

The purpose of this book is to explore what may be involved in the substitution of such learning for the kind that is currently practiced in most of our schools and colleges. This will necessitate a close examination of what language is, how it works, and how it is learned. Both the theoretical and the practical aspects of this new mode of learning will be reviewed from the point of view of the teacher and the learner alike.

A word must be said about science, for every effort will be made in this study to benefit from its recent findings in the field of language. Science is a public affair and deals with truths that are publicly verifiable. It is impartial, objective, comprehensive. The scientist bends over backwards in his efforts to suspend judgment, to show no preference for things as he might wish them to be; he tries to identify and describe things as they are. This exclusion of moral philosophy and social responsibility from his considerations, which the scientist not only permits himself but insists upon, is an easing of the burden which those who instruct the young dare not indulge in. In this study we shall accompany the scientists as far as they wish to go; it will frequently be necessary to digress and to go further, for language is a private as well as public matter, and the world as it is is not the only world the young should contemplate.

ACKNOWLEDGMENT

The names of all those whose ideas, advice, experience, and collaboration are reflected in this book would make a very long list. I acknowledge with pleasure my indebtedness to many colleagues, old and young, and in particular the following:

Theodore Andersson, University of Texas
Frederick D. Eddy, Georgetown University
Charles C. Fries, University of Michigan
A. Bruce Gaarder, U.S. Office of Education
Howard B. Garey, Yale University
William P. Holden, Connecticut College
Marjorie C. Johnston, U.S. Office of Education
Susanne K. Langer, Connecticut College
Harry L. Levy, Hunter College
Archibald T. MacAllister, Princeton University
Dorothea McCarthy, Fordham University
Kenneth W. Mildenberger, U.S. Office of Education
Edward S. Noyes, Yale University
Charles E. Osgood, University of Illinois
William R. Parker, Indiana University
Wilmarth H. Starr, New York University
Mary P. Thompson, Modern Language Materials Development Center

Olga Scherer-Virski
Donald D. Walsh, Modern Language Association
Rulon S. Wells, Yale University

I wish to thank Yale's Master of Arts in Teaching Program for the opportunity of visiting language classes at all levels of learning, in many different types of schools and colleges. Much of the content of this book is the direct result of observations made during these visits. I wish also to thank the Modern Language Association of America and the Carnegie Corporation of New York through whose generous aid an advance issue of this book was made possible. To no one am I more grateful than to my wife for her patient and competent assistance in the preparation of the manuscript.

N. B.

LANGUAGE AND LANGUAGE LEARNING

THEORY OF LANGUAGE

1

Language, like sleep, is not a substance but a process; in practice it is known to everyone, yet its theory all but defies formulation. In order to develop such a theory we should take into account three levels of analysis, considering first the play of phenomena upon the senses, then the concepts we can recognize as common to certain groups or classes of these phenomena, and finally the formal logical or mathematical system with which these concepts seem to agree. Though parts of the picture are clear with regard to language, the subject as a whole still awaits a genius who will be able to unify its vast complexities.

Everybody speaks a language. Wherever we find man we find him speaking, from the second year of life on. Data for the development of the first level of a theory of language have been available on every hand for uncounted centuries. As for the second level, many concepts dealing with language were recognized by early civilization and were reflected in the invention of phonetic alphabets, in the formulation of rules of grammar, and in inquiries into the relationship of words to meanings. New concepts of this kind are still being formulated.

One of the latest and most important, that of the phoneme, has been extensively explored only in our own century. Others have long been recognized but are still only vaguely understood, for example, meaning, thought, and linguistic change.

The formulation of the third level of language theory by relating concepts to logical or mathematical systems is limited by the gaps in the second level, yet some attempts to do so have met with success. In this book we shall be interested chiefly with the first and second of these three levels.

Analysis of a language event

A supreme difficulty in the stating of a theory of language lies in the fact that so many different fields of study are involved. Any sample of language in action chosen at random from the infinite number available will make this clear. Let us take for consideration a situation such as this: A is sitting at a desk in an office writing a letter. There is a knock at the door. A calls out in loud tones, "Just a minute."

He goes to the door, opens it, and perceives B, who says, rather apologetically, "I'm sorry to disturb you. . . ."

A interrupts by saying, "Not at all. Come right in." In this example the same event—a speaker addressing a hearer—is repeated several times. It will suffice to analyze it once in detail.

As A sits at his desk, the kaleidoscope of consciousness in his head is given a sudden new configuration by the sound of B's knock. Out of a composite of emotional reactions, reorientations, and intentions, one of these finally comes to dominate: A's wish to signify his presence on the other side of the door and to ask B to wait until he opens it. This intention is almost simultaneously transformed—we may say coded—into certain of the English words available to A to convey this intention. The muscles of A's vocal apparatus thereupon perform a highly complicated sequence of movements that produce and modulate the sounds that make up these English words. As these sounds are uttered (the process of *phonation*) they are perceived by A's own ears and almost instantly the waves he has set in motion cross the air that separates him from B and strike the latter's eardrums. There an almost imperceptible movement is made that dispatches to B's brain a sequence of neural impulses that are then interpreted as the words spoken by A, and decoded in a form similar to the intention that had taken shape in A's head. The message has passed through a number of easily distinguishable stages: a mental state, an encoding process, a physiological reaction, a purely physical event, another physiological reaction, a decoding process, and finally, another mental state. (See the diagram on page 4.)

To analyze even as simple and banal a specimen of language as this, we must refer to at least three major fields of study, each a fully developed discipline in its own right: physics, psychology, and descriptive linguistics. And when these three sciences have dealt fully with the matter, other questions will still have to be answered. Why does a speaker choose the words he uses? Where do they come from? How does he come into possession of them? How do their choice and use affect the interpersonal relationship between speaker and hearer, and vice versa? Answers to these questions will involve us in a contemporary and historical view of the individuals concerned in the speaking and in the speech community of which they are a part. We shall eventually be dealing with the whole significance of language in human affairs, and many different branches of learning will be called upon for aid in clarification.

Such a broad enquiry will have dealt with at least the principal phases of what lies at the core of language, the spoken word, but it will have left aside at least three other kindred considerations of first importance in the present study. For one thing, at the point of encoding we must note that the English code may be replaced with any one of hundreds of others, all entirely competent to the task. For another, at the point of phonation a number of substitutes can replace the sound waves generated by the vocal organs, the principal one of these, of course, being the picturing of these sounds in writing. Thirdly, the universal availability and great flexibility of language put at the disposal of man an additional medium for one of his most characteristic activities: the creation of fine art. Just as the making of tools and utensils and dwellings often results in productions that reach a high level of refinement and aesthetic value, so does the use of language frequently attain to the level of fine art, the art of words.

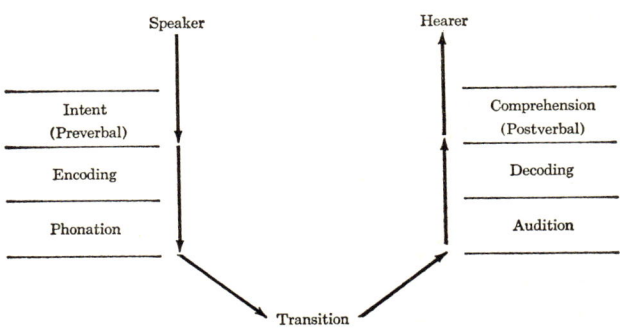

A LANGUAGE EVENT

Science has made a thorough study of language at the point of transfer from speaker to hearer, when it assumes the form of sound waves. These waves can be captured, examined, and measured at will. They have a pitch, depending on the frequency of vibration, an intensity, depending on the amplitude of vibration, and a quality, depending on the number and relative intensity of overtones. Many things have been done with language in this physical form. It can be recorded on drums and discs and on tape and film. It can be viewed in action by the sound spectroscope and recorded for further study by the sound spectrograph. It can be transformed into electrical impulses that travel by wire and into radio-frequency waves that encircle the earth. Language in this form has become a major interest in laboratories of experimental physics; these have provided us with much new knowledge about the nature of language and with many instruments for its transfer and preservation.

At the stage at which words are spoken (phonation) and heard (audition), physics also applies, for mechanisms are still at work here, although the machines are physiological rather than mechanical. Life has entered the picture. A special branch of physics, called phonetics, studies this transition from the animate to the inanimate, and the reverse. It is concerned with the manner in which the vocal apparatus produces the sounds of speech and how the hearing mechanisms perceive them.

Nature of the code

The next point of interest is the nature of the language code being used. The number of sounds that the speaking apparatus can make and that the ear can recognize as being distinguishable from all the others is very great. What sounds are actually used in any given language? Which ones make a difference to the hearer? Do some sounds occur more frequently than others? Do the sounds combine into clusters that tend to stick together? Is there any system in the formation of these clusters and in the order of their appearance? Do these clusters differ with any regularity in the functions they perform? Answers to these questions lie in the province of the descriptive linguist, and his findings have supplied us with information of great interest and value. It turns out that the number of different sounds used in any one code is relatively small and that the number of sounds *that make a difference* is even smaller, a fact that led to the concept of the phoneme (a term that will be fully discussed in chapter 2).

It turns out also that the formation of sound-clusters and their order and function are highly systematic and that the system is so strictly standardized for all the speakers in a given speech community that a mere handful chosen at random will reveal the workings of that particular code in every detail. The descriptive linguist marks off his field of enquiry with considerable severity. He is interested in how things are said but not in the content of what is said or why it is said or how it should be said or how the speaker learns to say it or indeed why he wants to talk at all. For the most part he limits his interest in meaning to a single consideration: does a change in sound produce a change in meaning?

Sign and symbol [1]

So far what we have talked about relates to waves and mechanisms, to teeth and tongue and mouthy sounds. But all this is not language until we take into account what the sounds represent. In themselves, speech sounds are utterly trivial, yet their very triviality contributes to the success of their essential function: to stand for something else. The two words *sign* and *symbol* relate to this function and, although a most important distinction can be made between them, they have in common that they are double-ended, with one thing at one end and another at the other, and that the filament that joins these two must pass through an active brain. Whatever is a sign or a symbol for something else has to *be* that sign or symbol *to* a living animal.

The human brain does many things, but certainly one of its most important activities is to transform physical realities, both within and without the individual, into the buzzing, purring, sibilant sounds of speech—and back again. To follow the pathway from one end to the other of any sign or symbol will inevitably lead us inside the brain, which is the special province of psychology. Since science can fill in only a part of the total perspective we are seeking, it will frequently be necessary, as we discuss what happens within the organism, quite frankly and courageously to philosophize.

Whether or not a given word is a sign or a symbol is not a question of the word itself but of its use. All words may be called symbols, in the sense that their importance lies not in themselves but in the fact that they stand for something else. In this sense words perform the duty of acting as proxies that is characteristic of all the observable phenomena in other symbol systems, for example, sounds in music, movements in the dance, or gestures in religious rites. But without ceasing to use words as proxies, human beings use them in two basically different ways, and we may employ the terms *signs* and *symbols* to

---

[1] Here and in the subsequent pages I have followed very closely the ideas set forth and the terminology employed by Susanne K. Langer in her *Philosophy in a New Key*, chapters 2, 3, 4, and 5.

distinguish between them. When we use words as signs, we refer to what is or is expected to be in the immediate environment. "Sit in this chair" or "Come with me" exemplifies a *sign* use of language, and we often employ gesture to accompany or even take the place of words used in this way. This *sign* use of words is a behavior pattern we share with the animals, for they respond constantly to signs and often learn to respond to the sound of words that refer to something in the immediate environment.

But human beings also use words to refer to what is not in the environment at all. If we say, on hearing footsteps at the front door: "There's the postman," we use the word *postman* in its sign function. But if we say: "I'll write you a letter tomorrow," we refer to nothing in the immediate environment, but to the concept of a letter that is held in the mind of the person to whom we are speaking. Words so used are not signs but *symbols*, and this is by far the commonest use of words by human beings, though for the animal such use of language is impossible.

To cite another example, a blind person may lecture for an hour on his relationship with his seeing-eye dog, while the latter lies quietly only a few feet away. During this hour, the lecturer will have mentioned the dog many times, giving complete details of the training period that both had to go through and using many of the words he normally uses in talking to his dog. Then, with only a slight change in voice dynamics, he will say the words that bring the dog to his side ready to guide him out of the lecture hall. During the lecture, words have been employed in their *symbol* use, to which the dog does not respond. The same words in their *sign* use command his immediate attention.

Words as signs are of course very important to the learner, both of the mother tongue and of a second language, and the pursuit of this importance would lead us quickly into the very nature and validity of knowledge. For our purposes it will be sufficient to develop in greater detail the difference between signs and symbols, for although the sign use is the gateway to language and permeates it in many ways, it is in its symbol use that language truly comes into its own and that meaning is conveyed without dependence upon the local environment.

Let us consider another example of both sign and symbol use of language in order to emphasize the logical distinction that can be made between them. To begin with, let us use a word to refer to what is plainly to be seen by speaker and hearer. At one end of the sign filament we may have an object that is seen, a furry animal with pointed ears, long white whiskers, and a tail, curled up on a rug before the fire. At the other, issuing from the speaker's lips, a sequence of sounds beginning with a catch at the back of the mouth, continuing with a simple vowel sound, and ending with the quick pressing of the tongue against the roof of the mouth. A radical transformation occurs between one end and the other of this phenomenon, and it takes place in the cortex of the brain. There is nothing about the object in question to indicate why these sounds rather than any others should be chosen to represent it, and this leads to an important conclusion about speech sounds: they are purely *arbitrary*. In spite of this arbitrariness, every talking member of the speech community, good or bad, old or young, important or unimportant, makes the same series of sounds when confronted by this object and asked what it is.

If we trace the pathway of the sign filament in the opposite direction, that is, as it functions in the hearer rather than the speaker, we find that the sequence of sounds described above makes an impact upon the eardrums, is transferred as nervous impulses to the brain, and is there converted into an auditory image which is matched with the visual image of the furry object as perceived by the hearer viewing the total scene before him.

At this point we may make a truly remarkable observation about the matching of the auditory and visual images by the hearer. An animal receiving an auditory sign invariably relates it to the environment which he sees immediately before him. This is the typical animal response to signs, a behavior pattern that relates to the immediate in time and place. The human intelligence, though wholly capable of this same kind of behavior and practicing it all day long, is also capable of a further refinement of this behavior that is totally denied the animal. The human can hold the auditory image in the mind and react to it as such, without seeking to relate it to the immediate environment. This is the *symbol* use of language, and it is due to the fact that the human being can call up and react to his conception of a cat without either seeing one or expecting to see one. This behavior pattern is, in fact, the normal human response to speech. From the point of view of logic, a sign has a three-point pattern: the meaningful term (the word *cat*), the object meant (the animal asleep on the rug), and a mind that relates one to the other. But a symbol has a four-point pattern: the meaningful term, the object meant, the conception of the object that is held in the subject's mind, and the mind itself that relates these three. (See the diagram on page 10.) A further significant conclusion results from these observations: *Only the human being can symbolize in words.*

A conception can also play the part of the stimulus in the symbol function and produce as its response another conception. This is exemplified in the simplest word association. I may summon up the conception *dog* and, by free association, find myself pairing this with *cat* or *food* or *tired* or *eared*. This symbolization from one conception to another is the essential, unique, and continual task of the human brain. By far the greater part of any individual's overt language behavior is in the form of talk, yet this is but a small sector of his total language behavior, most of which is completely internalized and forever beyond the scales and graphs of science.

Signs, of course, are by no means restricted to words. Whatever is seen or tasted or smelled or felt may serve equally well as a sign for something else. The same is true of symbols, though with a far different pattern of distribution. Symbolization in animals appears to be restricted to the higher primates, to be but a minor element in their total behavior, and *never to be connected with vocal behavior*. (W. N. Kellogg and L. A. Kellogg tell of a chimpanzee to whom a bag of hay symbolized something to fear, another to whom a pebble was something to find comfort in, and a third to whom a pair of trousers symbolized the eventual return of its absent owner.) Human beings,

THE LOGIC OF SIGNS AND SYMBOLS

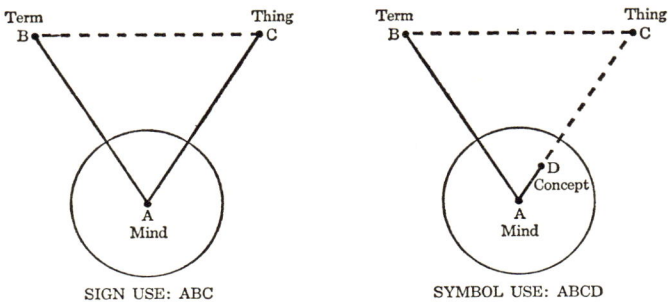

The solid lines represent direct or concrete relationships; the dotted lines represent indirect or abstract relationships.

on the contrary, symbolize incessantly when awake and not infrequently when asleep. The greater part of this symbolization has to do with language, yet very important sectors of it have only a tenuous connection with words, such as visual images, the belief and behavior patterns of rite, ritual, and myth, and—the least verbal of all—music and mathematics.

Visual and verbal forms

Since verbal and visual images are by far the most numerous and most general, it will be well to distinguish clearly between them. A visual image—a *presentational* form—is characterized by a simultaneity of perception. If I look at a picture of a cat, I see the whole cat at one glance, and I can immediately report on its size, color, kind, attitude, activity, and numerous other details. A verbal image—a *discursive* form—of the same cat comes to me in a stream of vocables that arrive one after the other over a measurable period of time; I must retain them and fit them together as they come if I am to be able to give as accurate a report as I can after the visual presentation. This linear reformation or projection of reality is quickly compensated for, because I am so accustomed to dealing with things and processes in this fashion, and I know that if I should touch the cat it would not give me the impression of beads on a string. But language is forever liable to this projection none the less; such is the very essence of discourse.

A further important distinction between verbal and visual forms is apparent if I look closely at the units that in each case contribute to the total impression. The verbal units each have specific areas of reference that remain with them if they are withdrawn from the context in which they are used. The word *whisker* still stands for a whisker and *tail* for a tail, in this context or any other. This is by no means true of the lines and shades and colors that denote the same details in the visual image; separated from their context, their symbolic function is lost.

Still another special quality of verbal units is that they must obey strict rules concerning their form and their sequence as they are presented. We may thus identify *morphology* and *syntax* as special characteristics of verbal forms, both of which are lacking in visual forms. By this contrast it is clear that forms perceived by the eye are on the one hand more precise: the effective accuracy of a passport photo would be very hard to duplicate in words. Yet on the other hand visual forms lack the ability to permit generalization. Verbal forms can never be as minute and unmistakable as visual, yet they gain vastly in the universality of their application.

Individual and community: parole *and* langue

We have said that a verbal symbol is double-ended, with typically a real object at one end and the conception of this object by the brain at the other. The speaker-hearer can symbolize concerning anything at all in his external or internal environment. Now the systematic study of the environment surrounding a speaker-hearer is the special province of the cultural anthropologist, who finds much to contribute to and to profit from in a careful scrutiny of the speaker-hearer-environment relationship. The importance of this relationship becomes clearer if we refer again to the typical speech event described on pages 2–3. Recall that it involved two people, A and B, talking together about something. The "something" is none other than the environment surrounding the speakers, and by extension this environment becomes the cultural milieu in which they find themselves. The cultural anthropologist studies the kinds of things men think and do to a great extent in the same way when they live together in a community. This study focuses upon such matters as rite and ritual, myth, family ties, education, work, play, food, property, dress, and, most especially, speech.

Participation in these patterns of learned and shared behavior takes place to a surprising extent beneath the threshold of awareness; one learns and conforms with scarcely a thought about the learning and conformity. Yet an individual transplanted into a community from one that is radically different stands out in a thousand ways as being what he is, an outsider. Speech is at once the cultural pattern most strictly adhered to by all the members of the group and the most difficult for the outsider to simulate in a convincing way. Language, central in its importance for its own sake to community life, is also the medium through which the greater part of the other cultural patterns are learned, participated in, and transmitted.

These facts remind us that language is both a private and a public affair, manifesting itself in the behavior of both individuals and groups and displaying a remarkable interdependency, in origin and function, among its component elements. In one sense, language is always individual behavior; everything connected with language reduces itself in the last analysis to what someone says or hears. Yet the very nature of language requires that the individual behavior patterns conform almost exactly with those of everyone else in the speech community, so that a given language seems to exist not in the speech of any one individual, but in that of the whole community. Again we have a double-ended structure, with the individual's behavior at one end and the immense repository of communal language at the other. The two ends of the structure are, of course, absolutely interdependent. No individual invents language; he takes it as he finds it and does remarkably well if any of the slight originalities or deviations he may propose can be said to have the most minor effect upon the communal speech. At the same time, the communal language does not remain fixed, and the phenomenon of linguistic change unquestionably is related to the use of the communal reservoir of language by individuals as they speak and listen. The first to perceive this interdependency with great clarity was Ferdinand de Saussure, a linguist of the late nineteenth century, who proposed the word *parole* for the individual manifestation and *langue* for the social or group manifestation, the two being subsumed under the term *langage*.

Meaning

Of all the problems connected with a theory of language, none is more general, more involved, or less well understood than that of meaning. "What does this mean?" and "What do you mean?" are queries that continually come to the mind and to the lips of every user of language. To give an answer is itself often difficult enough; to analyze the operation whereby the answer is given is utterly dismaying because of its enigmatic complexity. Yet the attempt to do so must be made, and, fortunately, some of the finest contemporary minds have given the problem their best thought, not without results.

Again, De Saussure makes a valuable distinction between what we may call the code of language and its meaning. Rulon Wells, in his article "De Saussure's System of Linguistics," page 7, rephrases this insight as follows:

> Speech (la parole) is made up of two linear sequences, each of which is articulated, that is discrete. The members of the one sequence are *tranches de sonorité* which are in turn sequences of one or more phonemes. . . . The other sequence composing speech is a sequence of meanings. A meaning is not a physical thing but a concept.

We should note that meaning is by no means restricted to words. An unlighted house means no one at home. The sound of a bell means someone at the door. An acrid odor means the toast is burning. A sharp taste means no sugar in your tea. A surface that yields to the touch means the melon is ripe. These are all sign functions and may operate perfectly well with little or no verbal accompaniment. The following discussion deals principally with meaning as it is attached to words, and these, though they occasionally serve as signs, function most of the time as symbols.

The meaning of *meaning* may be rendered less elusive and ephemeral if we distinguish between a series of binary terms that attach themselves to this word in English and that burden it with rather more than its fair share of symbolism. First, meaning has both a logical and a psychological aspect. Logically, a term must be capable of bearing a meaning; psychologically, it must be employed in a meaning relationship by a living mind. Dictionaries give us plentiful lists of logical meanings; they become psychological when a speaker or a hearer puts them to use.

An essential pair of words, *sign* and *symbol,* have already been discussed at some length. At this point, let us note that the meaning of a sign lies outside the mind that employs it, whereas the meaning of a symbol lies within that mind, and is subject to the myriad modifications that the present circumstances and past history of that mind may bring to bear upon it. Closely connected with a symbol is another pair of great importance: *concept* and *conception.* Since the meaning of a symbol is so personal, there would be little likelihood of any two people being sure that they were referring to the same object unless there were a common denominator of identity in their separate meanings. To this common denominator of identity may be given the name *concept,* which is all that a symbol conveys. Concepts are publicly agreed upon, standardized, and relatively limited and constant; our conceptions are our own. The terms *langue* and *parole* of De Saussure accord very well with this distinction.

So far we have talked only of isolated words. Meaning takes on a new and vastly more important aspect when we speak not only of a *term* but of a series of terms strung together in a *proposition.* By itself, a term names something without saying or asserting anything about it. The inert units of lexicography take on life only when a speaker chooses them and combines them into the thread of discourse. The unit of discourse is not a word but a proposition, uniting the speaker to the environment. We quickly perceive that meaning as expressed in propositions can relate to and represent the highly complicated patterns of reality which we observe about us and hold them for consideration in the mind. We perceive also that meaning can be more or less clear depending upon the way in which propositions are constructed, that it can be negated when terms are chosen at random or ineptly, and almost miraculously enhanced, as in poetry, when artistry takes a hand in their selection and combination.

Meanings do not stay permanently fixed, in the sense either of *parole* or of *langue.* Every individual continues to increase and modify the items in his total stock of meanings as long as he lives. Much more slowly, the language itself changes. Every word in a language has a history and its meaning will have changed with this history; this historical meaning may or may not have value in its current cultural use. Enthusiasm for etymology occasionally needs to be tempered with a few reminders. For example, with all due respect to philology, nobody today actually thinks "God be with you" when he says "good-by," nor "the day of Odin" when he says "Wednesday," nor "yours without blemish" when he signs a letter "yours sincerely."

Finally, we may note two other terms indispensable to an understanding of meaning: *literal* and *figurative.* A term that has a literal denotation in a given context may be used figuratively in an entirely different context as a symbol for something that is logically analogous yet nameless. For example, we may say, "The bomb *burst* into smoke and flying steel," and also, "The children *burst* into laughter." The concept of an explosion is common to these two contexts, and is borrowed from the death-dealing event in the first to bring life and merriment to the second. This is the phenomenon of metaphor, and it permeates language everywhere. The context must guide us in deciding whether the literal or the figurative meaning is intended, yet as time goes on literal meanings are often weakened, metaphors fade, and what was once figurative comes to be taken as literal: "The poet was hounded by his creditors." Metaphor itself, however, is perennially active and continues to generate not only the humor and pungency of current slang but also the freshness and revelation of poetry.

The spectrum of language

If we were to cut through our entire speech community as a biologist cuts through living tissue and examine a cross section of it, we should find language everywhere and playing a great variety of roles. We should find it mingled with visual images and emotional promptings, busily forging the thoughts, uttered and unuttered, of every conscious person. We should find it in its spoken form among children as they play with sounds and learn the speech of the community, among adults as they meet by twos and threes and greater numbers in work, in ceremony, in study, in competition, and in relaxation, ranging from profound statements to cocktail-party chatter. We should find it in immediate transfer between persons often far apart in space and, in substitute forms, in delayed transfer between persons far apart in time as well as space. We should find it in use by the scientist at his desk and in his laboratory, as he struggles desperately to outwit metaphor and confine language within precise meanings that will represent as exactly as possible the tangible facts with which he deals. We should find it in the schools, serving as the mediating matrix through which learning takes place in all disciplines, and in language classes where it is being focused inward upon itself, to give the learner greater scope and control in its use. We should find it in the hands of the literary artist, being molded, refined, perfected by the selective and creative vigor of his inspiration.

If the steady flow of language as it passes by the fine point of the present moment could be diffracted into its major elements, like a ray of light passing through a prism, we should observe that it separates itself into three broad bands. These bands may be labeled audio-lingual, gestural-visual, and graphic-material; in simpler terms we may call them talk, gesture, and writing.[2]

THE LANGUAGE BANDS

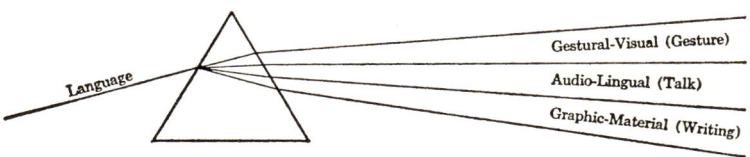

In the central band, the *audio-lingual,* language is on its own. In this area the speaker-hearer process can operate quite without assistance from the eye and may be carried on in the dark or, with mechanical aid, at distances far beyond the range of the natural voice. Phenomena in this band are, however, always linked to the present moment and involve an interpersonal relationship between speaker and hearer and also the situation in which they are.

The *gestural-visual* band runs parallel to the audio-lingual and includes, principally, the facial and bodily movements made by the speaker and perceived by the hearer. The phenomena in this band often reinforce those in the audio-lingual—the word *yes* may be accompanied by a vigorous nod of the head—but the fact that the central band can dispense with the gestural-visual gives the former an enormous advantage in range and flexibility. Gesture is, in fact, but a faint obbligato in the rendition of speech.

On the other side of the central band is a third, the *graphic-material,* whose relationship to the audio-lingual is very different from that of the gestural-visual. It, too, makes use of the eye, but to picture not the muscular movements that accompany speech but the spoken code itself. With materials and

---

[2] In this description I have followed in the main, though with some changes in terms, the analysis given in section 4 of *Psycholinguistics,* edited by Charles E. Osgood and Thomas A. Sebeok.

tools, the hand can depict with considerable fidelity the rapidly changing features that characterize the flow of speech sounds. Although orthography cannot reflect all the rich detail that embellishes the spoken code, it has, in compensation, an advantage not found in the other two bands: mobility in time and space. Like a series of action pictures caught by a camera and recorded on a film, written terms and propositions may be manipulated and stored away for use at another time, may be conveniently transported to a distant place, and may be selected and rearranged in different sequences with consequent modification in meaning and enhancement of effectiveness and style. It is usually the eye that must restore the graphic phenomena to a form that can be interpreted as auditory images by the hearer. The development of this third band has, as everyone knows, completely transformed the life of civilized man, but its complete dependence upon the central audio-lingual band must never be disregarded.

The origin and development of language

A theory of language must take into account not only its nature and function but also its origin, its diversification, its evolution, and its acquisition. All one can say with certainty about the origin of language is that it must have originated somehow, sometime, somewhere. So deeply hidden in the mists of the past are its beginnings that almost no serious writer of the present day gives the problem more than passing mention. Yet, in the light of current knowledge, certain statements can be made about the origin of language, for which one can claim only a greater or lesser degree of likelihood. The beginnings of language probably stand as a principal line of demarcation separating man from the other primates. The constant readiness of the ear to respond to stimuli from all points in the environment irrespective of the position of the body and of a source of light, added to the great variety, the universal availability, and the triviality of speech sounds, tended to make vocal signs the most direct and the easiest medium for symbolizing the multiform phenomena of life. Only in an animal already long accustomed to habits of vocalization and to various types of symbolization could language have developed, yet there are many facts based on the observations of the higher apes and of primitive cultures now in existence suggesting that these habits were indeed characteristic of early man. Symbolization in words probably developed along with and out of a medley of symbolizations in play, ritual, dance, and song. Once the knack of verbal symbolization was seized by a few members of a primitive tribe, it could have spread very rapidly not only within the tribe but to others as well. This phenomenon is to be observed in the human infant, for, once he has caught on to the trick of symbolization through language, he quickly generalizes the habit to deal with the environment he knows.

Of the two principal elements of discourse, vocabulary and syntax, the former could have grown out of the use of a word as a symbol rather than as a sign, with the attendant ability to conceive a meaning and hold it in the mind, and the latter could have grown out of a tendency to qualify and particularize the composite referents that cluster about a one-word sentence. Both of these developments seem to be swiftly repeated by the growing child in the early years of life. The theories of Otto Jespersen and J. Donovan, coupled with the reports of R. M. Yerkes and A. W. Yerkes and Kellogg and Kellogg on behavior in the higher primates, tend to substantiate at least the plausibility of the foregoing statements. A great debt is due Susanne K. Langer, who integrates these suppositions with her finely wrought presentation of the entire spectrum of symbolic transformations.

To discuss differentiation in language requires that we speak of *a* language rather than of language. For a single criterion by which one may distinguish one language from another, none is better than the empiricism "mutual unintelligibility." Like other rules of thumb, this one must not be scrutinized too closely. For example, there are many geographical areas in which sectors that are contiguous use language in a way that is mutually understandable, yet this is not true of sectors that lie at the extremities of the same area. This circumstance is reminiscent of the color spectrum, in which one has no difficulty in distinguishing red from orange, yet one cannot identify the exact point at which red ends and orange begins. The differences between languages are not uniform, for some are obviously more or less closely related, while others are totally unrelated. Systematic relationships between languages have been scientifically established, more often on the basis of vocabulary than on the basis of grammatical structure.

A review of all the languages of the world shows at least twenty families, with sometimes many scores of individual languages in each one. Two of these families, the Indo-European and the Semitic, were the only ones to receive a great amount of serious and sustained study prior to the present century, and many widely held hypotheses about language have had to be relinquished in view of the facts presented by a broader perspective. Undoubtedly the most valuable insight to emerge from this comprehensive view is the fact that the essence of language lies in the audio-lingual band rather than the graphic-material, that language is primarily what is said and only secondarily what is written. The application of this insight to the study of language and to the acquisition of a second language is certain to be revolutionary.

Living languages, like all other forms of life, are in a constant state of evolution. Much has been written about language drift and the laws of phonetic change, but contemporary scientists fail to find proof of any common direction of such changes. Enough is known, however, about the history of certain languages to make the fact of change universally recognized. Within a given language, modifications in vocabulary are much more rapid and more frequent than changes in structure, while within a given family of languages, over a long period of time, new members are born and older ones cease to live. There is ample proof that languages come into being, mature, run their course, and die, as Sanskrit has, though the effect of their having existed may endure long after their death. Some, like ancient Hittite, become wholly extinct. With languages as with people, to be dead in no wise means to be without influence, and certain of the dead have far greater influence than most of the living. The criterion by which a living language may be identified as such is relatively simple: Is the language in question the mother tongue in a living speech community? If so, it is a living language; if not, it is dead. There was a time, for example, when children learned at their mother's knee a language that was synchronous with the highly stylized oratorical and literary language of the Latin classics and from which the latter were skillfully fashioned. Such a circumstance has not been true for many centuries, and all we know of the central or audio-lingual band of Latin we must surmise from what remains to us through the mediation of the graphic-material band. This in no way diminishes the value of Latin for the present world but, in contrast with a living language, it clearly indicates a radical difference both in its present nature and in the discipline of its acquisition as a second language by the student of today.

Language learning

The learning of language is essentially a problem in psychology, individual, dyadic, and social. Given the language of the speech community and the innate physical and mental capacities of the newcomer to that community, what happens between the time of his ignorance of the local language and his eventual control of it, either partial or complete? The process is a type of learning that involves the establishment of a set of habits that are both neural and muscular, and that must be so well learned that they function automatically. Language learners divide themselves into two main classes, those who as infants are learning the mother tongue and those who, having attained facility in a mother tongue, are learning another as a second language or, in some cases, an additional one. There are many important comparisons and distinctions to be made between these two groups of learners.

In the case of the infant, there is a fascinating contest between his inborn potential for the use of *parole* and the community's highly systematized practice of *langue*. Of course, the latter always wins and imposes its will upon the loser almost completely. This outcome has long obscured the arresting significance of what the infant brings to this struggle. For within the newborn baby there is a vital force that finds delight in incessant verbal play, with the result that within a matter of months he "breaks the code" of the language being used about him, and within a few years he has completely mastered it in its spoken form. It is through the magic of language that man comes eventually to understand to an impressive degree the environment in which he lives and, still more surprising, gains an insight into his own nature and his own condition. Without language, this universal happening would be unthinkable. The human infant merits full credit for his contribution to this remarkable synthesis.

The individual who already possesses a mother tongue brings to the learning of a second language a very different set of physical and mental capacities. Partial, if not complete, command of one linguistic code has already been attained, and it can be both a help and a hindrance in learning the second. The conditions for learning, almost identical for all learners of the mother tongue, differ widely for the second-language learner. The greatest single difference is whether or not he finds himself in the "cultural field" of the language in question, by being either geographically within its borders or in direct contact with it in an authentic "cultural island" transplanted to a distant place. Another difference of great importance is the age of the learner, for this largely determines the extent to which he still retains the faculties that made it possible for him to learn his mother tongue. When those who study a second language do so within the official school system (already a specialized and somewhat artificial milieu) of their own language community, a special set of conditions for learning is imposed. To an intimate analysis of these conditions the chapters that follow are addressed.

Suggestions for further reading

Gardiner, Sir Alan H. *Theory of Speech and Language*. Oxford: Clarendon Press, 1932.

Langer, Susanne K. *Philosophy in a New Key.* Cambridge, Mass.: Harvard University Press, 1942; New York: New American Library, 1948.

Morris, Charles W. *Signs, Language, and Behavior.* New York: Prentice-Hall, 1946.

Osgood, Charles E., and Thomas A. Sebeok. *Psycholinguistics: A Survey of Theory and Research Problems.* Baltimore: Waverly, 1954.

Saporta, Sol, ed. *Psycholinguistics: A Book of Readings.* New York: Holt, 1961.

Wells, Rulon S. "De Saussure's System of Linguistics." *Word,* III, 1–2 (August 1947), 1–31.

LANGUAGE AND TALK

In the popular mind, language is what is written in books and learned in school. That the central band of the language spectrum, the audio-lingual, is primary and generative, while the other two bands, the gestural-visual and the graphic-material, are derivative, is an idea proposed for the first time by our contemporaries, and it has not yet gained wide acceptance. Yet even the five-year-old child who has never been in school exemplifies in every utterance the undoubted hallmark of the language community in which he has grown up. We are reminded by Leonard Bloomfield in *Language*, page 21, that "until the days of printing, literacy was confined to a very few people. All languages were spoken through nearly all of their history by people who did not read or write; the languages of such people are just as stable, regular, and rich as the languages of literate nations." By far the greater number of known speech communities speak their language without writing it; none has ever been discovered that writes its language without speaking it. The length of time that writing has been in use—five or six thousand years at the most—is trifling in comparison with the length of time spoken language has been in existence. Whether or not an individual becomes literate, the language he speaks remains throughout his life a dominant factor in his personality, the core of his inner thought, and by all odds the most utilized mode of contact with his fellow man. We may safely conclude that language always has occurred and always will occur chiefly in its audio-lingual form.

To the principal activity of this central band we may apply the word *talk,* a term that is sometimes used with an overtone of contempt, yet which has a reputable history and which is, on the whole, in acceptably good estate in current usage. Talk is as indispensable to the life of man on the human level as is sleep or drinking water on the biological level. Such an observation implies no denial of the value of literacy in modern life, but is rather an attempt to regain a perspective that an overemphasis upon printing has tended to obscure. Because the relation of writing to language, to language learning, and especially to literature will be far clearer if talk—the soil in which writing is inevitably rooted—is first understood, we shall examine this central band with some care.

When the study of descriptive linguistics broke away from its parent discipline, philology, and proceeded to apply the philosophy of science in its researches, it found in audio-lingual phenomena a fertile field for its enquiries. The events of which talk is composed occur in prodigious quantities, and they are highly regularized for everyone in the speech community, so much so that the entire system is discernible in the utterances of each speaker. Science is most successful when it can deal with happenings that are numerous and systematic, and the field of descriptive linguistics was not long in establishing itself as a science. It did so, however, by concentrating upon the sounds uttered by a living speaker and, for the most part, by leaving aside gesture, writing, meaning, and past history. The rewards have been great. A wholly new evaluation of language and of the world's languages has emerged from the study of the behavior of living speakers. As for languages that are written, it was soon discovered that the letters, syllables, and words that have traditionally represented the sounds of speech are so inadequate to the facts as to require replacement by more precise concepts and terms. Acquaintance with at least a few of these new terms is indispensable to an appropriate analysis of talk.

The phone

We may begin by defining the *phone*, which is any sound produced by the human vocal apparatus and audible to the ear. The study of phones and the manner of their production and perception is the province of phonetics, in which the descriptive linguist must be thoroughly trained and with which he begins his analysis of speech behavior. If, for example, he is studying a language unknown to him, he makes lengthy records in phonetic transcription of the phones he hears as he listens to a speaker of that language. The number of phones he will recognize in the new language will be extensive, but will by no means exhaust the reservoir of sounds that might be used. An economy in the use of materials available for speech is already apparent at the level of phonetic analysis.

The phoneme

The second important term to define is the *phoneme*, a concept that grew out of the realization that not all of the differences in the phones uttered by a speaker make a difference in meaning to the hearer. In the flow of sounds issuing from the speaker, certain groups or classes of phones technically different from each other, yet with a high degree of similarity, are interpreted by the hearer as being identical, that is, as implying no change in meaning. A phoneme, then, may be defined as a class of sounds that are all slightly different, yet all of which pass for the same when received by the hearer. In fact, the hearer is usually quite unaware of these slight differences. As an example of variation within the range of a given phoneme we may cite the pronunciation of the English word *up*. The speaker usually ends the word with the lips tightly pressed together. But occasionally the *p* is sounded; then the lips are pulled apart and a slight puff of air follows. These sounds are clearly distinguishable as phones, but they are considered to be members (*allophones*) of the same phoneme, for the meaning is the same in spite of the phonetic difference.

Another example of the phoneme is found in the *k* sounds at the beginning of the two words *keel* and *cool*. These sounds are not the same, and we can easily feel the difference in the point of articulation by pronouncing one after the other. In spite of this, no two words are distinguished from each other in English solely on the basis of a contrast between these two *k* sounds. In Arabic, on the other hand, there are words that are entirely alike except for these two kinds of *k*'s, which are thus the only means of distinguishing them. We say, then, that this difference is not phonemic in English, whereas it is in Arabic; in English one phoneme contains both kinds of *k*'s, but in Arabic they fall into separate phonemes.

To give an example of a contrast in sounds that is phonemic in English but not in another language, we may note the sound of *h* at the beginning of such a French word as *hais* in the expression *Je te hais* ("I hate you"). In French this word is usually pronounced without any aspiration at the beginning, yet an aspiration may occur, especially if the speaker is expressing strong feeling. But there is no change in meaning. Therefore there is in French only one phoneme. But all speakers of English are familiar with the difference between *is* and *his*, *it* and *hit*, and the like. The change in sound is precisely what it is in French, but since the change takes us into new meanings in English, we recognize that there is an added phoneme.

Another example of the same type is the pronunciation of the word *mismo* in Spanish. Sometimes the sound of *s* in this word is similar to an *s* in English, sometimes to a *z*. But this difference does not change the meaning, and no words are distinguished solely on the basis of contrast of the voiced and voiceless sibilant in Spanish. In English, on the other hand, many pairs of words, such as *pace* and *pays*, *dose* and *doze*, and *fierce* and *fears*, are distinguished only by a contrast of this kind. In Spanish, then, these two sounds fall into the same phoneme, but in English into two phonemes.

A given language uses only a limited number of phones, and

its total list of phonemes is even smaller, for each of the latter may comprise several allophones. Every language makes its own choice of the sounds available and displays a remarkable degree of stability in their employment. When languages are compared in this regard, two facts emerge that are of great importance to the learner of another language. The first is that the phones of one language never exactly coincide with those of another. Although certain phones in one's native language may closely resemble those in another, in general a new sound-system must be learned in mastering a new language. A second significant fact is that the types of differences that produce phonemic distinctions in one's mother tongue may not do so in another language, and vice versa.

There is a second dimension in phonemic analysis that appears when sounds that have a recognized status when considered as individual segments are strung together in a sustained flow of talk. When a single phoneme is examined in relation to a total constellation of sounds in which it may appear, the factors of pitch, loudness, rhythm, duration, and juncture are at once observed. (Only the last of these needs defining: it refers to the significant boundary that divides one word or one utterance from another.) These five factors are also considered qualities of phonemes, to which the name *prosodic* or *suprasegmental* is given, in contrast to the *segmental* phonemes first described. All these are of course of the greatest importance in talk as it appears in action and are particularly valuable to the literary artist when he creates and composes with sounds.

The nature of suprasegmental phonemes is easily seen in utterances that contain the same words in the same sequence, yet in one case make a statement and in another ask a question. "You're going home" is made up of the same segmental phonemes as "You're going home?" Yet the meaning is not the same, and what makes the difference—the change in pitch—is called a suprasegmental phoneme. The same phenomenon may be observed in the utterance: "The temperature hasn't gone down so far, so far," in which the first *so far* means "to that point" and the second *so far* means "up to the present moment." The difference in meaning is carried not by the separate sounds in themselves but in their intonation in the total pattern. An even more subtle distinction—very common in English—can be heard in such pairs of expressions as *big black snake* and *big blacksnake, crazy house* and *crazyhouse, blue bird* and *bluebird*. In each of these pairs there is a difference in meaning, and it is borne not by the individual phonemes but by the overall pattern they produce.

The morpheme

A third concept perceived and elaborated by the descriptive linguists is that of the *morpheme*, which may be defined as the minimum unit of spoken speech that can convey meaning. Like a syllable or a word, it may contain a single phone or a cluster of phones, yet it does not necessarily coincide with either a syllable or a word, as a few examples will show. *Soon, do,* and *man* are English morphemes that are also single syllables and single words. But if we add to *soon* the suffix *er*, or to *do* the prefix *un*, we add a sound-cluster that bears a new meaning and is a syllable but is not a word; if we add to *man* the sound of *z* (written *'s*) we add a sound that bears a new meaning but is neither a word nor a syllable. Yet *er, un,* and *'s* all count as separate morphemes. A morpheme is said to be either *bound* or *free*, depending on whether or not it can appear in discourse by itself. The word *unmanly* contains three morphemes; the first and the third are bound, the second free, for it can be used alone while the others cannot.

The linguistic scientist has not only identified concepts that represent more accurately than does traditional nomenclature the minimum units of talk, but he has also had some success in presenting a better view of their behavior when they enter into the more complex patterns of discourse. The two principal factors, form and order, that impose themselves upon linguistic units when combined into utterances are still examined under the headings of morphology and syntax, respectively, but a word is no longer assigned to a category such as "noun" or "verb" because of any quality within itself. Rather, it is said to belong to a certain class or type on the basis of its function in an utterance. An older analysis called the word *silk* a noun, with an adjective *silken*. Yet in the expression *silk stockings* the word *silk* can be replaced by *knitted* or *long* or *inexpensive*, none of which we would call a noun. A more refined analysis says that *silk* is something more than a noun. The study of many families of languages has made the newer concept necessary, for it has demolished the notion that all languages have the same basic grammatical categories.

What talk includes

At this point, in order to summarize in precise terms the phenomena that characterize the audio-lingual band, we may say that TALK:

a. REQUIRES A MINIMUM OF TWO PEOPLE. Of course, talk may be *practiced* by one person, and often is, both by the very young when they are experimenting with and learning speech sounds and their meanings, and by the adult when, for instance, he reviews his bank statement or hits his thumb with a hammer.
b. UTILIZES A LINGUISTIC CODE MUTUALLY UNDERSTOOD. Even if two languages are used, mutual understanding is no less necessary.
c. ASSUMES A COMMON AREA OF REFERENCE. The common area of reference may not always be easily identified, but talk assumes the predisposition to find one.
d. IS AN INTERCHANGE BETWEEN PARTICIPANTS. Both participants receive as well as give in talk.
e. RELATES EACH SPEAKER TO THE OTHER AND TO THEIR IMMEDIATE ENVIRONMENT. The vocal behavior of the speaker is always related to the response, real or anticipated, in the hearer, and vice versa. Thus the relationship is reciprocal or dyadic.
f. IS BOUND TO THE PRESENT MOMENT. Only with the aid of the graphic-material band can language escape from the present and the immediate; that it has been able to do so is, of course, one of the supreme facts of human culture.

g. INVOLVES ONLY THE VOCAL AND AUDITORY APPARATUS. Although activities in the audio-lingual band can dispense with the gestural-visual and the graphic-material, the reverse is not true; except for pantomimes or pictures, there is nothing in the gestural or the graphic that does not stem from and depend upon the audio-lingual. We talk constantly with persons whom we do not see, in our homes, at work, and by telephone; such conversations are typical of talk in its purest form.

h. DEALS INDISCRIMINATELY WITH WHAT IS REAL AND WHAT IS POSTULATED. The total environment that can be symbolized by talk includes not only the real world that surrounds the speakers but also the infinitely greater ideational world to which they have access simply because they are alive and human; talk as the meeting point of these two realms stands in need of much further study and elucidation.

If we speak metaphorically of a "molecule" of talk—that is, the absolute minimum that can be so called—we may say that its conditions are satisfied when one person talks to *and receives an immediate answer from* someone else about something (for example, "Catch anything?"—"Nothing."). This pattern of behavior is so universal and so germane to the human condition that its true significance has often been missed. Yet it is precisely what has been conspicuous by its absence in the majority of language classes in America.

The nonlinguistic features of talk

Given the systematization that pervades all speech and the conformity required of every speaker, one might wonder what degree of individual freedom is permitted within these fixed limits. Yet everybody speaks differently—else how could we recognize our friends at the other end of the telephone wire? The fact is that talk is a constant synthesis of two distinguishable factors that may be called linguistic and nonlinguistic. The quasi-identity of all spoken language in a given speech community is to be found in the first of these, individuality in the second.

Edward Sapir, in "Speech as a Personality Trait," studies these nonlinguistic features of talk and distinguishes five relevant levels which he describes as follows: (1) *voice,* the lowest and the most fundamental, (2) *voice dynamics,* that is, intonation, rhythm, continuity, speed, and so forth, (3) *pronunciation,* variations made upon the phonemes of the language, (4) *vocabulary,* selections made from the lexical pool, and (5) *style,* the arrangements made of the vocabulary elements. A variation of such features within a customary range is to be noted in any speaker as he addresses himself to different hearers in different circumstances. For an individual to make a permanent shift in the range of these nonlinguistic traits in his speech is a major operation, requiring strong motivation, definite objectives, and much time and effort. It is the common experience of the young as they progress through school, though much rarer in the adult. G. B. Shaw makes such an alteration the theme of his play *Pygmalion.*

Changes in talk through time

So far we have considered talk only as it appears in a cross section of the audio-lingual band, that is, in its synchronic aspect. There is another dimension, the diachronic, which may be studied by examining successive states at different points of time in the history of the language and of the individual speaker.

The recognition of certain facts about change in language marked the beginning of the modern scientific period in linguistics. The first of these was that all languages are and, as far as we know, always have been in a constant state of fluctuation; the second, that independent changes lead to totally different results; and the third, that certain changes (especially in sound) show a high degree of regularity. As a result of migration and the vagaries of politics, trade, and similar factors, there are always patterns of dialectical variation that do not diffuse equally throughout a speech community, with the result that dialects eventually drift so far apart that they become mutually unintelligible. Yet the different languages thus created continue to show evidences of a common origin. We frequently find forms that resemble each other because of a common ancestry, recognizable in words that are called cognates.

Philologists and linguists alike have accumulated a vast literature concerning details of linguistic change in many different languages. In summarizing a few significant facts, we may note that, with respect to sound, one phoneme may give way to another (the Latin *centum* became the French *cent:* the *k* sound changed to *s*), or it may disappear (the Latin *tabulam* became *table* in French, with the loss of the vowel *u*), or it may be transposed to another position in the sequence (the French *moustique* derived from the Latin *musca* with the diminutive ending *ito:* the sounds of *t* and *k* changed places)—or an entirely new one may be inserted (the English *empty* comes from the Anglo-Saxon *emtig:* a *p* sound has been engendered between the *m* and the *t*). We may observe a sound change in the process of development by listening to the pronunciation of a word such as *probably*, which is often shortened to *probly*, and not infrequently to *prolly*.

Changes of this kind are paralleled by comparable modifications in grammar, yet none of them can be called haphazard or degenerative. On the contrary, we might well expect evolutionary changes to take place when dealing with phenomena so closely integrated with a living culture. There are always many possibilities for change at any given state of a language, but it has so far not been possible to predict what specific change, if any at all, will take place.

We have been discussing change in language in its *langue* aspect. Of course, these modifications have their loci, both in origin and in practice, in the mouths of living speakers. The *parole* of each living speaker also undergoes a process of change as he learns his mother tongue and such additional languages as he may eventually acquire. The following chapter deals with some of these processes and their relationship to each other.

Suggestions for further reading

Bloch, Bernard, and George L. Trager. *Outline of Linguistic Analysis*. Baltimore: Linguistic Society of America, 1942.

Bloomfield, Leonard. *Language*. New York: Holt, 1933.
Chomsky, Noam. *Syntactic Structures*. 's Gravenhage: Mouton, 1962.
Gleason, H. A., Jr. *An Introduction to Descriptive Linguistics*. Rev. ed. New York: Holt, 1961.
Hockett, Charles F. *A Course in Modern Linguistics*. New York: Macmillan, 1958.
Politzer, Robert. *Teaching French: An Introduction to Applied Linguistics*. Boston: Ginn, 1960.
Sapir, Edward. *Language*. New York: Harcourt, Brace & World, 1921.

MOTHER TONGUE
AND SECOND LANGUAGE

3

In the first part of his *Democracy in America*, Part I, 1, Alexis de Tocqueville wrote, in 1835:

> We must watch the infant in his mother's arms; we must see the first images which the external world casts upon the dark mirror of his mind, the first occurrences which he witnesses; we must hear the first words which awaken the sleeping powers of thought, and stand by his earliest efforts—if we would understand the prejudices, the habits, and the passions which will rule his life. The entire man is, so to speak, to be seen in the cradle of the child.

Science has made much progress since 1835, but so far it has told us little more than did Tocqueville about the learning of the mother tongue by infants. Factual information on this subject might come from a corps of workers who were not only skilled in linguistics, in anthropology, in the psychology of learning, and in problems of human growth and development, but had themselves mastered a second language after learning their mother tongue. They would need to observe many hundreds of children growing up in the usual home environment in many different cultures and trace their progress through every waking hour of their first five years of life. Such a project would, of course, be next to impossible. The reports we do have, those of Jules Ronjat, Werner F. Leopold, Jean Piaget, M. M. Lewis, and Arnold Gesell, for example, valuable though they may be, are based upon observations made at home by the children's parents (a notoriously biased group) or in institutions, where the environment can never be that of a normal home. As for the individual himself, the revelation of the knack of language —how the verbal symbol functions—usually comes before the child is a year old, and his own reports, either at the time or later, can scarcely be taken into consideration.

Physiological aspects

Despite the serious gaps in our information about the learning of the mother tongue, some useful observations can be made with reasonable certainty. Every individual possesses three networks of nerve cells: the autonomic nervous system, which controls the lungs, the stomach, and other organs; the sensorimotor system, which enables us to perceive with our senses and to make muscular movements at will; and a third involving memory, language, volition, imagination, and symbolism. These are integrated into a single neural fabric, and the twelve billion or more cells that make it up—all the individual will ever have— are formed some months before birth. There is an area of the cerebral cortex (called Broca's area) in which the control of speech is centered. Integration between nerve cells takes place a little more slowly in this area than in some others, and nothing that can truly be called language appears in the child's behavior until toward the end of the first year of life; learning must wait upon physical growth. However, activity in the vocal-auditory regions begins at birth, persists, and is highly varied. It is, at first, "simply a kind of mass activity. The system does everything it is capable of doing, as if the motor neurons were firing off indiscriminately" (Charles E. Osgood and Thomas A. Sebeok, *Psycholinguistics*, page 128). At four weeks, the infant is heedful of sounds; at sixteen weeks, he babbles, coos, chuckles, gurgles, laughs, and pays heed to the human voice. At twenty-eight weeks, in addition, he crows and squeals; comprehension is evident. At forty weeks, mastication muscles and speech are observed to be maturing together, and by the end of the first year the child listens intently to words, understands commands, and usually has a repertoire of one or several word-sentences of his own.

Psychological aspects

The breakthrough into language comes with the child's first voluntary matching of an object in the environment with the vocal sounds by which it is currently designated in his speech community. The notion that the child accomplishes this by imitating those around him is an almost universally held lay opinion, and is perpetuated by many an unwary psychologist. How incorrect this assumption is has become clear to those who have taken the time to observe and report with care. A few quotations from the most reliable writers in this field may serve as a helpful corrective. Dorothea McCarthy writes in *Manual of Child Psychology*, page 501:

> There is a tremendous psychological gap which has to be bridged between the mere utterance of the phonetic form of a word and the symbolic or representational use of that word in an appropriate situation.

At the beginning of life, as noted by Osgood and Sebeok in *Psycholinguistics*, profiles of sounds produced by newborn infants show no differences over racial, cultural, or language groups. The babbling period that ensues some months later might well come and go without leaving a permanent record in the child's habits. Yet an event of great significance to the child invariably takes place: the chance association of sound and symbol in his random activity is reinforced by the behavior of those around him. The report in *Psycholinguistics*, pages 128–29, continues:

> Analysis of sound profiles at the babbling stage indicates that differences are evident between infants in different language groups. How do these differences arise? . . . The writers in-

cline to the notion that secondary reinforcement is a necessary and sufficient condition to explain this phenomenon.

Gesell and his associates observe in *The First Five Years of Life*, page 190:

> Spoken language appears first as a relatively independent activity, engaged in as play for its own sake, as an accompaniment to other types of behavior or as a social response without a specific communicative aspect. . . . Even as late as 18 months, "talking" continues to be largely a form of play, as an accompaniment to an action, rather than a surrogate for it.

Leopold in his *Speech Development of a Bilingual Child*, Volume I, page 22, writes:

> The diary at this point reveals my astonishment at the course which the development took. From the literature on child-language I had expected a stage of mechanical sound-imitation, with later induction of meanings for the words thus acquired. In Hildegard's case, the phase of mechanical imitation was completely lacking, meanings were always developed before sound-forms. The impulse for any kind of imitation was strikingly weak in this child.

Leopold's daughter was far more typical than he seemed to suppose. Lewis, writing in *Infant Speech*, page 80, says:

> Our only alternative is to recognize that the hearing of the adult word can merely stimulate the child to the utterance of his *own* babbling sounds and that from this the child may become trained to respond with a particular sound to a particular heard sound.

McCarthy summarizes the best thinking on the subject in the *Manual*, pages 494–95:

> Most present-day psychologists seem to agree with the opinion of Taine (1876) that new sounds are not learned by imitation of the speech of others, but rather that they emerge in the child's spontaneous vocal play more or less as a result of maturation, and that the child imitates only those sounds which have already occurred in its spontaneous babblings.

It is clear from these statements that the mind of the child, far from being a *tabula rasa* which passively receives the language patterns of the community as they are impressed upon it, is rather an active agent with a prodigious capacity for *parole*, and it is the interaction of his *parole* with the *langue* of the community as represented in the behavior of those around him that first leads him to the use of language symbolization.

There seems to be but one case on record in which this revelation first came to a mind mature enough to perceive its significance and able to recall the event later on. This is the experience of Helen Keller which she tells in her *Story of My Life*.[1] As she and her teacher were passing a well house on a summer day, the latter placed one of the child's hands in the stream of water gushing from the spout and in the palm of the other spelled out the word *water*. At that instant the child grasped the notion that words could stand for things. The mystery of language was revealed to her, and the prospect of a bright new world in which everything had a name made her eager to learn. An event somewhat akin to this must be experienced by every child as he begins to use his first words, but it takes place too soon for awareness or for any memory of it to be retained.

Development

During his second year, the child continues to increase his stock of one-word sentences, units that compress all the various parts of a complete proposition into a single morpheme. This is pure semantic or vocabulary encoding; the "little" words such as articles, prepositions, adverbs, possessives, and the bound morphemes that indicate number, tense, possession, and the like—the grammar—will be added later. The verbalizing of wants appears toward the end of the second year; the narration of a simple experience develops between two and three years. The answering of even simple questions dealing with nonpresent situations presents difficulty as late as from two and a half to three years. At the age of three, long sentences including compound and complex structures are common; tenses,

---

[1] (New York: Doubleday, 1903).

moods, and parts of speech are distinguished, however imperfectly. Both in talking and in comprehending the speech of others, nonpresent situations are dealt with verbally. As for clarity of articulation, some children pronounce all their words sharply and clearly from the time they first begin to talk; others remain almost incomprehensible to outsiders until a relatively advanced age. The four-year-old verbalizes continually about everything, asks questions endlessly, and discusses his own behavior and that of others. Egocentric or autistic speech—talk that goes on without regard for a listener—looms large in his performance, and persists in diminishing proportions for a number of years. At five, questions are more meaningful; the child really wants to know. His imagination is no longer footloose, and fairy tales with excessive unrealities vex and confuse him. His knowledge of structure is essentially complete, and the child expresses himself in finished, correct sentences. All types of sentences appear, including hypothetical and conditional clauses. As a reminder for those readers who may have forgotten, here is a bit of dialogue taken down verbatim from the lips of a four-year-old and a five-year-old:

> FOUR. I know that Pontius Pilate is a tree.
> FIVE. No, Pontius Pilate is not a tree at all.
> FOUR. Yes, it was a tree, because it says: "He suffered under Pontius Pilate," so it must have been a tree.
> FIVE. No, I am sure Pontius Pilate was a person and not a tree.
> FOUR. I know he was a tree, because he suffered under a tree—a big tree.
> FIVE. No, he was a person but he was a very pontious person.

(This quotation, as well as other statements in the preceding paragraph, are from Gesell and others, *The First Five Years of Life*, pages 19–55.)

The observations by technical experts of the learning of the mother tongue corroborate in a striking way the words of Susanne K. Langer in *Philosophy in a New Key*, page 98:

> Young children learn to speak by constantly using words to bring things *into their minds,* not *into their hands.* They learn it fully whether their parents consciously teach them by wrong methods or right or not at all.

How much do children talk? Careful counting reveals what many parents have often suspected: the oral production of words by children is prodigious. There is, of course, a great range in personal differences in the quantity of spoken words that an individual produces, and this is no less noticeable in children than in adults. At the age of four, some children produce over a thousand words an hour, with four hundred words an hour a probable average for a representative group at this level. It is not unusual to find a five-year-old child using ten to fifteen thousand words per day. *What this means in terms of practice of a skill is highly significant for the older learner of a second language.*

If such a degree of control in the use of the most complicated grammar and syntax patterns can be attained *by everyone* within a space of four years at this immature age, how can one explain the strikingly lesser progress of students of a second language in our schools? Granting the positive effect of the "cultural field" in which the child grows up, the great potential of the child's motivation, and the immediate return he finds in practice, the facts suggest that the answer is partly to be found in a traditional lack of understanding of what language is and how it is learned. To learn how language is acquired and used, we must study language development in the infant and the child.

Bilingualism

Many individuals are exposed to more than one language in infancy and childhood and retain some effects of this exposure in later life. Little is known about bilingualism, but many individuals and many geographical areas are referred to as bilingual. The term itself, no less than *meaning* and *culture,* stands in great need of definition. If the scientists have told us little about the learning of the mother tongue, they have been able to give us even less satisfactory information about language development in infants who habitually hear an additional language. Such official reports as we have are either biographical studies of children by their own parents or broader surveys of areas in which the presence of adverse socioeconomic tensions or of a bastard form of one of the languages involved (such as pidgin English) distorts and obscures the facts of language learning of interest to us here. A notable exception is the report on *The Place of Welsh and English in the Schools of Wales* prepared under the direction of the Ministry of Education in England in 1953. This report states that bilingualism in itself is neither an advantage nor a disadvantage in the development of normal children. It has been claimed that children from homes where more than one language is spoken are often retarded. Even if it were proved (as it has not been) that such children are below standard in English vocabulary because of bilingualism, the lack of a few lexical items in the mother tongue at a given age may be a modest price to pay when, in exchange, one is in possession of all the structure and a sizable vocabulary of a second language. And in fact, the claim that bilingual children are at a disadvantage in intellectual development has recently been vigorously refuted in studies made under the direction of Wallace Lambert at McGill University in Montreal, Canada.

We should not expect anyone to maintain two languages in equal balance at all times, for the reason that the individual's language behavior is inevitably linked to that of the person with whom he is speaking and with the situation in which they find themselves. Depending on the shifts in these variables, one language or another will dominate. In the words of Einar Haugen in *The Norwegian Language in America,* Volume I, page 10: "It is a law of general validity that one's experience in one language must necessarily lag behind one's experience in another." Bilingualism cannot be defined as the ability to control two language codes, nor can it be considered as a stage eventually reached after prolonged experience with a second language. Rather, bilingualism implies the presence in the same nervous system of two parallel but distinct patterns of verbal behavior. These include not only the overt facts of vocabulary, structure, and phonology, but also the inner predispositions that guide the selection of the elements of discourse and separate sets of concepts to which meanings are referred. If, when in conversation in a second language, a speaker's language behavior, both overt and internal, is characterized by adherence to the concepts and the patterns of the second language rather than of the mother tongue, we may call the speaker—at least with reference to this cultural, linguistic, and semantic area—bilingual. This definition is the hope of the second-language learner. It means that he can, with suitable practice and training, look forward to becoming bilingual within a short time in the limited area of his experience in the second language. But he must also widen this area of experience to compare with that of a native speaker of the second language, if he is to become fully bilingual. A regrettable corollary of this fact is that though a given learner may, with proper guidance, become to a definite extent bilingual, yet the same learner, with improper guidance, may not become bilingual in so much as a single statement, even though his circumstances and his expenditure of time and effort are the same. This is without doubt the most trenchant criticism to be made of language teaching as it has traditionally been practiced in America.

Incomplete mastery of a second language

Between the frequently encountered circumstance of the monolingual in full control of only the mother tongue and the much less usual case of the true bilingual, there is a continuum of hybrid states in which speakers possess something less than complete command of two languages. Typical is the Ph.D. candidate who takes a "cram" course in order to pass his language examination, who knows a certain number of lexical and structural equivalents in the two languages enabling him to comprehend (in the mother tongue) a text written in the second language, but who is lacking in any knowledge of its phonology and any sensitivity to the predispositions that accompany its discourse, and is unacquainted with the concepts that people the minds of those who speak it. Typical also is the person who is born and raised in one country, then lives for a long time in another and becomes to a great extent bilingual except for obvious deficiencies in a single area, usually the sound-system. Even more typical is the product of our schools who has had desultory practice in hearing and speaking the second language, but who, hampered by the learning of vocabulary lists and constant translation from one language to the other, has been successfully prevented from acquiring a different set of verbal habits for the new language. The transition from no language to one language is universal, and is generally accomplished in the first five or six years of life. Clearly *all* can learn a first language, for all do. Could all learn a second language? We do not know. Where the conditions for learning are reasonably similar for both first and second languages, as in many bilingual areas, the answer seems to be yes. Even in the schools, with a proper understanding of the mechanisms involved and the necessary disposition and activity on the part of the learner, it is patently possible for him to become bilingual *within the area of his experience with the second language.* In the following chapter we shall look more closely at these mechanisms and dispositions—in a word, at the conditions for successful language learning.

Suggestions for further reading

Gesell, Arnold, and Frances L. Ilg. *The Child from Five to Ten.* New York: Harper, 1946.

——, and others. *The First Five Years of Life.* New York: Harper, 1940.

Lambert, Wallace E., and Elizabeth Peal. *The Relation of Bilingualism to Intelligence.* Washington, D.C.: American Psychological Association, 1962.

Leopold, Werner F. *Speech Development of a Bilingual Child.* 4 vols. Evanston and Chicago: Northwestern University Press, 1939–49.

McCarthy, Dorothea. "Language Development in Children." In Leonard Carmichael, *Manual of Child Psychology.* 2nd ed. New York: Wiley, 1954, pp. 492–630.

Piaget, Jean. *Le langage et la pensée chez l'enfant.* 3rd ed. Paris: Delachaux et Niestlé, 1948.

Weinreich, Uriel. *Languages in Contact.* New York: Publications of the Linguistic Circle of New York, No. 1, 1953.

LANGUAGE LEARNING

4

At a rapid survey of the quantity (not to mention quality) of the literature on teaching in America, the mind reels. By far the greater part of it must be dismissed as irrelevant once it is granted that this teaching is to be appraised in terms of the learning that is presumed to be its concomitant. For the fact that a great deal of animated and well-disposed teaching takes place, accompanied even by lively and well-intentioned study, is no assurance that any significant degree of learning will result. It may be stated as axiomatic, certainly as far as classrooms are concerned, that the experiences and reactions of the individual will affect his future behavior only to the extent that they have occurred under proper conditions of practice. What are some of these proper conditions and do they, or can they, obtain in our schools?

Types of learning

In an effort to bring the classroom, language, and learning into some sort of proximity, it will be useful to consider the theories of learning currently in vogue, even though the phenomena upon which the theories are based are the activities of animals or, if the subjects are human, not the performances of humans who are learning language. *Learning may be defined as a change in performance that occurs under the conditions of practice.* Two types of learning stand out as essentially in contrast, at least in their apparent structure, though they may occur simultaneously and proceed with reciprocal effect. The first of these goes by the name of classical conditioning and was made famous by Ivan Pavlov and his salivating dogs. The other is often termed trial-and-error or, perhaps better, instrumental learning. In classical conditioning, if a stimulus that produces a given response is accompanied (just preceded) by another stimulus, it will be found after many repetitions that the first stimulus may be omitted and still the response is produced. The second stimulus has assumed all the effectiveness of the first. Pavlov's dogs that salivated at the taste of food eventually "learned" to do the same at the sound of a bell.

The type of learning called instrumental is rather more complicated in its description. First of all, the subject is motivated by some sort of drive; he performs at random a number of behavioral acts, one of which results in a reward of some kind and a consequent lessening of motive or drive. After a number of repetitions he abandons all the random acts except the one that gains reward, and he performs this without delay. A hungry rat when put in a box will sniff at the corners, try to climb out, remain quiet and meditate, stand up on his hind legs, and perform other movements until finally, after some time, his activities lead him to depress a lever which gives him a pellet of food. On the hundredth trial he goes straight to the lever, presses it, and continues to do so as fast as he can eat.

One important difference in these two modes of learning is that in the classical-conditioning type, the response is elicited from the subject by manipulating certain events during the proceedings; in the instrumental type, the subject eventually learns the right response on his own. A point of similarity is that a response that is rewarded and learned may induce the learning of a second response that produces the first, even though no reward ever follows. A rat that learns to go to a food dish and eat when he hears a click will learn to press a lever that makes the same click, even though the lever-pressing does not produce food. This phenomenon is referred to as secondary reinforcement.

Theories of learning

Various interpretations are given to these generally recognized types of learning as attempts are made to induce, manipulate, and predict learning under laboratory conditions. These have led to a number of theories (no less than ten) that are at present popular and all of which are distinct if not antagonistic. Since the days of J. B. Watson in the 1920's, the behaviorists have rejected as irrelevant all responses that cannot be observed and recorded. They have assumed that the typist brings no more to an experiment than does the typewriter, the only difference being that the typist's machinery is more complicated. In contrast, the so-called Gestalt psychology proposes that the individual does contribute to perception (and, by extension, to learning) certain raw materials that interact with the phenomena received by the senses and that together these produce the forms, patterns, and wholes with which we feel ourselves to be surrounded. Without wishing to pronounce upon the relative merits of these theories, it is fair to state that both have made valuable contributions to the science of human behavior. Credit is certainly due the behaviorists for ridding psychology of a great clutter of old wives' tales about faculties, instincts, and the like. Credit is likewise due the Gestaltists for helping psychology to get beyond the rat box, in which, of course, it could not remain.

Are there factors that operate in the learning process that are important in all these theories? One would seem to be the nature and extent of learning which the subject already possesses, another his capacity to learn more. The age of the learner is important, as well as his urge to learn. His "mental set," that is, his awareness of the problem and what it entails, will also count. In addition to these factors, which the learner himself brings to the process, there are certain conditions of learning that will also greatly affect the final results. One of these is the nature of the physical circumstances in which the learning takes place, another the effectiveness of reward and secondary reinforcement. Of great importance is the amount and duration of effort required during a single period, the frequency of its repetition, and the time intervening.

Learning in the classroom

It is not enough to know how a given skill can best be learned, or what happens when one set of conditions is replaced by another set of conditions. The problem is rather how the learning of the skill in question can best take place under the conditions that exist or are likely to exist. More precisely, how can the circumstances of the classroom and the conditions for maximal learning be brought into harmony? In seeking a solution, we should not attempt to transform the classroom into "real life" (a bright and childlike wish that is, on second thought, absurd), but to identify the optimal conditions of learning that can exist within the limitations of a large room in a public building. A classroom must be taken for what it is: a situation in which twenty to thirty youthful human beings face in the same direction with one adult facing them. Thus they must remain for an hour or for a day, with their attention and behavior under the guidance and control of that adult. They are surrounded by windows and blackboards, desks and chairs. From time to time bells ring and activities and places change; then the slow advance is resumed in a slightly modified deployment. Whatever variants of this pattern may be found serve only to emphasize its basic sameness.

The goals of language learning

Language is a highly complicated activity, and it is wholly learned. It involves both neural and muscular tissue, and it has psychological, interpersonal, and cultural aspects that are indispensable to its acquisition and use. We may now consider what dominates the perspective when learning moves into the classroom and turns its attention to a second language. *The single paramount fact about language learning is that it concerns, not problem solving, but the formation and performance of habits.* The learner who has been made to see only how language works has not learned any language; on the contrary, he has learned something he will have to forget before he can make any progress in that area of language. If his prior training has conditioned him to require that he "know what he is doing," an analytical explanation may help to relieve this concern which, in turn, may be acting as a block to learning. When a track is blocked it should be cleared at once; clearing the track, however, should not be identified with advance along the track toward a destination.

The question, then, is what *is* the destination, what *is* to be learned? Are we to take a classroom, put in it teacher, students, and books, add a little leaven of curriculum planning, then set the mixture aside to see what happens? Or are we to prescribe in advance what the learning shall be? If the answer to the latter question is yes, then we must plunge at once to the heart of the matter, which involves nothing less than a second performance of one of the most complicated types of learning.

We have our choice of two goals. We may, on the one hand, seek to establish in the learner, within the limits of his experience, a coordinate system of two languages in which not only the overt patterns of behavior that characterize the new language, but also the mental processes that accompany it, shall have equal status with the mother tongue, yet be entirely separate from it. Or we may, on the other hand, be content to establish in the learner a compound system, in which some features of the new language are learned, yet for the most part, and especially with respect to the internalized processes, the mother tongue is not relinquished, but continues to accompany—and of course to dominate—the whole complex fabric of language behavior.

It is precisely here that the issue is drawn. If the goal for the learner is a *compound* system, then our present methods and our present textbooks are entirely adequate. If the goal for the learner is a *coordinate* system, then a ringing challenge is sounded, a radical transformation is called for, a new orientation of procedures is demanded, and a thorough house cleaning of methods, materials, texts, and tests is unavoidable. It is the purpose of this study to explore what goes with the decision to establish in the learners in our classrooms a dual system of verbal symbolism in which mother tongue and second language are coordinated but not compounded. Bilingualism within the limits of possibility is clearly implied.

The coordinate system

The learner's activities must at first be confined to the audio-lingual and the gestural-visual bands of language behavior; only later will he become active in the graphic-material band. No less important than his overt, observable behavior are the internalized activities that normally accompany language. His external behavior will include the mastery of phonology, of patterns of order, of form classes, and of vocabulary. His internal behavior will be a matter of auditory images, of the predispositions and anticipations that are synchronized with the stream of speech and the concepts to which the verbal symbols in question refer.

From the start the learner plays a dual role in vocal language, first as hearer, then as speaker. Recognition and discrimination are followed by imitation, repetition, and memorization. Only when he is thoroughly familiar with sounds, arrangements, and forms does he center his attention on enlarging his vocabulary. In learning the control of structure, what he may at first do as a matter of conscious choice he will eventually do habitually and unconsciously. Throughout he concentrates upon gaining accuracy before striving for fluency.

The speaker-hearer-situation relationship is adhered to at all times. The memorization of word lists, lexical equivalents, and paradigms plays no part whatever in his early tasks. The learner will not actually be harmed by memorizing paradigms; nor will he be by cleaning the classroom windows or waxing the floor. At this point all three activities will advance his language learning about equally. The *parole-langue* aspects of language are reflected in his learning as a speaker one satisfactory mode of expressing a given intention, while as a hearer he learns to recognize several common variants that are essentially synonymous. He learns to understand much more than he attempts to reproduce.

This program of learnings does not banish either English or grammar, but it is very specific about their proper function. English is not to be used by the learner as a *speaker*, though it is occasionally useful to him as a *hearer*, both to identify areas of meaning before sounds in the new language are given and to compare and differentiate patterns in the two languages. The essential point is that *the learner never speaks in English*. Grammar is not a matter of rules and examples extracted from the graphic-material band, but of pattern practice on models chosen in the audio-lingual band. A student learns grammar not by attempting to say everything he will eventually want to say, but by familiarizing himself with structural patterns from which he can generalize, applying them to whatever linguistic needs he may have in the future. Little children constantly say things they have never heard because they have quite unconsciously recognized and learned patterns that they then have at their disposal for the expression of their intentions. This use of analogy can be made a potent ally of the learner of a second language. Pattern practice, which opens the door to analogy, may be called the antithesis of paraphrasing. In the latter, an attempt is made to keep meanings almost constant and vary words; in the former the attempt is to keep words almost constant and vary meanings.

After the student has acquired a suitable degree of audio-lingual command, he learns the traditional system of orthography in which these sounds are represented on paper—as he learned the orthography of his mother tongue when he began his schooling—and also learns to write in this system himself. Reading and writing are introduced some weeks or months after hearing and speaking have begun, and continue to lag at a considerable distance behind the advance in the latter skills, using for materials only the speech patterns that have already been learned. In many languages, though by no means all, the learner will be disturbed at the anomalies in the system of spelling by which the sounds he has learned are traditionally recorded. A few comparisons with English, a champion offender in this regard, may soothe him.

The learner's activities may be briefly summarized as follows: he is to hear only authentic foreign speech, he is to hear much more than he speaks, he is to speak only on the basis of what he has heard, he is to read only what has been spoken, he is to write only what he has read, and he is to analyze—if he does so at all—only what he has heard, spoken, read, written, and learned. What the learner must *not* do may be summarized as follows: (a) he must not speak English, (b) he must not learn lists of English–foreign-language equivalents, and (c) he must not translate from the foreign language into English. All these activities will nullify his efforts to establish within himself a coordinate system of two languages, and will instead only collapse the structure into a compound system with English dominant.

In the selection and preparation of material for the learner to use, there need be no appeal to authority or to logic, merely to the authentic patterns of speech. The difficulty of finding texts and speakers that will serve as models for the learner has been greatly exaggerated. In dozens of countries the world over, every hour of every day, announcers and speakers address audiences over the radio and in public gatherings, and succeed not only in making themselves universally understood by the members of their speech communities but in being reasonably acceptable to all. As speakers, these listeners would of course be widely divergent, but as hearers their response is surprisingly similar. Language may be out of focus on the unfamiliar side, as in the case of a speaker who does not know the language well; it may also be out of focus on the familiar side, as in the case of native speakers in informal contact who habitually reduce the clarity of their speech signals to the minimum required for comprehension. "Jeet jet?" is readily accepted as meaning "Did you eat yet?" On the other hand, the radio announcer, the public speaker, and the stage actor are all obliged to keep their language sharply in focus so that every listener may understand. The learner, and especially the classroom learner, is entitled to hear language clearly in focus as he learns.

Speech systems

The stream of speech may be likened to counterpoint in music: a number of flowing patterns, each with a degree of independence, constantly interweave to form, simultaneously, other patterns that are still more complicated. Certain strict regulations govern their change and development, in order that each may have individual freedom and yet not hamper the freedom of the others. In speech four separate systems are constantly operating at once: the sound-system, the arrangement system, the form system, and the selection of words with regard to meaning. The learner must, of course, deal with all of these in order to understand or to say anything, but he may concentrate upon mastery of one of them at a time, keeping the others temporarily at a minimum. In learning the sound-system he at first practices sheer mimicry, then recognition and discrimination. At this point he does not deal with sounds individually, but in complete meaningful expressions, which enable him to perceive and imitate stress, intonation, pitch, and rhythm. After extensive practice of this kind he ceases to emphasize the learning of sound-patterns and concentrates upon the order and forms of words. Later he may return to the problem of sounds and work with them alone to improve his production of them according to his individual needs, whether by descriptive analysis, comparison of similarities in the two languages, exercises for the sake of pronunciation only, or any combination of these. Eventually he will work with the production of sounds when reading from a printed page and practice the oral reproduction of long sentences and paragraphs.

Words: form and arrangement

After a sufficient mastery of the basic patterns of structure, the time comes for emphasis upon the learning of vocabulary items as such. It is necessary to classify these according to the role they play in the stream of speech. There are four principal classes: those that designate things, actions, qualities, and functions. *Thing* words, easily recognizable as nouns, are inseparably connected with matters of number, gender, and article. *Action* words, also known as verbs, involve problems of person, number, and tense. *Quality* words, usually called adjectives, recall the matters of position, number, and gender. *Function* words are the "little" words that show relationships, the bound morphemes that show person, time, ownership, and the like, and also "replacers" (pronouns) that help to avoid monotonous and awkward repetition.

In the first exercises that deal principally with the form and arrangement of words, the learner listens to and repeats utterances of the following types: statements, rejoinders, polite formulas, questions, and directives, in negative as well as affirmative form and with appropriate "replacers." It will not be forgotten that the form of these exercises always embodies the principle of the "molecule of speech," in which people talk to each other about a selected situation, and that the learner alternately plays the role of speaker and hearer. As the systematic presentation of structure progresses, the exercises employ interrogative words and questions embedded in larger structures, proposals that include the speaker, and nouns and adjectives used as modifiers, together with expressions of time and number, cause and result, place and means, purpose and concession, ownership, comparisons, and exclamations. At a subsequent stage, the learner deals with completed acts, changes of voice, action in past and in future time, expressions of necessity and condition, and especially equivalents in the new language for such English words as *should* and *ought*.

Throughout these exercises designed to acquaint him with and give him control of forms and sequences, the learner will have been dealing with only enough vocabulary to give these exercises substance. When these patterns have become familiar, habitual, and automatic, he may begin to devote a major part of his effort to increasing his vocabulary. The acquisition of vocabulary is planned in a systematic way, and not left entirely to chance encounter in the speech and writings of others.

The study of words naturally follows their division into the four classes already referred to: things, actions, qualities, and functions. The pattern-practice exercises for the learning of structure will inevitably have employed most of the "little" words in the function class, such as auxiliaries, prepositions, conjunctions, interrogative words of time, place, and ownership, and markers of particularity (articles) and degree. To these will have been added the "replacers" referring to individuals such as *I, mine,* and *ours,* to classes such as *both, all, few, many,* and those of indefinite reference, *everyone* and *nobody,* as well as the new language equivalents of the English *do* and *so,* as in "I always do" and "I think so." Examples of another group of important "little" words are *some, any, too, either, yet,* and *any more,* which emphasize the presence or absence of a quantity, a negative, or an addition.

After this there remains the vast area of "content" words, the sort that dictionaries are made of. The learner must be warned that the area of reference that is symbolized by a given word in one language almost never matches that of its dictionary equivalent in another language, that the meanings are often very different, and sometimes wholly different. (For example, we may find in the dictionary the French word *pièce* given for the English word *room.* Yet *pièce* has meanings in French that have nothing to do with *room,* and *room* has meanings in English that are quite unrelated to anything the French mean by *pièce.*) The choice of content words for the learner to study is guided first of all by the situations and circumstances in which he is, then those he is likely to encounter in the immediate future. Since the learners we are concerned with will continue for some time in academic surroundings and pursuits, of immediate concern is a vocabulary enabling them to study the culture and literature of the country whose language they are learning.

The learner in the classroom

The four most visible and tangible factors involved in classroom learning are the learner, the teacher, the book, and the physical surroundings. While the last two tend to remain in a relatively stable state, the first two are variables. A close look at the role of the teacher will be reserved for another chapter; for the moment, we shall be concerned chiefly with the learner. The amount of former language learning and habits of language learning which the learner brings to the classroom is immense. Given his psychological and physiological development and the environment in which he finds himself, it is unrealistic to suppose that second-language learning can be for him a mere repetition of the processes of learning the mother tongue. Not only are all the sound-patterns and structural patterns of his native tongue familiar to him, he performs in them rapidly, automatically, with complete ease and confidence. He has learned them all without awareness, except for the few cases in which the logic of inference has led him to the use of forms not tolerated by the *langue* of the community—he must not say *runned*, but *ran*. In addition, he has learned to read and write his first or native language, and of course thinks that reading and writing are what language really *is*. Certainly, for him, when it comes to learning, language is something in a book. He has spent untold hours diligently studying English "grammar," that is, identifying the parts of speech, parsing written sentences, memorizing lists of prepositions and conjunctions, learning an unwieldy nomenclature, and striving for "correctness" in diction, in punctuation, and above all, in spelling. It has never occurred to him that pronunciation, word order, stress, or intonation might be parts of grammar, or that these might have any connection with what a statement means. He does know about learning new words and has made serious efforts to increase the number of those he recognizes and sometimes to use them when he writes. Since reading, writing, parsing, spelling, nomenclature, and correctness constitute what he has learned about English grammar in school, it is quite natural for him to suppose that he will deal with these in his study of a foreign language, except that most of the words and some of the rules will be different. Meanings, and of course the "basic grammar," will always remain the same.

What he does not know is that the sound-system and the structural system of the new language are different in nearly every detail from those in his mother tongue, that meanings in the new language will never be identical with those in English, and that there is no more a universal grammar than there is a universal diet. Nor does he realize that he must practice the sound-patterns and the structural patterns of the new language over and over, just as he did in learning the mother tongue, making them automatic and habitual, before he really knows them. He is often quite unaware that he can learn to coordinate English and the foreign language in his head without bringing them into contact at every instant. His greatest difficulties are probably these: he does not realize what his task is; there is always available to him in English an easier way of doing whatever he will attempt to do; and despite his best efforts, a certain amount of interference and distortion will often be induced in his performance in the new language by the mere presence in his head of the words and patterns of the mother tongue. Whatever may have been his experience with the learning of English grammar in school, an entirely new concept of grammar now awaits him. It must be explained to him that in his new circumstance grammar means the stream of speech issuing from a speaker's lips, the recognition of the similarities and differences in these sounds, their complicated forms and arrangements, their intricate relations to each other and to the things they represent, and his eventual production of these sounds in a controlled and meaningful way. He is entitled to have these facts made clear to him at the start, for he will learn more if he begins with this awareness of the nature of the problem, of its chief difficulties, and of the degree of achievement he may look forward to within a given time.

   Second-language learning may be begun at any age, but the nature of the learning will vary with the age of the learner. As a child, the learner has a muscular and neural plasticity that permits him more readily to adopt the new speech habits; his world is limited and he finds the constant reworking of familiar experience in terms of the new symbolism quite to his liking. But the value of his learning is predicated upon a guarantee of its continuity. To be meaningful, the foundation he has laid must be built upon, and not in a haphazard but in an orderly fashion.

The older learner no longer has the muscular resilience of childhood, nor does he so easily comply with the discipline of required practice. But he may compensate for these handicaps by the strength of his motivation, by mature insight into the value of the learning process, and by having specific goals that serve to focus his efforts. If due consideration is given to psychological, pedagogical, and economic problems, much is to be said, when every prospect pleases, for a start at the age of eight. But if a beginning is made at this age, the modeling and the programing must be above reproach and long-term continuity assured.

Conclusion

A discussion of learning is not complete without some remarks about error, which bears a relationship to learning resembling that of sin to virtue. Like sin, error is to be avoided and its influence overcome, but its presence is to be expected. Errors in language are likely to be due to one of the following causes: (a) the student may make a random response, that is, he may simply not know which of many responses is the right one; (b) the student may have encountered the model but not have practiced it a sufficient number of times; (c) distortion may have been induced by dissimilar patterns in English; or (d) the student may have made a response that follows a sound general rule but, because of an anomaly in the new language, is incorrect in this instance. The principal method of *avoiding* error in language learning is to observe and practice the right model a sufficient number of times; the principal way of *overcoming* it is to shorten the time lapse between the incorrect response and the presentation once more of the correct model.

The learnings we have listed will enable the student to establish a bridgehead in the new language territory, to provide for himself there, and to explore and become acquainted with his new surroundings. But it must be remembered that he is now in another speech community and in another culture. Before him lie all the areas of experience in the new community, and the knowledge of these is the true reward for his adventure. He will never cease his learning of language, for every new situation will be saturated with verbal content, much of it equally new to him. This applies not only to the acquisition of vocabulary, which is practically infinite, but also to structural forms as they assume their myriad configurations both in the mouths of speakers and in writing. It is the remarkable power of written words that they can re-create living situations far removed in time and space, and provide the reader with a vicarious experience of these situations. To be sure, pictures can do this also, but our concern here is the symbolic transformation of experience through discourse. Fortunately, the classroom lends itself well to activity of this kind. The responsibility for the choice of reading materials appropriate to the interest and capacity of the learner and faithful to the ethos of the new language community is not to be taken lightly. This choice is largely the teacher's, and to an examination of his role in the language learning process we now turn.

Suggestions for further reading

Agard, Frederick B., and Harold Dunkel. *An Investigation of Second-Language Learning.* Boston: Ginn, 1948.

Delattre, Pierre. "A Technique of Aural-Oral Approach: Report on a University of Oklahoma Experiment in Teaching French." *French Review,* XX (January and February 1947), 238–50, 311–24.

Fries, Charles C. *Teaching and Learning English as a Foreign Language.* Ann Arbor, Mich.: University of Michigan Press, 1945.

Gouin, François. *The Art of Teaching and Studying Languages.* New York: Scribner, 1892.

Köhler, Wolfgang. *Gestalt Psychology.* New York: Liveright, 1929.

Mallinson, Vernon. *Teaching a Modern Language.* London: Heinemann, 1953.

LANGUAGE TEACHING

5

If a scientist were bold enough to apply his methods of analysis and his terminology to the succession of events in a classroom, as if he were observing the contents of a test tube, he would be likely to identify the teacher's role as that of a positive catalyst. It is the function of such a body to enter into and speed up a reaction that would take place only very slowly without its presence. A catalyst is usually recoverable intact when the process is over, though its physical properties may be somewhat altered. On the whole this description fits the teacher rather well. If our scientist should continue by reminding us that there is also a second type of catalyst, called negative, the result of whose presence is to *hinder* the reaction, we should probably dismiss him as un-American. This reminder is not irrelevant, however, because the behavior pattern that is the goal of language learning is so intimately dependent upon teacher-learner interaction that the role the teacher plays is more critical than in almost any other subject. It is through the exercise of his role as model, interlocutor, and coach that the teacher eventually establishes in his students the control of the language skills that is for them a prime objective.

The position of the language teacher

The foreign-language teacher of today is in a predicament. On the part of the academic world, the business world, the military, and the public at large, knowledge of another language is unquestionably approved of and sought after. Language study occupies an important place in the general curriculum, and one may state that, by and large, the better the school, the greater this importance is likely to be. At the same time the majority of students who elect to study a foreign language in their freshman year in college enter with a less extensive preparation than they did some decades ago. Criticism by those who have spent from three to six years as students in foreign-language classes in school and college is frequently negative and often tinged with bitterness, the chief complaint being that during these courses they neither spoke nor heard the language in question. Teachers of foreign languages are continually called upon by administration officials and by colleagues in other fields to defend and justify the amount of time and energy spent on language learning. The writings of their technical journals clearly reveal on the part of foreign-language teachers themselves many doubts and uncertainties about right goals and right procedures.

If it may be said that the foreign-language teacher is not fully confident about his task, it is equally true that his task is frequently misunderstood by others, even those closest to him in his work. Language learning involves motor skills as well as intellectual activities, and the foreign-language teacher must develop in his pupils not only ideas and perceptions and values, but also complicated patterns of muscular coordination and habit formation such as are in no sense required for the study of mathematics or history or a science. Neither do such problems exist in the study of one's mother tongue, for these muscular habits have been fully formed in the first five years of life. As an example of this lack of understanding, we may cite a passage by Maurice P. Hunt and Lawrence E. Metcalf in their book, *Teaching High School Social Studies*. While presenting a well-reasoned argument for the improvement of teaching in their own discipline, these writers state that "learning which involves primarily the acquisition of non-thoughtful responses is not consistent with the needs of democratic citizenship,"[1] thus neatly tossing foreign-language learning out the window, surely without malice, but in unpardonable ignorance. As we have seen, *the acquisition of non-thoughtful responses is the very core of successful language learning,* and Congress itself has pronounced such learning to be in our national interest.

This predicament of the foreign-language teacher—or indeed any teacher—cannot be properly appreciated without looking closely at the nature of his task and seeing him in relation to the general character of the school world in which he operates. Furthermore, no serious treatment of any educational problem proceeds very far without finding that the roots of the matter lead directly to broad cultural issues that are deep and all-pervading. For these reasons it will be useful to sketch very briefly the history and status of both teacher and school as they appear in formal education in our country.

Teacher and practitioner

To teach is to show, and in this basic sense teaching is a facet of human life everywhere. The inculcation in the young of the belief and behavior patterns of the culture into which they are born is indispensable to the evolution of man. Education is as important to the Bushman and the Eskimo as to ourselves, and for them it bears an obvious relationship to the welfare of the community. In the great civilizations the informal education of primitive life has of course continued, but it has come to be accompanied by a formal education in learnings deemed important for all, the most general and enduring of these being the ability to read and write the communal language. On a more advanced level, learning by being apprenticed to practitioners of religious ritual, healing, law, and the various arts and crafts appeared early in many societies, and in some fields, especially law, this custom persists with us today. For the most

---

[1] (New York: Harper, 1955), p. 21.

part, however, formal education in our society is carried on by persons who are not actively engaged in the discipline in question, but who *teach about* this activity. Usually we do not find mathematics taught by engineers, nor poetry by poets, nor economics by brokers and bankers, nor science by researchers from a nearby laboratory. This trend away from the teacher as a practitioner of his specialty reaches its nadir in the currently popular doctrine that the teacher need not even command a passive knowledge of his subject, but is expected merely to know and like children and be able to manage a classroom successfully.

The unique demand made upon the teacher of a foreign language is only too obvious. Aside from the teacher of music or dancing or art, he is often the only member of his faculty who is required to have a practitioner's knowledge of the discipline he teaches, while in the intellectual areas of his subject no less is expected of him in ability and training than of any teacher in the other academic subjects. To make things more difficult, the demands are now being increased. Teaching by those who merely knew *about* the language they taught has been tried and found wanting. The need is for teachers who are thoroughly at home in the language skills they presume to teach.

American schools: development

This reversion to the concept of the practitioner as the most desired type of teacher does not easily find its proper place in the decentralized and heterogeneous organization of our schools. If we remind ourselves of a few pertinent facts about the latter, it will not be difficult to see why this is so. It is all but impossible to make valid generalizations about American schools, for almost anything either good or bad can be said of them. The magnificence of the finest and the meanness of the poorest (the journey in space from one to the other is often brief) scarcely seem to belong to the same planet.

The free public school did not come into being immediately after the surrender of Cornwallis at Yorktown. The Constitution made education a matter for the states to handle, and the country was a half-century old before the first state, Massachusetts, established an agency for enforcing the law of 1827 requiring every large town to maintain a free high school. As one example of an attitude current in the early nineteenth century, we may recall that Edward Everett, president of Harvard from 1846 to 1849, thought there was no more right to free schooling than there was to free tailoring. Schools in which rich and poor could mingle on equal terms date from only shortly before the Civil War, and, as the century advanced, more and more were created as communities attained a sufficient size and a stable life. In most areas the education of children in the public schools has always been paid for by the owners of real estate in the local community. If the community cannot collect adequate real estate taxes, education suffers. Wealthier communities provide far better schooling than poorer ones, and bid openly against each other for the best talent available, leaving the less fortunate communities to make out as best they can. It is thus an accident of geography whether a sound program of studies or a shabby one is available for a given child. One may wonder about the "equality of opportunity" in such a system.

Since colonial days religious values, frontier values, and business values have in succession dominated the over-all patterns of American thought. At no time has there been general agreement in theory on the aims of our schools. Two principles that color our attitude toward formal education have never been reconciled: one, the social value of the mind trained by discipline to understand the world, and the other, the value of a simple mastery of the three R's followed by an immediate frontal attack upon life itself. A suitable schooling for the future gentleman and scholar has always been available for those properly qualified, but along with the recognition of the worth of a sound academic training, we have never ceased to place a high evaluation upon those whose success was due to learning acquired in the school of hard knocks. As Harold J. Laski reminds us in *The American Democracy*, page 325: "To expect a nation which wrested civilization from nature to be interested in education merely for the sake of the play of the mind would be folly."

American schools: orientation

We may discern four essentially different aims for our schools outlined by those who would direct formal education toward the establishment of a new social order: those who would make it the guardian of the "American tradition" (this last never exactly defined); those who consider universal education impossible and who would train only the elite; those who encourage the inculcation of our national mythology through which the truth of the matter will reveal itself to the perspicacious few; and those whose concern is predominantly religious and who would minimize general learning and concentrate upon spiritual and moral values.

This uncertainty of orientation is accompanied by other difficulties that stem from the nature of our school system, in which those who possess the ultimate legal authority frequently lack the ability or the training or the desire—if not all three—to exercise that authority properly. There are in America some fifty thousand school districts, each under the control of a local school board that is legally responsible to no one. This group decides with finality upon the appointment and dismissal of personnel, upon salary schedules, the content of the curriculum, and all matters involving expenditures, future plans, and general policy. A certain measure of control over the decisions of this board is sometimes exercised by a board of finance that may refuse the approval of funds, and by state and federal authorities that may withhold available funds unless stated conditions are met. In this system the decentralization is certainly extreme. Administration of the public schools is very similar to administration in business and government; in the independent schools full authority and responsibility are usually placed in the hands of a single administrative officer. There are more than thirty million schoolchildren in our schools and more than a million adults who teach them, most of the latter being women. There are five distinct types of schools in America: the public schools, in which more than three-quarters of the population between the ages of six and sixteen is enrolled; an inferior counterpart of this for Negroes in the South; private schools for Roman Catholics; private schools for Jews; and private schools for the well-to-do. There is but one general requirement: every child who is well enough must attend school somewhere.

Americans are for the most part transplanted Europeans, and by and large our citizenry must trace its ancestry back to the peasants, the bourgeois, and the nobility of Europe. The composite nature of our society cannot be understood without reviewing the character of the successive waves of immigration that crossed the Atlantic, and especially around 1914, when the arrivals were roughly in the proportion of a thousand peasants to one member of the middle class and a thousand of the latter to one nobleman. For many reasons, formal education does not occupy as high a position in our culture as it does in the countries from which our citizenry came. Differences are at once apparent when we consider the amount of our national income spent on formal education, the position of education in the organization of our federal government, the standards we set for teacher competence and student achievement, the evaluation by society of the teacher as an individual, and the reputation of our teacher-training institutions in the academic world. To be poorly paid has always been the teacher's lot nearly everywhere. But the position of formal education as reflected in public expenditures (as a nation we spend more for alcohol and tobacco than we do for education), in the organization of federal activities, and in the attitude of other institutions of learning toward teachers' colleges gives the thoughtful enquirer serious pause. There are no official national standards for achievement by students and as yet no widely accepted national standards for teacher competence. In some cases such standards are set by the states, but this is an inadequate substitute in view of the national need. In the organization of the federal government, education is sandwiched in between health and welfare, surely a curious reflection upon our national attitude toward its importance.

We often hear of America as the country of universal education. That every child would be glad to receive a formal schooling if he could get it is a widely held adult attitude not so generally held by adolescents, especially when they observe schooling held up to ridicule in entertainment programs and popular magazines. A school typically contains four types of students: those who are able and willing to follow the prescribed regimen, those who are able but *un*willing to do so, those who are unable though willing enough, and those who are unable and unwilling, and do not pretend otherwise. The teacher is likely to find all four groups represented in any class he enters.

Given this degree of diversity, of confusion, of varied orientation in our schools, it is not difficult to see why those who undertake the rigorous training that will enable them to practice what they teach are often disillusioned when they discover that those who share the circumstances in which they contract to make their training effective—administration, colleagues, and students alike—are either indifferent or inimical to what they have to offer.

This condition of our schools is at present silhouetted against a background of crisis, a crisis that is partly material, partly intellectual. The material crisis is the less serious and is sure to be resolved within a reasonable time. This phase of the matter is, in a word, housing. Twenty years ago the long-range prophets talked only of a falling birthrate for the second half of this century. But some elemental forces have been at work that had not been counted upon, with the result that there are now many more little Americans than anyone had dreamed of. Yet we tend to take in our stride problems that relate to bricks and I beams, glass and laminated wood. Housing will be provided.

Far more serious is the question of whether the drift toward socialization in our schools is to continue (with the schools assuming more and more the functions of the family and the church) or whether education as an intellectual experience is to be reaffirmed. We are deluding ourselves unless we see the issue in these terms. Some overtones of this phase of the crisis may be heard in an article in *The School Executive* by Clinton R. Prewett, who, after noting the barriers to good teaching that take the form of classroom interruptions, overcrowding, clerical work, noise, and money-gathering, advises administrators to "become a little more people-conscious," to "think in terms of people instead of rooms, paper towels, or floor plans," to "remember that educational practices are improved more by teacher growth and development than by curriculum innovations." [2] But the great need of formal education in America is not only for additional buildings, a curriculum with increased intellectual content, and teachers better trained in their subjects. Its great need also is to understand itself, to see itself as the variegated and amorphous organism that it is, inextricably rooted in our social structure, and keenly sensitive to all the latter's aspirations, blunt practices, and regrettable follies.

Problems facing the teacher

Properly sensitized and in a receptive mood, any observer becomes aware, vaguely or acutely, of the foregoing components in the ethos of the American school as he walks through the playground, the hallways, and the classroom. How do these various factors affect the teacher as he deals with them day by day in the routine business of helping the young to learn? How many students and of what kind file into his classroom on the day the course begins? What goals does he set for himself and them at this important moment of departure? What methods will he use and what materials will be available to him in achieving these goals? What are the physical surroundings in which he is expected to teach? What activities must he engage in to keep up to pitch his skill as a practitioner of his subject? What does he contribute to and receive from the professional organizations of which he is or should be a member? What should he do about the tests for college entrance?

STUDENTS

To begin the answers at the focal point of teaching, we may remark that the foreign-language teacher is, ideally, someone of good character who likes to work with people younger than

---

[2] "Let's Remove the Barriers to Good Teaching." *The School Executive,* May 1956, pp. 83–85.

himself, who is thoroughly at home in his students' mother tongue and in the language they are learning, and who is well acquainted with the school world in which the learning is taking place. His students, ideally, are those who have the necessary motivation, who are reasonably homogeneous in ability and previous training, who prosper under the conditions of learning imposed by a classroom, who perform well under the stress of measurement, and who live up to their promise and capacity.

Ideals are seldom encountered in reality, yet certain selective factors tend to place language teaching in more favorable circumstances than might at first be supposed. Since a foreign language is usually an optional subject, it profits from an automatic screening of those who choose it—especially with regard to interest and ability—which cannot operate in required courses. In an elective system, something impels a student to select one course rather than another, and it is likely to be a lively motivation that can be very significant in his success as a learner. Another helpful fact is that most of the leading colleges (though only about 14 per cent of *all* B.A.-granting colleges) require credits in foreign-language study for entrance, with the result that a large number of those who elect such courses are oriented toward college. Because of these selective factors, language classes tend to be composed of the ablest learners in a student population and those most interested in further advanced study. The extent to which these observations are true is soon made plain to anyone who spends a little time in the corridors, the lunch room, and the language classes of any given school.

At the same time, since foreign-language study is usually *not* required for a school diploma, many students may be "guided" into, out of, or away from such a course by the school counseling service. It goes without saying that those who give such counsel assume the responsibility of possessing an intimate knowledge of the areas in which language learning differs from other disciplines if they are to counsel wisely.

Many first-year language students in both school and college are in the course on trial, largely because there exists no satisfactory prognostic test that will select those most likely to succeed or not to succeed in the learnings that are proposed. The course itself is obliged to function as an index of success in further study. (In Connecticut, for example, there were in 1954 in the public high schools 4300 students in first-year French, 2800 in second-year French, 700 in third year, and 160 in fourth year. Thus a third of those who enrolled studied the language for one year and then dropped it.) The lack of an acceptable prognostic test is linked to the fact that there is no general agreement as to the learnings that a language course should contain, and without such agreement the construction of the test remains virtually an impossibility. The lack of unanimity on aims in the foreign-language field is of course related to the uncertainty about aims in formal education in general. Agreement in the discipline of language learning is especially difficult because of the nature of the subject matter, which involves both facts and skills, and on the proper proportions and sequences of these we do not find teachers generally in accord.

CURRICULUM

From the point of view of curriculum, the succession of learnings offered to a student is often not well planned. All too frequently the proposed learnings display little discernible continuity as the student passes from one institution to another or from one level to another. In his second or third year, he is likely to find himself either floundering beyond his depth or treading the same old mill, if indeed he is not completely disoriented because neither the learnings nor the conditions bear any resemblance to what he has experienced before. The most critical point in the transition scale is the junior high school. In its intermediary position, this institution assumes the responsibility for continuing the learnings for those who come to it with some preparation as well as for initiating learnings that are to be built upon as students advance to the senior high school. As far as language learning is concerned, many such schools have given little evidence of being aware of their responsibility in either direction, let alone taking action to fulfill it.

Hardly less important is the transition from school to college, because for most students the full value of a language course lies in continuing in college a series of learnings begun at the secondary level. Teachers on both sides of this dividing line are well aware of the importance of an integrated continuity; when this is lacking it is chiefly due to the almost infinite disparity of secondary school courses, to the variety of emphases at the college level, and to insufficient information about what a given student's learnings have been in the past or are likely to be in the future.

The indeterminate status of objectives is of course reflected back upon methods and procedures in the classroom. Method involves decisions concerning the selection, quantity, timing, and emphasis of learnings. Ideally, method should reveal at every point full awareness of the nature of language and the nature of learning, of the relationship of the mother tongue to the second language, of the dichotomy of facts and skills, of the limitations and advantages of classroom conditions, and of the ultimate outcome of present activity. In many a language classroom it requires the closest scrutiny to discover even traces of such awareness in the methods being employed.

TEXTBOOKS

The teacher often finds himself in a helpless situation, for the textbooks available to him are inadequate, yet he has neither the time nor the facilities nor the responsibility for creating his own teaching materials. This is patently a professional responsibility to which the leaders have so far given little consideration. One source of inadequacy in textbooks is the naïve thought that preparing a language text is virtually the same as preparing a work of literary research, in which individual acumen and personal effort are highly prized. Overlooked has been the fact that a textbook must represent the composite effort of experts from many fields if it is to be an instrument that will help the student learn.

With all due regard for effective personal authorship, it must be admitted that, as a professional group, language teachers have abdicated their position as arbiters of what and how their students shall learn from books and by default have yielded the editorial and critical function in this area to those who print and distribute texts. The issue here is sharp and unpleasant, but it cannot be avoided. Are teachers themselves to decide what they will teach, or will the decision be made by a group of persons whose conclusions are reached on the basis of ultimate financial profit? No far-reaching or permanent improvement can come about in foreign-language teaching until those who are responsible again establish their authority over the nature and content of the tools they put into their students' hands.

Since it is clear from the nature of the materials available that the language learner's needs with regard to books have seldom been understood, and far less often responded to, it may be useful to comment briefly on this subject. A learner needs three distinct types of printed materials: exercise books, reference books, and selected readings. An exercise book is a highly personal affair that must be adjusted to the learner's circumstances and calculated progress, and should be used by one student only. If it can be designed so as to fall to pieces precisely at the end of June, all the better. By that time, whatever value it may possess will already have been transferred to the learner's head. The exercise book should be inexpensive, unbound, and replaceable at the student's expense if lost or mutilated beyond use. Economically, a series of such books would be no more costly than many of the books currently popular as language texts.

Reference books are in another category, and should be designed quite differently. The learner is entitled to have at his disposal a systematic presentation of the learnings he has acquired, set forth according to an analysis of the entire subject and not in the sequence followed by him at the beginning. Such books may be prepared for much use by many learners and have no need to reflect the individual's early progress.

The third type of book, selected readings, also has a distinct set of requirements. Such books should contain the works of authors who wrote for other than a classroom audience and whenever possible should be used as originally printed. If they are edited for the classroom, no English should be introduced except possibly in a vocabulary. The printing of a text with two languages simultaneously in sight does untold damage to the learner by defeating the prime purpose of his efforts: the development of a coordinate system. Footnotes and glosses in the original language help the learner most, as do quite frequently certain omissions of a special kind. Deletions for the sake of brevity, such as the author himself might make, are not only permissible but many times desirable; deletions and substitutions because of "vocabulary difficulty" tend to result from a serious misunderstanding both of meaning and of difficulty and should rarely be allowed; deletions on moral grounds, when the original is not deemed offensive in its own tongue, are a product of monocultural myopia and are not to be taken seriously.

These three types of materials should never be bound in the same volume. The learnings expected in the acquisition of a new language are far too disparate ever to be thought of—especially by the learner—as containable in a single package. The important distinctions between visual and verbal forms, to say nothing of the differences in the three language bands, are all but obliterated in the type of book that presumes to be the single answer to everything.

In the preparation and use of printed materials, the nature of meaning—the lifeblood of symbolism—should constantly be kept in mind, for the learner must deal with not only what is capable of bearing meaning, but what has meaning *for him.* He is entitled to use materials that not only give him ample scope for attaining competence in the audio-lingual band before attacking problems in the graphic-material band, but also provide for continued activity in the former as advance is made in the latter.

PHYSICAL SURROUNDINGS

The physical surroundings in the classroom should be such that the learner can play his part alternately in the speaker-hearer relationship, with a series of situations to relate to, sufficient opportunity for repetition, and appropriate progress through the various skills until they have been mastered. By way of environment, actuality usually provides as a working unit one classroom containing one class and one teacher. Not always, however, for allowance must be made for the added presence of students who are obliged to spend a free period in a room where a class is being held, for the presence of two and sometimes three teachers when teacher training is in progress, and for the use, in lieu of classrooms, of hallways, auditoriums, common rooms, basement areas, churches, and other public buildings rather more frequently than taxpayers are aware of. Usually provided also are blackboards, bulletin boards, pictures, cupboards, and books, and upon these the teacher depends for effective material aid nine-tenths of the time.

But actuality often does not provide a most precious ingredient for successful language learning: background silence. The student needs to hear from three to five times as much of what a speaker says in the foreign language as in the mother tongue. The disastrous effect upon learning of the sounds of passing traffic, of noises in adjacent rooms and hallways, and of interruptions by the loud-speaker of the school's public-address system is incalculable. Such handicaps are not wholly inescapable. When it became apparent some decades ago that sound movies were destined to replace silent films, every movie theater in America was made acoustically acceptable within a matter of months. In recent years the menace of noise in our classrooms has grown steadily worse, and little relief is in sight.

To reverse the ideal for a moment and note the conditions in the environment most likely to *negate* the teacher's efforts, we may imagine him in charge of a class of thirty-five to forty pupils representing a wide range of ability and differences in previous learnings, ask him to teach from a book he did not select or help select, deny him daily access to a duplicator for making copies of teaching materials, schedule this class each day in the last period before lunch, assign it to a different classroom each day of the week, none of which has more than a few square feet of blackboard space and all of which open out upon a truck throughway. Let no one think this set of conditions so rare as not to be met with time and again in our public schools. Let no one think either that the relationship between these negative factors in the physical surroundings and learning is not just as often sympathetically understood by colleagues and administrators alike, and all reasonable efforts made to deal with them. Perhaps the most realistic formula for improvement is a very simple and very possible one: make all as good as the best that can be found.

A new aid to language teaching is the electronic device that records and immediately reproduces the sounds of the voice. Magnetic tape recorders can store up and re-create with great fidelity the phenomena of the audio-lingual band, and they thus open up for exploitation a new and valuable adjunct to efficient and useful learning. That any mechanism could replace one of the partners in the speaker-hearer relationship on the psychological level is of course absurd—the difference between animate and inanimate is rather too great for that. But in the modeling, repetition, and practice areas of language learning, so important in the acquisition of skills, mechanisms can relieve the teacher of much fatigue and provide the learner with the necessary patterns for imitation.

THE TEACHER'S PROFESSIONAL ACTIVITIES

Like Antaeus, whose strength diminished when he lost touch with the earth, the language teacher, in order to retain his skill, must frequently renew contact with the culture in which the language he practices is spoken, if not in its homeland at least in one of its cultural islands. The language teacher is usually well aware of this, and when the needed contact is not remade, it is due far less to lack of willingness on his part than to the restraining circumstances, usually financial, in which he finds himself. Release of time from his position, sufficient financial resources, and programs of transportation and exchange—all matters beyond the individual's immediate control—are necessary if the teacher is to renew and retain the language skills so laboriously gained.

It is important to see the foreign-language teacher in relation to the professional group of which he is—at least potentially—a member. The tradition of the "three professions," divinity, medicine, and law, has been greatly augmented in its adaptation in American society, and language teachers are quite justified in thinking of themselves as a professional group. Yet we may well ask, Who belongs to this profession? How does one become a member? Who are the leaders? Is there a body of basic principles that all subscribe to? Is there a stated ethical code? For what conduct is a member disbarred? The unhappy fact is that no one knows the names of all those who belong to this profession. There is no stated oath or creed and as yet no qualifying examination that is a requirement. There are no criteria by which to judge malpractice. As a profession, language teaching may be compared to a structure with an imposing ceiling and no floor. Ideally, a profession centers upon a value system that prizes the cultivation and application of a body of thought above the goal of financial gain. It is characterized by organizational structure, pride of membership, difficulty of admission, interprofessional exchange of ideas and intraprofessional understanding, joint meetings held at regular intervals, publications that disseminate new information among its members, and an accepted code of conduct that cannot be transgressed with impunity. Language teachers have a profession that has many of these characteristics, but that is crisscrossed by diverse organizations seriously overlapping each other, that does not confer membership according to proved ability, and that has no stated code of ethics, much less a means for enforcing one in practice. A great burden of responsibility for the welfare of all the members of this profession falls upon the leaders of the various organizations and the heads of departments in colleges and universities. Without their willing it, and often without their full awareness, the decisions they make and the policies they follow are directly reflected in the statements that go into college catalogs, in the practices to be found in both school and college classrooms, and in the examinations that students must pass in order to advance from one level to another. These leaders have not been unmindful of this responsibility, and the decision of the Modern Language Association in 1947 to reword its constitution so that it would include an official concern for language teaching is a landmark of first importance. Why so many of those who are primarily interested in literature and literary research should so long have thought that language majors and candidates for advanced degrees simply materialized out of the blue must remain a mystery.

An important readjustment in values at the college level is implied in the decision of the Modern Language Association. It is no secret that individual advancement in the college hierarchy has long tended to depend rather more upon degrees and publications than upon effectiveness in teaching. One may hope for the day when even in higher education there will be general recognition of the fact that the imparting of knowledge to the young is no less important than its pursuit and redaction.

EXAMINATIONS

The lack of a professional code of ethics is especially regrettable in the matter of examinations. A later chapter is devoted to tests and measurements, but here we may note that the present use of tests for college entrance involves moral problems that are not generally understood. The tests taken by the greatest number of candidates for college entrance, those prepared by the College Entrance Examination Board and the New York Board of Regents, are constructed, administered, and evaluated on the assumption that they measure achievement in a corpus of learnings agreed upon and adhered to by language teachers. In the nature of things, the tests can present but a brief and representative sampling of the contents of the corpus. These tests function adequately so long as the teaching is firmly centered in the curriculum corpus agreed upon. When teaching is not so centered, but is deflected by or shifted bodily over to the study of the samplings culled and set forth in these tests, two highly unfortunate results follow: the tests can no longer function properly, and the students are wrongfully deprived of the rewards to which they are entitled in return for their efforts. It has been proved many times over in practice and thoroughly substantiated by scientific experiment described in the *College Board Review* [3] that the time spent in cramming for these tests results in no appreciable improvement in scores and in none

---

[3] John W. French, "An Answer to Test Coaching." *College Board Review*, No. 27 (Fall 1955), pp. 5–7.

whatever that is not notably increased by disregarding the tests entirely and spending the same amount of time in studying the subject.

This misuse of tests is clearly a matter of what the teacher does in the classroom. Yet his predicament cannot be understood unless we recall that more often than not such tests are his only index of the learnings he is expected to teach, that he is strongly motivated by the desire to help his students put their best foot forward, and—saddest of all—that his professional status is not infrequently measured by his superiors in terms of his students' scores on these tests. Too often there is little positive correlation between the assumptions upon which the testing agencies operate and the practice of teachers as they direct the work of students in their classes.

These are serious matters that merit thoughtful study by both testing agencies and teachers' organizations. Rightly understood, there can be a very positive effect of measurement upon teaching; without such understanding, the teacher is only too prone to skirt the quicksands of dishonesty. Getting the student into college is not the same thing as preparing him to do well in a given course when he gets there. The grooming of students solely to pass tests is a type of fraud that could not be indulged in by an engineer, or his bridge would fall, nor by a doctor, or his patient would promptly die. Those who work in a profession that is immune to pragmatic sanctions must adhere to an ethical standard of the highest order if they are to live with their consciences.

OTHER SHORTCOMINGS

Other shortcomings of the language-teaching profession are well known and have often been cataloged. There are American-born teachers whose competence in the language they teach is slight and who know too little about the structure of English and about the learning of a second language. There are foreign-born teachers who teach their mother tongue and who do not know enough about American schools and colleges nor about what it is like to learn their language as a second language when English has been learned first. There are teachers in schools who send their students on to college with no facility whatever as hearers or speakers of the language they have been studying. There are teachers in colleges who conduct their classes in English to the disillusionment and disgust of the increasing number of students who enter college well prepared to take such courses in the foreign language. There are courses at both levels in which all efforts are turned toward learning grammar rules and translating from the foreign language into English. There are teachers in both schools and colleges who are so insistent upon the learning of language itself that ideas and appreciations receive scant notice if any, while at the same time other teachers so overload their elementary courses with literary history and interpretation that their students resign in understandable despair. No language course should be given that does not include some examples of literary art, just as no language course should have its primary aim obliterated by an overemphasis upon literature. The willing horse should not be denied the glory of a noble rider—nor should he be ridden to death.

Undoubtedly the weakest point in the language teacher's understanding of his task is the reasoning that leads him to say: "But if I do not have my students translate into English what they hear and read, how can I be sure they have grasped every meaning?" This most naïve of all statements reveals a serious misunderstanding of both the nature of language and the nature of meaning. It seems to say that meaning is a prerogative of the mother tongue, and to deny that every language has a uniqueness and a self-sufficiency that make it absolutely independent of any other. Yet the language under study has a right to be known and evaluated on its own merits, without being constantly coupled with and compared with and overshadowed by another. If by the stating of ideas and observations in the mother tongue one could be assured of an immediate and complete grasp of meaning on the part of all listeners, the proposal might indeed have appeal. But the mere act of making clear statements in the mother tongue is in itself no assurance that all students will understand, a fact attested to by teachers of English and history. Of course there are levels of language difficulty, and the restatement of ideas in modified form often results in an improved grasp of meaning. The mistake is to think that this must be done in the mother tongue. On the contrary, it is the foreign-language teacher's greatest challenge that meaning proceed at its maximum without destroying the coordinate system of language which it is his primary obligation to inculcate.

The strengthening of these weak points will of course require much rethinking about aims and methods and much rescheduling of the student's progress. But there is one inescapable conclusion resulting from this rather painful study that cannot be too heavily stressed. With the same body of students now enrolled, the same amount of time in the curriculum, the same corps of teachers with the competence they have, and a new insight into the language teacher's role in classroom learning, an improvement of truly impressive proportions could be attained in a very brief time. Competence is a priceless ingredient of good language teaching, and the American-born teacher must work long and hard and unremittingly to attain and keep it. But competence in itself is but half the story, as the indifferent success of many a foreign-born person teaching his mother tongue to Americans makes only too clear. The other half of the story is to know what to do with the competence one has. An enormous potential for the improvement of language teaching lies in the margin of difference between the competence possessed by the average teacher and the use to which he puts that competence in his classes.

Suggestions for further reading

Birkmaier, Emma M. "Modern Languages," *Encyclopedia of Educational Research.* 3rd ed. New York: Macmillan, 1960, pp. 861–88.

Georgetown University, School of Foreign Service. *Reports of the Round Table Meetings on Linguistics and Language Teaching.* Washington, D.C.: Georgetown University Press, 1951 to date.

Jespersen, Otto. *How to Teach a Foreign Language.* New York: Macmillan, 1904.

Laski, Harold J. *The American Democracy.* New York: Viking, 1948.

MacAllister, Archibald T. *The Preparation of College Teachers of Modern Foreign Languages.* New York: Modern Language Association, 1963.

Parker, William R. *The National Interest and Foreign Languages.* 3rd ed. Washington, D.C.: Government Printing Office, 1962.

UNESCO. *The Teaching of Modern Languages.* Paris: UNESCO, 1955.

LANGUAGE AND CULTURE

6

When individuals communicate through language, understanding tends to follow in direct proportion to the similarity of the conceptions they weave about the words being exchanged between them. Misunderstanding often results from the use of words that can convey more than one concept. To a cobbler, for example, a *shoe* is made of leather and covers the foot; to a railroad worker it is made of metal and presses against another metallic surface, causing friction. To *baste* may mean to sew together with long loose stitches, it may mean to moisten with melted fat or gravy, it may mean to beat with a stick. This multivalent character of many words is the essence of the pun and the source of much humor in literature and in real life. The humor fades, however, when such a word is used as a key word in serious discussions without preliminary agreement about the concepts involved, and becomes highly ironic when the users shift nimbly from one concept to another without warning and even without awareness. The trustworthiness of language symbols in their role as a system of communication is, in such a case, called into serious question.

The meaning of culture

An important word of this type is *culture*. At heart it bears the simple domestic notion of growth in animals and plants. It was long ago extended by metaphor to apply to persons subjected to education and training, and in the nineteenth century it was recognized as bearing not only the absolute meaning of refinement of mind, taste, and manners in an individual, but also of intellectual attainments, especially as exemplified in the relics of artistic endeavor, representing whole phases of a civilization. To these two very different areas of reference—biological growth and intellectual refinement—the social scientists of the twentieth century have added a third meaning: the sum of all the learned and shared elements that characterize a societal group.

These last two meanings are sharply opposed, for culture in the sense of *refinement* is accompanied by the creative, selective, and eliminative factors that are essential to art, while culture as a term for the *learned and shared* elements of communal life reflects the objective and comprehensive attitudes of science. It is natural for the humanist to interpret the word *culture* mainly in terms of its *refinement* meaning and equally natural for the scientist to attach to the same word chiefly the meaning *way of life*. Clearly the word may bear both concepts, yet it cannot mean either or both indiscriminately if it is to be understood. Failure to make the necessary distinction in advance is likely to produce communication similar to that between two interlocutors in which the first repeatedly uses the word *execute* in the sense of *carry out,* while the second uses the same word to mean *put to death* and develops his side of the interchange accordingly.

The "cultured" language teacher

Culture in its *refinement* meaning has long been attached to language teaching. The language teacher is presumed to be a cultured person and the learner is presumed to enhance his own culture as he learns a second language. The culture of the foreign country whose language is being studied, as reflected in its literature, art, architecture, music, dance, and the like, is the subject of much consideration and is often treated at length in speech through *realia* (pictures, newspapers, clothing, and other cultural articles) and in other ways. Valuable as all these meanings and uses of the word *culture* unquestionably are, they must on no account be confused with the meaning that the word has for the scientist. Since we cannot fully understand the nature of either language or language learning unless we examine carefully the relation of language to the total way of life of the group, we shall find it profitable to explore briefly the concept which the scientist attributes to the word *culture*, leaving aside entirely for the moment its connotation *refinement*. To do so follows directly from our earlier definition of the *molecule of speech*, for the speaker and the hearer must perform in and refer to a situation, and this, by extension, leads directly to the communal life, or culture, in which the language being spoken has its roots.

The scientific meaning of culture

A few summary statements may be made that suggest what lies at the core of the scientist's concept of *culture*. The adage "All men are brothers" is another way of saying that the genus *homo* has only one species, Homo sapiens; this in turn is another way of stating the biological fact that the normal mating of any pair from the entire group can produce offspring and the psychological fact that the offspring can learn any language or adapt to any culture. Whatever may have been his genetic heritage, the infant brings to the learning of language and culture —granting individual differences—neither more nor less than any other child of whatever race or color; the one requirement for membership in any culture is to be born in it and to remain in it for the first twenty years of one's life. Every culture imprints a value system upon the individual who grows up within it. Culture is taught by the old to the young and learned by the young from the old. By far the greater part of this teaching and learning of cultural traits, as well as their practice, takes place well below the threshold of awareness. The discrete elements of culture divide themselves into two principal classes: material and nonmaterial. Belief and behavior tend to display clearly discernible designs or patterns that cluster around certain focal points of thought and activity, which may be referred to for want of a better name as *situations*. Typical situations are the getting and eating of food, the fabrication and use of tools, the preparation and occupation of lodgings, the interaction of the sexes, the comprehension and use of time and space, the wearing of clothes and ornaments, defense and recreation, worship and learning, reactions to the vital events of birth, sickness, and death, symbolic transformations such as language, rite, or myth, and attitudes and beliefs about life's meaning as reflected in the value system of the individual and the group. Some cultural situations appear to be universal; others that might seem inevitably universal turn out not to be. A culture engenders a "field" which has a perceptible effect upon all within it, especially with regard to the learning and practice of the patterns that are typical of it. The transplanting of the essential character of a cultural field to a geographically distant cultural island is not only possible but common, as may be seen in the foreign "colonies" in many large cities of the United States. Every individual the world over belongs to a culture, and his patterns of thought and action are the result of his relationship with it. Let no American doubt that he, too, lives in a culture, as well as the Bushman and the Samoan. Baseball, Coca Cola, and peanut butter are as authentically and universally American as the igloo is Eskimoan.

Language is the most typical, the most representative, and the most central element in any culture. Language and culture are not separable; it is better to see the special characteristics of a language as cultural entities and to recognize that language enters into the learning and use of nearly all other cultural elements. The detailed facts of culture cannot properly be evaluated in isolation but must be seen as integrated parts of the total way of life in which they appear. Cultural integration, however, when it shortens its focus in order to scrutinize case histories, tends to lose sight of certain general concepts not discernible in the individual person. Every language makes a relatively narrow choice of the vocal sounds that are available for speech, and in the same way every culture makes a restricted choice of the possible modes of human living. Every societal group has a culture uniquely its own, just as it has a language that is completely individual and self-sufficient. Just as there are often many dialects of a given language, so are there often many subcultures of a given culture. The view that language is the keystone in the structure of a culture is stated by Edward Sapir in *Culture, Language, and Personality*, page 1, thus:

> Language is an essentially perfect means of expression and communication among every known people. Of all aspects of culture, it is a fair guess that language was the first to receive a highly developed form and that its essential perfection is a prerequisite to the development of culture as a whole.

A cultural anthropologist who wishes to study a chosen culture must know its language and spend a period of time living in the cultural area. His procedure is to talk with many people, to make tactful soundings in order to gain confidence and not offend, and to take copious notes on all that he hears and observes. As he does so, he has certain key questions in mind and will try to discover:

Who is busy and who is idle.
What people talk about most.
What people value most.
Who runs things in the home and in the community.
Who the heroes are.
What is taboo.
What the character of the religion is, and whether the gods are kind or cruel.
What folk tales everyone knows.
What modes of artistic expression are allowed and encouraged.
What conduct wins general approval and what merits scorn and ridicule.
What is considered fair and what unfair.
What is considered funny.

What procedures accompany the exchange of goods and services.
What the important kinship ties are.
What games are played and what pastimes enjoyed.
What the role of music and dancing is.
What the important feasts and celebrations are.
What rites and ceremonies are observed at birth, adolescence, betrothal, marriage, and death.
What the rules concerning courtship are.
What people do to "get even" if they feel that they are injured.
What is done about the treatment of disease.
Who fights, how, and about what.
What the tacit assumptions and unquestioned practices are.

The answers to these and similar questions will reveal in outline the character of the culture that is being studied. Above all, the observer must note not only the exterior, observable patterns of behavior but the interpretation put upon them, their symbolic meaning in the minds of those who have grown up within the culture and are practicing members of it. For example, the black smudge worn on the forehead on a Wednesday early in spring is more than a dirty face; to the initiate it has a deeply religious meaning.

The facts and insights that result from such a study are things our students are interested in knowing. They are also things they must know in order to understand the history and the literature, the laws and the value system of the people whose language they are learning. In his essay *Mere Literature,* Woodrow Wilson seeks to draw a sharp line of demarcation between the scientist and the humanist, yet in so doing he presents a moving summary of the objectives of cultural studies that can be subscribed to by scientists and humanists alike: [1]

> In narrating history, you are speaking of what was done by man; in discoursing of laws, you are seeking to show what courses of action, and what manner of dealing with one another, men have adopted. You can neither tell the story nor conceive the law till you know how the men you speak of re-

---
[1] (Boston: Houghton Mifflin, 1896), p. 11.

garded themselves and one another; and I know of no way of learning this but by reading the stories they have told themselves, the songs they have sung, the heroic adventures they have applauded. I must know what, if anything, they revered; I must hear their sneers and gibes; must learn in what accents they spoke love within the family circle; with what grace they obeyed their superiors in station; how they conceived it politic to live, and wise to die; how they esteemed property, and what they deemed privilege; when they kept holiday, and why; when they were prone to resist oppression and wherefore—I must see these things with their eyes, before I can comprehend their law books.

When we inspect the currently available textbooks that presume to review the culture of the people whose languages are most frequently studied in our schools and colleges, we are forced to the conclusion that both authors and publishers have operated without benefit of the anthropologist's concept of the word. Aside from culture in the *refinement* sense, these books present, in picture and in print, little more than the colorful, the quaint, and the inoffensive. They often give details of geography, climate, and economic life but do not relate these to the most important characteristics of the culture. Only a selected number of surface appearances are considered, and there is no attempt to give a cross section of what is in fact to be observed or to explore the meaning which behavior has for the individual through an analysis and interpretation of the value system that is the heart of his culture.

Culture in the classroom

It is clear from the analysis we have made of the "molecule of speech" and the nature of meaning that the teacher must relate language to culture if a coordinate system is to result from the learner's efforts. This is the conclusion of Robert Politzer, who says in the Georgetown University *Report of the Fifth Annual Round Table Meeting on Linguistics and Language Teaching*, pages 100–01:

> As language teachers we must be interested in the study of culture (in the social scientist's sense of the word) not because

we necessarily *want* to teach the culture of the other country but because we *have* to teach it. If we teach language without teaching at the same time the culture in which it operates, we are teaching meaningless symbols or symbols to which the student attaches the wrong meaning; for unless he is warned, unless he receives cultural instruction, he will associate American concepts or objects with the foreign symbols.

Are we then to require that teachers of foreign languages take courses in cultural anthropology and that they devote a part of every class and every course to formal presentations from this discipline? If not, then how is the teacher to impart information that will be of interest and value to his students? Just as accuracy in phonology is best acquired as an incidental by-product of the learning of actual conversations, and as syntax and morphology are best learned not by analysis but by imitation and practice, in the same way knowledge of culture is best imparted as a corollary or an obbligato to the business of language learning.

Many successful language teachers habitually begin their classes with a five-minute presentation in the foreign language of a subject that has not been previously announced. The content for this simple and effective device may often be a topic that brings out identity, similarity, or sharp difference in comparable patterns of culture. For example, consider three holidays in France and the United States. In both countries Easter is essentially the same in concept and observance, but Christmas is markedly different in many ways, and the American Thanksgiving has no counterpart in the French calendar of festivals.

The point of view from which to present such topics should not be that of the deity observing the terrestrial sphere, nor a historian viewing the total experience of a civilization, nor an architect surveying the blueprint of a complicated structure. Rather, the point of view should be that of a young person of the age and status of the students being addressed, and the perspective should be that of such a person as he goes about his daily tasks.

The following list of topics (by no means exhaustive) may

be considered as items for such "hors d'oeuvres" in the language classroom.

GREETINGS, FRIENDLY EXCHANGE, FAREWELLS. How do friends meet, converse briefly, take their leave? What are the perennial topics of small talk? How are strangers introduced?

THE MORPHOLOGY OF PERSONAL EXCHANGE. How are interpersonal relationships such as differences in age, degree of intimacy, social position, and emotional tension reflected in the choice of appropriate forms of pronouns and verbs?

LEVELS OF SPEECH. In what ways are age, provenance, social status, academic achievement, degree of formality, interpersonal relations, aesthetic concern, and personality reflected in the standard or traditional speech?

PATTERNS OF POLITENESS. What are the commonest formulas of politeness and when should they be used?

RESPECT. Apart from overt expressions of deference and discipline, what personages and what cultural themes, both past and contemporary, are characteristically held in sincere respect?

INTONATION PATTERNS. Apart from the selection, order, and form of words themselves, what overtones of cadence, interrogation, command, surprise, deference, and the like are borne exclusively by the dynamics of pronunciation? (For example, the French *Vous vous en allez ce soir* may be pronounced in such a way that it is clearly either a statement, a rejoinder, a question, an order, or a sentence read by a child from a book.)

CONTRACTIONS AND OMISSIONS. What words or sound are normally telescoped into contractions (for example, *can't*) or frequently dropped altogether (for example, the French *ne*) in spoken speech?

EXPLETIVES. What words and intonation patterns are commonly used to enliven one's speech by way of commentary upon one's own feelings or actions, those of the person addressed, or the nature or behavior of other elements in the immediate situation?

TYPES OF ERROR IN SPEECH AND THEIR IMPORTANCE. What errors is the speaker of English likely to make in the new language?

What is the relative seriousness of these errors in the new culture? (For example, in French, a mistake in the gender of a noun is deeply disturbing, but the failure to make a past participle agree, if noticed at all, is readily condoned.)

VERBAL TABOOS. What common words or expressions in English have direct equivalents that are not tolerated in the new culture, and vice versa?

WRITTEN AND SPOKEN LANGUAGE. Aside from richness of vocabulary and complexity of structure, what are the commonest areas of difference between spoken language and writing?

NUMBERS. How are numbers pronounced, spelled, represented in arithmetical notation, written by hand, and formally printed in ways that are peculiar to the new culture?

FOLKLORE. What myths, stories, traditions, legends, customs, and beliefs are universally found among the common people?

CHILDHOOD LITERATURE. What lyrics, rhymes, songs, and jingles of distinct aesthetic merit are learned by all young children?

DISCIPLINE. What are the norms of discipline in the home, in school, in public places, in the military, in pastimes, and in ceremonies?

FESTIVALS. What days of the calendar year are officially designated as national festivals? What are the central themes of these occasions and what is the manner of their celebration?

HOLIDAYS. What is the usual rhythm of work days and days off? What do young people do with their days off?

OBSERVANCE OF SUNDAY. How does Sunday differ from weekdays with regard to what an individual does or does not do, may or may not do?

GAMES. What are the most popular games that are played outdoors, indoors, by the young, by adults?

MUSIC. What opportunities are offered the individual for training and practice in vocal and instrumental music?

ERRANDS. What are typical errands that a young person is likely to be asked to do, either at home or in school?

PETS. What animals are habitually received into the home as pets? What is their role in the household?

TELEPHONE. What phrases and procedures are conventional in the use of the telephone? What is the role of the private telephone in the home? Where are public telephones to be found and how is the service paid for?

COMRADESHIP. How are friendships and personal attachments likely to be formed and what provisions are made for fostering comradeship through clubs, societies, and other group organizations?

PERSONAL POSSESSIONS. What objects are often found decorating the bureau and walls of a young person's bedroom? What articles are likely to be discovered in a boy's pocket or a girl's handbag?

KEEPING WARM AND COOL. What changes in clothing, heating, ventilation, food, and drink are made because of variations in temperature?

CLEANLINESS. What is the relation between plumbing and personal cleanliness? What standards of public hygiene and sanitation are generally observed?

COSMETICS. What are the special conditions of age, sex, activity, and situation under which make-up is permitted, encouraged, or required?

TOBACCO AND SMOKING. Who smokes, what, and under what circumstances? What are the prevailing attitudes toward smoking? Where are tobacco products obtained?

MEDICINE AND DOCTORS. What are the common home remedies for minor ailments? What is the equivalent of the American drugstore? How does one obtain the services of a physician?

COMPETITIONS. In what fields of activity are prizes awarded for success in open competition? How important is competition in schools, in the business world, in the professions?

APPOINTMENTS. How are appointments for business and pleasure made? What are the usual meeting places? How important is punctuality?

INVITATIONS AND DATES. What invitations are young people likely to extend and receive? What formalities are involved? What is the counterpart of "dating" in the United States?

TRAFFIC. How does vehicular traffic affect the pedestrian? What are the equivalents of traffic lights, road signs, crosswalks, safety islands, parking meters, hitchhiking?

OWNING, REPAIRING, AND DRIVING CARS. Are young people interested in gasoline motors? Are they knowledgable about them? What is the role of the car in family life? What are the requirements for obtaining a license to drive?

SCIENCE. How has modern science affected daily living, inner thought, conversation, reading matter?

GADGETS. What mechanical devices are commonly found in personal use, in the home, in stores, and in travel?

SPORTS. What organized and professional sports are the most popular and the most generally presented for the public?

RADIO AND TELEVISION PROGRAMS. How general is the use of radio and television and what types of programs are offered, especially for young people?

BOOKS. What are the facts of special interest concerning the printing, punctuation, binding, selling, and popularity of books?

OTHER READING MATTER. In addition to books, what types of reading matter, such as newspapers, weeklies, magazines, and reviews, are generally available and where can they be bought or consulted?

HOBBIES. In what individual hobbies are young people likely to engage?

LEARNING IN SCHOOL. What course of study is usual for an individual of a given age and academic orientation when compared with that of a student in similar circumstances in the United States?

HOMEWORK AND LEARNING IN THE HOME. What is the importance of homework in formal education? What is taught at home by older members of the family?

PENMANSHIP. What styles of handwriting are generally taught and used? What kinds of writing tools are available at home, in school, in public places? What are the conventions concerning the writing of dates, the use of margins, the signing of names?

LETTER WRITING AND MAILING. How do letters customarily begin and end? How are envelopes addressed? Are there typical kinds of personal stationery? Where are stamps bought? Where are mailboxes found?

FAMILY MEALS. What meals are usually served *en famille?* What is the special character of each meal, the food eaten, the seating arrangement, the method of serving dishes, the general conversation?

MEALS AWAY FROM HOME. Where does one eat when not at home? What are the equivalents of our lunchrooms, cafeterias, dining halls, lunch counters, wayside inns, restaurants?

SOFT DRINKS AND ALCOHOL. What types of nonalcoholic beverages are usually consumed by young people and adults? What is the attitude toward the use of beer, wine, and spirits? What alcoholic drinks are in frequent use at home and in public?

SNACKS AND BETWEEN-MEAL EATING. Apart from the normal trio of daily meals, what pauses for eating or drinking are generally observed? What is the customary hour and the usual fare?

CAFÉS, BARS, AND RESTAURANTS. What types of cafés, bars, and restaurants are found and how do they vary in respectability?

YARDS, LAWNS, AND SIDEWALKS. What are the equivalents of American back yards, front lawns, and sidewalks in residential and business areas? What is their importance in the activities of young people?

PARKS AND PLAYGROUNDS. Where are parks and playgrounds located and with what special features or equipment are they likely to be provided?

FLOWERS AND GARDENS. Of what interest and importance are flower shops, house plants, gardens for flowers and vegetables in town and in the country?

MOVIES AND THEATERS. Where are moving picture houses and theaters to be found? What procedures are involved in securing tickets and being seated? What can be said of the quality and popular appeal of the entertainment?

RACES, CIRCUS, RODEO. What outdoor events are in vogue that correspond to our auto or horse races, circuses, and similar spectacles?

MUSEUMS, EXHIBITIONS, AND ZOOS. What types of museums, exhibitions, and animal displays are generally provided and what is their role in the education of the young and the recreation and enjoyment of adults?

GETTING FROM PLACE TO PLACE. What facilities for travel are

provided for short distances about town or from one city or part of the country to another, by bus, rail, or airplane?

CONTRASTS IN TOWN AND COUNTRY LIFE. What are some of the notable differences in dwellings, clothing, manners, shopping facilities, public utilities, when life in town is compared with life in the country?

VACATION AND RESORT AREAS. What areas have special climate, scenery, or other natural features that make them attractive for vacation?

CAMPING AND HIKING. How popular are summer camps, camping, hiking, and cycling trips, and what organizations are especially interested in their promotion?

SAVINGS ACCOUNTS AND THRIFT. In what ways do banks or other organizations provide for the deposit of small amounts of money by individuals? To what extent and in what ways are young people encouraged to practice thrift?

ODD JOBS AND EARNING POWER. What kinds of chores and odd jobs are young people expected or permitted to do? If these are paid for, how is the individual reimbursed? To what extent are regular paying jobs made available to younger persons?

CAREERS. What careers have strong appeal for the young? How important is parental example and advice in the choice of a career? What financial help is likely to be forthcoming for those who choose a career demanding long preparation?

It is culture in this technical, scientific sense that has been so misunderstood and so inadequately presented in our classrooms. Once the necessary distinctions are made and this meaning is clearly conceived, its usefulness and worth to the youthful student are only too apparent. There is litle danger that culture in its other two meanings of *refinement* and *artistic endeavors* will be slighted; all the influence of literature and textbooks, travels and traditions will inevitably orient both teacher and student in this direction. The focal point of the presentation of culture in all its meanings should be the view of life as seen from within the new speech community, especially by individuals who are in circumstances comparable to those of the student. The teacher, by means of the incidental talks suggested above, by means of behavior traits as speaker and hearer that are authentic and typical in the new community, by establishing in the classroom a cultural island made up of both material and nonmaterial elements, and especially by identifying and commenting upon references in literature that are culturally significant, may convey to his students the concepts which make language learning invaluable and are at the same time accompanied by many other important learnings.

Suggestions for further reading

Benedict, Ruth. *Patterns of Culture.* Boston: Houghton Mifflin, 1934.

Kluckhohn, Clyde. *Mirror for Man.* New York: McGraw-Hill, 1949.

Kroeber, A. L. *Anthropology Today.* Chicago: University of Chicago Press, 1953.

Sapir, Edward. *Culture, Language, and Personality.* Berkeley, Calif.: University of California Press, 1956.

Scherman, Katharine. *Spring on an Arctic Island.* Boston: Little, Brown, 1956.

Thomas, Elizabeth M. *The Harmless People.* New York: Knopf, 1959.

Wylie, Laurence. *Village in the Vaucluse.* Cambridge, Mass.: Harvard University Press, 1958.

LANGUAGE AND LITERATURE

7

Language and literature need to be compared and contrasted for the benefit of both; if there are areas of difference, these must be definable, and it is our purpose now to identify and describe such differences from the point of view of the language classroom. If seemingly inadequate and arbitrary definitions of literature are proposed, their aim is less to define literature than to distinguish between it and language. The risk of implying that the two may be mutually exclusive is not absent, yet a little reflection reminds us that a dichotomy between language and literature is as absurd as a dichotomy between child and man. There is no sharp line of demarcation, but a continuum. Literature presupposes language, though the reverse is not true; childhood without manhood is commonplace, but manhood without childhood is unthinkable.

What is literature?

In our century, America has witnessed a departure in the academic world from traditional emphasis upon intellectual training in favor of gross efforts toward what is termed social adjustment. The study of literature as well as of language has been a reluctant companion to this trend, often finding itself frustrated and ineffective for lack of being understood, and consequently in greater and greater need of understanding itself. What *is* literature? Is it everything in print? Is it whatever reading is countenanced by respectable people? Is it the noble pageant of the "great" books? Is it the finest flower of esoteric delight, culled and savored in secret by the happy few?

Literature is best thought of, along with music, painting, and sculpture, as one of the fine arts. What, then, is a fine art, and indeed what is art? To assist us in distinguishing art from non-art, no statement is more useful than that of George Santayana in his *Life of Reason:* [1]

> [Man's habitat] must needs bear a trace of his presence. . . . These vestiges of action are for the most part imprinted unconsciously and aimlessly on the world. They are in themselves generally useless, like footprints. . . . Sometimes, however, man's traces are traces of useful action which has so changed natural objects as to make them congenial to his mind. Instead of a footprint we might find an arrow; instead of a disordered room, a well-planted orchard—things which would not only have betrayed the agent's habits, but would have served and expressed his intent. . . . Any operation which thus humanizes and rationalizes objects is called art.

A wide variety of human activities may thus be termed art, and certainly the selecting, modifying, and disciplining of vocal sounds into language is one of the most universal and important. If we accept this definition, it is clear at once that science, too, is an art, though remaining very close to one of the two extremes between which art lies: utility and spontaneous fancy. In seeking to establish the truth about the composition and history of things, science has minimized preference—which is the origin of value—and stressed objectivity, impersonality, certainty, and the compilation of neutral facts, with the result that it has given man a remarkable command over his environment. The fine arts, in contrast, though they have never abandoned usefulness, have

---

[1] (New York: Scribner, 1954), p. 301.

always given a prominent place to aesthetic value—and therefore to the irrationality of individual preference—and to imagination.

Literature as a fine art

The distinction between language and literature is then, at bottom, a distinction between art and fine art. If art may be said to be equally interested in the true, the good, and the beautiful, the same proportion is not observed in the fine arts, in which aesthetic values far outweigh moral values and the pursuit of truth is largely ceded to philosophy and science. In literature, then, as in any fine art, we shall look chiefly for the immediate pleasures and positive values of aesthetics rather than for the negative values and remote rewards of morality or the intellectual certainty and practical utility of truth. If we say that language is oriented essentially toward a restatement or symbolic transformation of experience, we may say that literature is oriented toward the conscious creation of an illusion of reality. This illusion may well be devoid of any wish to distort or betray reality, yet the value system according to which its choices are made is less closely related to the totem-taboo dialectic that appears to underlie all cultural behavior and more closely related to the individual resonance to beauty we call aesthetics.

Fine art is a matter of medium, purpose, and design. But the arts differ among themselves in that music, for example, may be concerned almost exclusively with its own medium, sound, while literature, though ever eager to exploit the intrinsic resources of its medium, words, must give the greater part of its attention to the flux of human events to which its symbols refer. The word *literature* is itself somewhat misleading, for its etymology suggests that literature is confined to the graphic-material band, which of course it is not. The tradition of oral literature long antedates writing and persists today, while in all written literature concern for the audio-lingual counterpart of the graphic symbols is an important ingredient of success.

Relationship of literature to language

Literature is wholly and inevitably rooted in language, and it is no surprise to rediscover in literature certain features that are peculiar to and basic in language. No more than language can literature separate itself from the "speaker-hearer-situation" trichotomy. As in the simplest dialogue, the intent—even though only latent—and the means of conveying a message must be assumed, and the message must be about something. A dream in itself cannot even be called language, though, once verbalized, it might well become literature. As the speaker's verbal behavior is inevitably conditioned by that of the hearer, so the artist's creative acts are influenced by the real or the presumed response evoked in his audience.

When science uses language, it does its utmost to minimize the difference between the concept which the verbal symbol may be counted upon to bring to all minds and the conception which the individual mind is prone to weave about that concept. In literature, quite the other way. In it, imagination, which comes into play as a concept expands into a conception, is highly prized, and while the universality assured by concepts is an important value in literature, it is the flight of individual fancy, which needs only to be rooted in concepts, that brings the greatest reward.

To see language and literature in the sharpest possible contrast, we may compare the former to the exuberant, unpatterned cacophony of a symphony orchestra during the brief moments of tuning up and the latter to the rhythmed, melodic harmony and counterpoint that respond to the beat of the conductor's baton immediately afterward. The musicians and their skills, the instruments and their capabilities have not changed; what has been added is order, selection of the severest kind (a false note, a note out of time, even a second's worth of unwonted timbre spells disaster), design, and, within the capability of the medium, meaning. So it is when language becomes literature. Intent, selection (and its counterpart, rejection), design, and meaning, manipulated by a single mentality, now dominate what was a few moments before diffuse, though talented, and though locally effective, was in the total pattern chaotic.

LITERATURE IN THE LANGUAGE CLASSROOM

We may at this point consider the questions: Why literature in the language class at all? Is it not better to give the student a thorough grounding in the language skills before he attempts the study of literature? Language classes can and indeed do flourish as if literature did not exist or had never existed. And there are many college teachers who bluntly say, "Let the language skills be taught and taught well in the schools; we will provide the study of literature when these students come to college." We may reply that if courses are rightly planned and the proper proportions kept, there is no reason why language skills cannot be taught along with the study of literature, and all the more successfully for the natural companionship of the two. It is frequently said that formal education should prepare the student *against* the life he is later to lead no less than *for* it. Surely an aesthetic experience in literature is one in which the most universal participation may be expected. Everyone uses words; who will be Philistine enough to deny that everyone, at least according to his interests and capacity, should have some knowledge and experience of the fine art of words, as we find it expressed in literature?

There are language classes in which it is indeed assumed that one of the goals of learning is the appreciation of literature, but that the student is first of all and most of all to be provided with the skills and tools with which he may at some later date study literature. It is undoubtedly an error to take the eventual literary experience for granted. Rather, it is in the class itself, in the traditional atmosphere of formal education and under the guidance of a trained teacher, that the study of literature should be launched.

On no account should literary history be substituted for literature itself. These are two different things, the latter being a fine art and the former more nearly a science. In the language class, only an intimate acquaintance with works of literature is justifiable.

As language teachers introduce literature into their courses they cannot be too careful about what they choose for their students to read. What passes for literature in a great many cases would be given short shrift by most competent critics. It is likely that many of the works frequently read as literature in the languages taught in our schools today would be impossible to justify on any grounds other than crass expediency. One of the most serious professional obligations in our field is the establishing of criteria that will relegate to the scrap heap a vast quantity of printed matter that masquerades as literature in language classes.

THE COMPREHENSION OF LITERATURE

What does the reader bring to the study of his first literary work in a foreign language? (Its value to him is directly related to the background, the attitude, and the linguistic capacity with which he approaches it.) Acquaintance in the mother tongue with the plot, characters, atmosphere, and general significance of a story may well be an excellent preliminary step to the study of that story in the new language. This is comparable to the clarification of what the words stand for in an expression in the mother tongue before giving its equivalent in the language being learned. The relating of the two takes place at the psychological level that is for the most part preverbal, and is in no sense the same as translating, or matching one word with another.

By what steps may the language student gain what can be called knowledge on a literary level of a work of literature? By the same steps he presumably uses in reading a literary work in English. Reading between the lines—and this is most important in literary study—presupposes an accurate and comprehending reading of the lines themselves. In any story there will be first of all a plot in which something happens to someone, at some time and in some place. If answers to the simple questions "where" and "when" are not immediately obvious, that is good reason for the teacher to bring them up. If nothing happens, but all is atmosphere, mood, introspection, or background detail, this too is important and calls for observation and comment. Who are the characters? In what terms does the author present and describe them? What do they do or say? What is the manner of their speech and dress, their conduct toward people and affairs? What is the problem with which the characters are to deal, and how soon and in what terms is it made explicit? How does the sequence of events move on to a climax and a conclusion? How does character reveal itself or change as events proceed? In all this the author will naturally leave much to be inferred, but at the beginning it is of first importance to comprehend and restate, with whatever brevity and simplification seem appropriate, what the author says.

But there is a second step of even greater importance. The literary artist's words and statements will of course be disappointing to the reader who takes them merely at their face value. The author wishes not only to demonstrate and to prove, but to impress and persuade, and he counts upon the power of metaphor to make his words convey much more than they actually say. It is this quality that distinguishes literary writing from scientific writing, and it is in this area, where conceptions are woven by the reader about the concepts which the words convey, that the teacher plays a challenging and delicate role, one which calls for his full adherence to the author's intent and the student's need. His success is in no small measure dependent upon the care and thoroughness with which he has fulfilled his obligations in step one.

As a third step we may ask the question, "How well has the author accomplished what he set out to do?" No reader who has taken the first step and who has been encouraged and guided through the second is likely to remain entirely neutral when this question is asked. He will have enjoyed the experience of following the author's presentation or he will not, he will agree with the ideas set forth in the story or disagree, and he will have value judgments to give of the author's performance as an artist. Of course it is a prime responsibility of the teacher to provide the student with the means of making these criticisms *in the foreign language.*

Are these steps to be taken without recourse to the mother tongue? Most emphatically, yes. For a wholesale reversion to English at this point is not only an inglorious admission of defeat on the part of the teacher but a betrayal of the very principles upon which the study of contemporary language is founded. Psychologically, it is the re-establishment of a compound system in the learner's head, a short-circuiting of the bilingual process which the student has been at pains to develop. In a word, it is effectively, even though inadvertently, disloyal. If the student simply cannot "understand," then it is not a destructive tidal wave of English that is called for but a revision by the teacher of the degree of difficulty, the pace, and the minuteness of the literary study he proposes.

The selection of literature

To list the characteristics that are desirable in literary selections is one thing; to identify individual works in which they are found is quite another. This is true not only because of the limitations which the language learner necessarily presents as a reader, but far more so because of the complicated nature of any piece of literature. René Wellek and Austin Warren remind us in their book *Theory of Literature,* page 17, that "a literary work of art is not a simple object but rather a highly complex organization of a stratified character with multiple meanings and relationships." Because of his limited ability in language, the learner for some time profits most from pieces of modest dimensions and without special difficulties in structure or vocabulary. This does not mean that literary works chosen for his use should be "simplified," a Procrustean act that does unwonted violence to the author's intent and lulls the reader into a false sense of security. It might seem that plays, since they are intended principally for presentation within the limits of the audio-lingual band, would be ideal material for study by the language learner. Experience proves that this is not so—which is after all not surprising, for though plays give the illusion of conversation, they do not in fact represent the way people talk, as comparison with a tape recording of any dinner conversation will quickly show. On the other hand, there is general agreement, based on experience, that the short story is one of the literary genres best suited to the special needs of the language student. In it there is a common meeting ground for artistic integrity and the limited ability of the youthful learner. Yet poetry, plays, and longer prose should not be ruled out. Young people respond readily to emotional appeal, and they love a yarn; these facts must not be lost sight of when the choice of literary works is made.

Good taste is a characteristic of maturity, both chronological and psychological. The man of thirty who is transported by Bach's *Art of the Fugue* must remember that there was a time in his musical development when he did not so immediately or thoroughly enjoy this music. The devotee of Molière or the Sartre enthusiast must be willing to wait until his students possess that degree of mastery of language without which the attempt to assimilate such authors is futile. By the same token, however, he must be sure that his students experience something more than mere language if the principal goal of their efforts is to be achieved.

There is an important principle in aesthetics—one can hear overtones of it in the phrase *de gustibus non disputandum est* —which holds that beauty is not beautiful unless the observer finds it so. It is the task of the teacher to select literary works which, though they may not immediately appeal to students, will end by affording them both the practical and pleasurable returns to which they are entitled. In order to formulate and develop good taste, a teacher must "lead" his pupils in the choice and treatment of literary materials, but not at so great a distance that mutual contact is broken off. In literary selections chosen for the language class it is reasonable to demand utility for the learner, exemplary use of the medium employed, and aesthetic satisfaction from the content and its presentation. What is generally esteemed in the literary world, what the teacher likes, what the students like, and what lends itself to the special tempo and the specific needs of the moment mark off the limits within which the choice of literary works for the language classroom is to be made.

As a part of the academic world, the language class must ever be mindful of the importance of literature, while the literature course must be careful not to destroy learnings which the student has labored to attain. The return to English, to translation, to the idea that language is in essence what appears on a tombstone or a printed page, to the notion that somehow the student is incapable of grasping meaning in anything but his mother tongue, is a devastating revelation of the teacher's ignorance of his discipline. Both language and literature are parts of the verbal symbolization of experience we call discourse, and whoever teaches in these areas must see that their basic oneness is reflected in the activities required of the student.

Suggestions for further reading

Foerster, Norman, and others. *Literary Scholarship.* Chapel Hill, N.C.: University of North Carolina Press, 1941.

Morize, André. *Problems and Methods of Literary History.* Boston: Ginn, 1922.

Northeast Conference on the Teaching of Foreign Languages. *Reports of the Working Committees.* 1957.

Santayana, George. *The Sense of Beauty.* New York: Scribner, 1896.

Vigneron, Robert. *Explication de Textes, and Its Adaptation to the Teaching of Modern Languages.* Chicago: University of Chicago Press, 1934.

Wellek, René, and Austin Warren. *Theory of Literature.* New York: Harcourt, Brace & World, 1949.

OBJECTIVES OF THE LANGUAGE COURSE

8

We must decide at the start whether the intention is, on the one hand, to learn the new language in terms of itself or, on the other, in terms of its restatement in the student's mother tongue. If the latter, we are limited to the results of a compound system, in which the mother tongue is never relinquished. Language symbols are "decoded" from one system to another, and comprehension, meaning, and value are all in terms of the student's first language. In a word, he never leaves home. If the former, then the ultimate objective must be language as the native speaker uses it, both publicly and privately, and all that this use involves concerning sounds, graphic symbols, meaning, and cultural values. There must be some knowledge of a second language as it is possessed by a true bilinguist.

Decoding vs. bilingual learning

In our country today there is a place, altogether respectable, for learnings that include no more than the decoding process. For example, many a person enrolled in advanced studies finds himself in need of gleaning essential facts from books and articles in his field that are available only in a foreign language and also finds himself without the time required for an authentic course of language study. For such a student, a course in decoding is legitimate and, from the point of view of efficiency, desirable. There should be no illusions about the nature and results of such learnings. Above all, there should be no confusion between this type of course and one that presumes to lead the student along the linguistic paths of a new language. Rather, there must be the sharpest distinction between a course whose avowed objective is decoding and one whose goal is the learning of a new language.

Kinds of objectives

For an authentic language course, there are different kinds of objectives that claim attention, and these include the personal and the national, the utilitarian and the aesthetic. Some objectives are immediate, others long-range. A list of objectives is usually set forth in the college catalog or the school syllabus; these lists often resemble only vaguely what is experienced in the classroom itself. It seems right that both individual and national needs should be kept in mind in defining the objectives of language learning and also that both useful and pleasurable ends should be given full consideration. It would also seem possible to define objectives in such a way that what is publicly avowed can be seen in process of actual attainment while the student is at work.

FALSE SHORT-RANGE OBJECTIVES

Short-range and long-range objectives are often very different, but they should be related and the relationship made obvious. What connection there may be between the conjugation of an irregular verb and the advancement of international understanding is all too easily lost on the language learner at an early level.

The teacher's duty to link the immediate with the long-range is often deflected by false objectives, and it may clear the air if we note at once some of the mirages and will-o'-the-wisps that so easily lead astray. First among false objectives is the mere "knowing" of so many hundreds or thousands of words in the new language. Inquiry as to what is meant by "knowing" usually reveals that they have been paired one by one with English equivalents—something that bears no resemblance whatever to the mental processes of the speaker of the new language. And even if the words are "known" in terms of being distinguishable from other words of the new language, the knowledge of words alone is nil without an adequate control of structure to fit them into discourse. Any statement about knowledge of vocabulary in the new language must be accompanied by a statement concerning the nature of this knowledge and in addition by a list of the structural patterns in which the student can use these words. Better still would be a list of the situations in which the learner may be placed vis-à-vis a native speaker and acquit himself with credit.

Another false objective is the often repeated exhortation to "finish the book." If there were a magic that would equate the number of pages worked over with the quantity of learning acquired, the phrase might have some meaning. But there is no such magic, and we falsify the state of affairs by assuming that so much assigned and studied is so much learned—a striking example of the difference between teaching and learning. The falseness of this objective results largely from a conception of structure learning as linear, starting usually with the article and ending with the literary subjunctive. No such neat separation of forms, no such logical progression from one thing to another, is to be found in language in action. Linguistic forms as we use them do not arrange themselves as they appear in grammar books any more than butterflies arrange themselves in an open field in the way a naturalist displays them in a glass case. When language is in action, there is always a speaker. He is always somewhere, speaking to someone, about something. *Unless the facts of persons and places are taken into account as well as linguistic facts, we do not have the full dimension of language.* When the student is not trained to do with the elements of language what the speaker of that language does with them, his learnings are of little use. As an objective, "finishing the book" is far too remote from the behavior patterns that are in fact desired.

A third type of false objective is a high score on a standardized test. When high scores result from good training in language learning, nothing could be more desirable. But the nature of these tests is such that if the high score itself is taken as the objective and students are coached in the taking of the tests, measurement easily becomes inaccurate and language learning is seriously impaired. (See chapter 15 for a discussion of these tests.)

The most serious of all false objectives is translation. There is a place in the scheme of things for translation as a legitimate objective, but that place is not in the early levels of language learning. Translation is at once too difficult a task and too damaging to the learner to be a part of his activities until he has reached a high level of achievement in the second language. Nothing will short-circuit the language-learning process more quickly and turn a coordinated system into a compound system more effectively than premature attempts at matching one language with another.

LEGITIMATE SHORT-RANGE OBJECTIVES

What then are the immediate objectives that are legitimate? The first is training in listening comprehension. Although language sounds originate in the voice box of the throat and are modulated into recognizable speech by movements in the mouth, it is the ear that dominates the learning and use of speech sounds. Ear training must come first. The second objective is the reproduction by the tongue and adjacent organs of the speech sounds the ear has learned to recognize. It is to be understood that the sounds are not selected for drill in isolation but are learned as they occur in the normal patterns of discourse. A third objective is reading, that is, the recognition of speech symbols, not as sound waves striking the ear, but as graphic signs on a printed page. Along with this is a fourth objective, writing, the ability to reproduce these graphic symbols in accordance with accepted standards in the new language. These immediate objectives imply three others: first, control of the structures of sound, form, and order in the new language; second, acquaintance with vocabulary items that bring content into these structures; and third, meaning, in terms of the significance these verbal symbols have for those who speak the language natively.

It is well to remind ourselves of the great differences, both physiological and psychological, that distinguish each of these skills from the others. One network of organs functions in hearing, a different set in speaking, a third in reading, and still a fourth in writing. All these work in harmony in normal language behavior, yet one of them may receive training while others remain undeveloped. The person who can understand a language but cannot speak it is familiar to all, and every child is adept at hearing and speaking his mother tongue long before he can read it and write it.

LONG-RANGE OBJECTIVES

When focus is shifted from the foreground to points at a greater distance, the long-range objectives appear in sharp outline. One of these is the great promontory, literature, the art of words, which looms so large in the academic world within which the learnings we are discussing take place. Another is cultural insight; by *cultural* we mean all the belief and behavior patterns of the societal group as they appear in arts and crafts, in tales and myths, in work and play, and in religion and everyday life. Neither an appreciation of literature nor cultural insight is fully attainable unless the learner has won his way past the foothills of the language skills. Having done so, not only are these major objectives within his reach, but from them he may get a better perspective of his own language, culture, and literature. The new vantage point permits an appraisal of their true character that is denied anyone who has not made this journey. Furthermore, like an astronomer measuring the stars or a mariner plotting his course, he now has two points rather than one from which he may calculate the achievements and contemplate the problems of humanity. In every language course worthy of the name, each of these objectives, with appropriate sequence, proportion, and emphasis, must play an important and discernible role.

From these immediate and long-range objectives there are outcomes that benefit the learner as an individual while he is a student and in later life. His returns are in the development of skills, attitudes, and sensibilities. The first represent what he may know and be able to do with regard to the way the foreign people use the language. The second represent his informed and sympathetic appraisal of the cultural patterns of the new country, especially when they differ from his own. The third comprise such humanistic ideals as enjoyment of the literature and other art forms of the foreign country, a keener awareness of the qualities of his own language and culture, and a deeper insight into the nature of meaning and the role of verbal symbols in the functioning of the human mind.

As these personal learnings increase, we add to the pools of potential that serve our national needs in the economic, the military, the diplomatic, and the academic worlds. Such are the objectives and the outcomes that should orient any course in second-language learning. They should be constantly in the minds of those who plan such learnings and those who benefit from them.

Suggestions for further reading

Carroll, John B. *The Study of Language.* Cambridge, Mass.: Harvard University Press, 1953.

Mallinson, Vernon. *Teaching a Modern Language.* London: Heinemann, 1953.

Saporta, Sol, ed. *Psycholinguistics: A Book of Readings.* New York: Holt, 1961.

UNESCO. *The Teaching of Modern Languages.* Paris: UNESCO, 1955.

CONTINUITY FOR THE LEARNER

9

Human interest in language being what it is, getting a student through the initial stages of learning a second language is relatively easy. What is hard is planning the sequences of learnings which come afterward. There are, of course, many reasons for this. To a great extent, the weakness in planned continuity for the language learner is related to the heterogeneous make-up of the American educational system. In our country there is no centralized national organization to which a school or college can turn for dependable recommendations about the content and sequence of language courses. Such agencies, to which one might look for guidance concerning standards, objectives, methods, course content, and continuity from one year's work to another, have traditionally been frowned upon and discouraged in America. A federal bureau of standards that can recommend the design of electric light fixtures or the size of liquid containers, yes, but such a bureau for standards of educational procedure, no. (Of course no manufacturer is obliged to follow these standards; they are merely there if he wishes to make use of them. Somehow this point is lost sight of when educational standards are considered.) In so far as there have been recommendations about the study of foreign languages by educational organizations that presume to speak with a national voice, the advice until recently has been: foreign languages are not worth the time spent on them; the sooner the whole matter is neglected and forgotten, the better. The language teachers' professional organizations have of course been heard from, but the most important and influential of them, the Modern Language Association, publicly reaffirmed its interest in language teaching only recently; between the years 1917 and 1947 it was officially interested only in research and scholarship. To be sure, two agencies have been continually at work whose activities have a nationwide effect upon foreign-language teaching: the College Entrance Examination Board and the textbook publishers; however, neither of these can be said to have either the competence or the desire to offer official guidance in matters of curriculum or continuity. For the first time in recent decades, awareness of all the problems involved found a most comprehensive and penetrating expression in William R. Parker's 132-page booklet, *The National Interest and Foreign Languages*, a discussion paper first published in 1954 (it has since been revised twice).

Almost simultaneously, from quite another quarter, the national conscience spoke forth in FLES (pronounced to rhyme with *chess*), which stands for Foreign Languages in the Elementary Schools, a postwar phenomenon of country-wide proportions whose existence was officially recognized in 1952 by the Office of Education in Washington, D.C., and the Modern Language Association in New York. Caught in the cross fire of Parker's discussion paper and the FLES programs, responsible officers acknowledged the need for a revision of our stated national attitude, as may be seen in *Modern Foreign Languages in the High School* (1958), edited by Marjorie C. Johnston, and "Modern Foreign Languages in the Comprehensive Secondary School" published in the *Bulletin* of the National Association of Secondary-School Principals, June 1, 1959. The National Defence Education Act of 1958 has been increasingly effective in broadening and strengthening our language programs at all levels of instruction. As a result, we now find new and vigorous action in many areas of language learning, and with this an increasing need to provide for steady and consistent growth as the student's competence improves.

Factors in continuity

The problem of continuity needs to be considered, first of all, from the point of view of the learner. As the student moves up the educational ladder he changes in many ways and finds himself at work in a number of different kinds of environment. He begins by being in an elementary school, later he finds himself in one of several types of secondary schools, and eventually he becomes a part of a college community. At any given moment, he is at a certain grade level or year level, with a certain degree of achievement. He possesses a set of abilities and interests that are characteristic of him at this point, and he fits into a schedule designed for his age. In the second place, continuity involves subject matter, which must be presented to the learner not only with due respect for his capacities and interests, but also with concern for the sequence in which the skills are to be learned, for the proportion of time allotted to each at various levels, and for the spiral presentation of structure and the widening circle of vocabulary—with the total integration of all of these continually in mind. Thirdly, in each type of school the language learnings are a part of a larger curriculum which is organized in ways that are suitable to and characteristic of a total pattern of school life. Often, there are marked changes as the learner moves from one to another.

Is it possible to plan a schedule of learnings that will successfully involve all these manifold factors? How can effective continuity take into account the many differences in the student himself, in the classrooms which he attends, and in the areas of the discipline he is studying?

Kinds of learners

Fortunately, amid all these variables, it *is* possible to find some constants and to single out certain factors that simplify what at first seems hopelessly complex. We have seen that there are in reality only two kinds of courses, one leading to decoding, the other to a degree of bilingualism. Given the diverse ages and interests of the students concerned, how many kinds of learners present themselves in a language classroom? Again the answer is *only two*: those who are at the age of eleven or twelve or younger, and those who are older.

Certain differences distinguish these two kinds of learners. Children accept language behavior as a normal part of their activities, while their elders, especially adolescents, do so far less readily. Children accept a new language system without feeling an urge to relate it word by word to the mother tongue, whereas the older student has a strong tendency to do this. Children readily engage in language exchange without feeling a need to analyze what they are saying, something that their elders have long since learned is very important in school. Children retain what they have heard and repeated without a sense of insecurity, even though it has not been written down; older people have been thoroughly conditioned in our educational system to a dependence upon reading and writing. Finally, children are much nearer than their elders to an age in which everyone has a full capacity to learn any language or any culture. As the curve of learning by imitation declines with increasing age, the curve of learning by analysis rises.

As is well known, FLES programs of second-language learning for children are now in progress in many schools. FLES is essentially an adaptation of the supreme psychological fact of the learning of the mother tongue: that any normal child can learn any language with nothing to go on save what he was born with and the language in action of those about him. If we recognize that the learner of a second language already knows one language well, and that the learning is not to take place in the home, nor within the culture in which the language is in current use, how much of the certainty that the child will learn the mother tongue still applies in this new and different learning situation? It turns out that the degree of certainty is surprisingly high, provided that the right conditions are created and the right things done. From a study of many programs that vary considerably with regard to starting point, time schedule, course content, and continuity, there emerges a pattern that appears to typify the best that may be observed and recommended.

There are many considerations that suggest the third or fourth grade as an optimum starting point. On the one hand, the child of eight has already become familiar with the school world in which he is to spend so much of his time. He has already become literate in his mother tongue—an intellectual achievement of immense significance—and has by now a sharpened sense of awareness of the business of learning. On the other hand, he is still young enough to enjoy talk for its own sake, to imitate new sounds with an almost mirror-like accuracy, and to accept and use new expressions without feeling a strong urge to take them apart or to compare them word for word with the mother tongue. Time will bring about changes in these factors, and the beginning of a second language may as a result be more difficult if he postpones his start until later years.

There is general agreement that the best time schedule for the elementary school program is a fifteen- to thirty-minute class daily, occurring in regular school hours and as early in the day as possible. Language achievement at this level is necessarily limited in extent but is of a special quality not attainable later, and will be enhanced or negated according to the learnings that follow in subsequent years. The chief concerns with regard to continuity are that the skills of hearing and speaking must not be permitted at any point to become dormant, that the learner be given full credit for accomplishment in these skills (traditional measurement in terms of grammar and translation are wholly inadequate for this), and that these acquired skills be fully integrated with those of reading, writing, and structure control that will of course be encountered as learning proceeds. The learner's participation in the new language experience is in terms of his involvement in the threefold interplay of hearer, speaker, and situation. This is done by making only the slightest use of the mother tongue, by resolutely avoiding the traditional analysis of grammar as well as translation from the foreign language into English, and by requiring that the skills of reading and writing be made to wait until the learner is sufficiently secure in hearing and speaking the new language; this usually means in the elementary school about two years' experience before reading and writing are begun, and then the material read and written must consist of what is thoroughly familiar to ear and tongue. Visual aids, especially pictures, are effectively employed at this level, but audial devices are of limited usefulness in FLES. Children do not readily accept the substitution of a machine for a person in the give and take of talk. This fact should give pause to those who recommend courses on television for children in the elementary school.

The preparation of material to be used in FLES classes is a serious and difficult matter of great complexity. It requires the collaboration of experienced and expert teachers whose efforts must be modified and reinforced by constant reference to three adjacent disciplines: descriptive linguistics (with regard to language), psychology (with regard to learning), and cultural anthropology (with regard to meaning). Not much that is currently in print for use in FLES meets these requirements.

To qualify as a teacher of these classes one must of course understand and like children and should have a sufficient degree of language competence to model the learnings that are desired. He or she must also have made a special study of the discipline of second-language learning and must have an acquaintance with the American school world at the elementary school level. FLES teachers now in service usually either are specialists who have trained for teaching positions of this kind, or are high school (occasionally, college) teachers who can readily accept the protean transformation required by the change in level. Some are classroom teachers at the elementary level who have acquired the necessary language competence and have received training in the teaching of a second language to children.

The outcomes of FLES are of at least three kinds: language achievement, shifts in attitude (toward those who speak the new language), and individual growth. The first of these is readily apparent and accessible to measurement. The second and third are no less apparent, but when we wish to measure and express changes in attitude and in personality we lack the devices and the neat symbols that seem adequate when we are dealing with language achievement. For the time being, evaluations of FLES concerning attitudes and the improvement of self will probably have to be content with anecdotal records.

Important as it is for teaching language at the elementary school level, FLES is no less so for having shed much light upon the nature of language learning at the secondary and college levels. The basic elements found in FLES coincide with those of any language course at any level founded upon an understanding of second-language learning in formal education. Anyone with an intimate knowledge of the possibilities and achievements of the FLES programs soon realizes how thoroughly the language courses as traditionally taught at the upper levels must be revised, not only if justice is to be done to the products of FLES, but also if these advanced courses are ever to accomplish even a modest share of what is claimed for them. A wholly new understanding of the language skills and the order in which they may be mastered; of the harmful effects of book, grammar, and translation when ineptly used; of the radical difference between the learning of Latin and of a contemporary language; of the importance of a model to go by, a person to talk with, and a suitable situation to talk about; of the relationship of talk to writing and of language to culture—all these are concerns of FLES.

Streams and levels in school language learning

As we look at the total perspective of continuity in which FLES now plays and will continue to play an important role, we become aware of the need for a comprehensive plan that will include the span of years from the elementary school to the senior high school. It is of course idle to think that any proposed general plan will fit all, or even nearly all, local circumstances. But this fact should not be allowed to deter the elaboration of a possible and recommendable design that may then be studied and adapted with necessary modifications at the local level. In the United States at present and in the foreseeable future, there are and will continue to be three principal points at which a program for effective learning of a second language may be started. These are: grade 3 or 4 in the elementary school, grade 7 (the threshold of the junior high school), and grade 9. The beginning of a second language in college is "schoolwork" that must somehow be done at college level; it must follow the program outlined for schools as best it can. The beginning of a *third* language in college is an entirely different matter. This is a responsibility the colleges have always willingly accepted and they will continue to do so. But they have every right to expect that the learnings in the second language shall have been of substantial quantity and quality.

If language study is to begin at these separate points and continue until the outcomes are fully rewarding, we must recognize three streams or tracks: grades 3 to 12, grades 7 to 12, and grades 9 to 12. As we know from observing the preschool child, the subject matter of language learning can be suited to the age, ability, and interest of the learner. The basic patterns of phonology, morphology, and syntax are identical, whether the speaker is six years old or sixty. Since similar amounts of language learning are to be acquired at different ages, in different schools, and in differing lengths of time, some word other than *year* is needed to express in common terms the learnings attempted and the results achieved.

The word *level* is proposed as such a term, and subject matter may be divided up into a number of such levels, any one of which contains elements that may be learned under a variety of conditions. Implied is the assumption that the start is a serious one whenever it is made. The familiar terms *elementary, intermediate,* and *advanced* indicate a general feeling that there is a language foundation composed of distinguishable levels, upon which further work in either language or literature may be based.

If we put together the concept of levels and the various grades at which the learnings may take place, we arrive at the following outline for precollege work:

Stream A

GRADE $\left.\begin{array}{c}3\\4\\5\\6\end{array}\right\}$ FLES (I)

Stream B

$\left.\begin{array}{cc}7\\8\end{array}\right\}$ II GRADE $\left.\begin{array}{cc}7\\8\end{array}\right\}$ I

Stream C

9	III	9	II	GRADE 9	I
10	IV	10	III	10	II
11	V	11	IV	11	III
12	VI	12	V	12	IV

In an attempt to give the word *level* a precise definition, we may say that it contains the amount of learning that can be achieved in an upper grade of the secondary school in classes that meet five times a week and that are at least forty minutes in length. We assume that the teacher is fully competent and that the class is composed of around twenty able and willing learners. There are good reasons for thinking that the content of a level so defined can be learned by college students in a semester, provided the same requirements are met, especially if they are learning not their first foreign language but an additional one. There are also many reasons for thinking that a level can be accomplished in the junior high school in the seventh and eighth grades together. In addition, there are good reasons for thinking that the first level can be accomplished in the elementary school if the pupils are in the language class during the third, fourth, fifth, and sixth grades, reciting daily, and learning through the use of materials that contain the linguistic content of what is used in the upper schools, but that differ, of course, in vocabulary and idea content.

We should note that one of the most important characteristics of the level as conceived of here is that it has a dual nature, since it is composed partly of code and partly of meaning. In whatever stream the learner may be working (that is, whatever his age may be) the code element will be the same for any given level. He may thus expect to encounter, at the appropriate time, such linguistic matters as the singular and the plural, the present and the past, the affirmative and the negative, the active and the passive, the interrogative and the command, the conditional and the relative, no matter how old or how young he may be. It is the *meaning* element that will differ from one stream to another, and the meaning content of learning materials must respect the chronological age, the psychological development, and the intellectual interests of the student to the greatest possible degree.

Let us suppose that in an ideal course in language learning there are, in all, six levels, and that at the end of the first two—whenever that may be completed—we place a marker and call the preceding levels the *basic course*. At the end of the fourth level we may place another marker and call those levels the *language requirement*. At the end of the sixth level we may place a third marker and say that it indicates the fulfillment of the *advanced requirement*, this being in general equivalent to what is currently known as an advanced placement program. Such a detailed plan is at present being actively considered by many groups of teachers and administrators in different parts of the United States. Whether or not we can in fact fit our learner's needs into such a program remains to be discovered. It appeals to many as a proposal or hypothesis that merits an honest trial until we know whether or not it is practicable.

The close inspection of such a perspective immediately poses a prime question: What is meant by the basic course? Certainly at the present time, there is no clear answer to be given. It may well be found within the boundaries of a "good to excellent" control of the phonology and of the most frequent forms and structures in the target language, on the one hand, and, on the other, of the realities of the learning situation that characterize the framework of formal education within which the language teacher must work. In such a course it is wise to emphasize a representative sampling of all the norms of face-to-face communication and to be less concerned about completeness and depth in any one linguistic area. Naturally, the receptive skills will be more amply developed than the productive skills. If the two-level basic course seems to fall somewhere between the very difficult and the impossible, it should be remembered that there are now many more things in the teacher's favor than there were before. There is a vast ground swell of public support for second-language learning. Teachers are now being better trained, materials are constantly being improved, and many technological aids, especially the tape recorder, are widely available. It would appear reasonable and well advised to make every effort to create such a course in view of present circumstances.

It may help us better to understand the nature and content of the basic course if we review what we may expect of our learner in terms of language competence at the end of each of the levels we have described. At the end of Level I, he is able to repeat the contents of a brief incident as he hears it spoken phrase by phrase and then is able to retell this incident after repeating it in this way. He can participate in a conversation about any one of a variety of situations. He can read aloud a printed text or write it from dictation. He can rewrite a simple narrative, making changes in time or point of view. He can do orally and in writing a wide variety of exercises that involve changes in number, gender, word order, tense, replacement, negation, interrogation, command, request, comparison, or possession. At the end of Level II, he is in control of all the elements of the sound-system, and can recognize and use those patterns of expression that are most frequently found in face-to-face exchange. He can comprehend through listening and reading any subject matter comparable in content and difficulty to what he has learned. He is able to write all that he can say. He has first-hand knowledge of brief samples of cultural and literary prose, and he is able to converse in simple language about them. When he has this degree of achievement we may say that he has completed the basic course.

At the end of Level III, the learner may be expected to demonstrate a continued accurate control of the sound-system and a wider acquaintance with the types of utterances that are characteristic of spoken language. He can read aloud from a text that is comparable in content and style to what he has learned. He can understand through listening a variety of texts prepared for comprehension by the ear. He can write from dictation a text he has previously studied for the details of its written forms. He can comprehend through reading all but the low-frequency patterns of syntax and the unusual vocabulary in printed texts of reasonable difficulty. He has first-hand knowledge of one to two hundred pages of reading matter of a cultural and literary nature, and he is able to discuss them orally and to write acceptable sentences and paragraphs about their contents.

In Level IV he can read aloud almost any nonfamiliar text, and can write from dictation passages of literary prose, sometimes after a preliminary reading and sometimes without such a reading. He can converse with a fluent speaker on a topic such as a play seen, a novel read, a trip taken, or a residence lived in. He can read a text and in writing summarize its contents and comment on the ideas expressed. In a page or two of text, especially selected for the purpose, he can discover and comment upon a certain number of points of usage and meaning that are culturally significant. He can receive oral instructions about an assignment to be written: its nature, its contents, to whom addressed, its form, its length, its style of presentation; then write it. He will have read several hundred pages of literary selections including novels, plays, short stories, and poems, as well as other writings chosen for their cultural importance. At this point we say that he has fulfilled the language requirement.

The content of Levels V and VI must vary to meet the needs of individual students. For many, a minimal course that will maintain and strengthen the language control that has been achieved, meeting perhaps twice a week and, if necessary, with no outside preparation, can be recommended. This will enable students to keep alive the skills they have perfected and will make the resumption of full-time effort in language learning much easier in adjusting subsequently to a college program.

For most students, a course involving the usual schedule and curriculum is best.

Those students whose work is exceptionally satisfactory and who can afford the time required can do in the twelfth grade the type of work that is now done in many colleges in standard courses for freshmen. Happily, in recent years there has been a concerted effort on the part of many schools and colleges to develop a program of this kind, not only in languages but in all academic subjects. A modest but increasing number of students now participate in the so-called Advanced Placement Program. This program, administered by the College Entrance Examination Board, outlines material for study and gives examinations that enable a successful student to be given upper-class status (and sometimes receive degree credit) in a subject as if he had done the work as a regularly enrolled freshman. In our field the program is, very properly, linguistic, cultural, and literary, and, rightly understood, it can only strengthen and be strengthened by a wisely progressive series of language learnings upon which it is based. It must not be thought, however, that in setting up criteria for content and measurement for Levels V and VI this program is at the same time making recommendations for the content and methods of teaching at earlier levels. The trained athlete can perform many feats of strength and dexterity which the novice cannot attempt without risk of injury. Again a warning must be sounded about the danger even through inadvertence of transforming a slowly developing coordinate system into a compound system by asking that it do too much too soon.[1]

Implications

Remembering the character and content of the basic course and recalling that it requires in all cases at least two years and often more, we perceive the supreme necessity of its being programed as a continuous, unified whole. Not only should

---

[1] The description in the foregoing five paragraphs of competence by levels follows closely the statements made in *Language Instruction: Perspective*

there be the most careful integration in the materials themselves, there should also be a comparable relationship in classroom procedures and techniques in both levels. This is especially true when the learner finds himself working under the direction of two or more different teachers and in quite different types of schools. If the learner is following Stream A, it is of the utmost importance that the Level II in which he works in the junior high school be especially designed to complement the Level I of his elementary school years. It is also clear from these recommendations that if streams are to be mixed and those who have started at different grade levels are to work together in the same class, this cannot be done until Level III, that is, after a basic course suited to one stream or another has been completed.

The continuity of the levels as thus described implies that the student should stick to one language through Level IV before *abandoning* it in favor of another. This of course does not preclude *adding* another language if it is desirable and possible to do so. The learner's program should be so articulated that, with appropriate review, he may continue in September at the point where he stopped the previous June.

To ask these things is to ask that elementary schools know what secondary schools are going to teach the pupils they send them, and that secondary schools know what learnings elementary pupils have had before they receive them; it is to ask that high schools and colleges exchange the same sort of reciprocal information. If this seems like asking too much, let us recall that it is, in effect, precisely what *is* done, except that it is done in a roundabout way by the use and abuse of placement tests, entrance examinations, and college catalogs. Instruments designed to give information to students about courses and to teachers about student achievement are made to serve as guides for curriculum content and classroom procedure at successively lower levels. *It is a professional responsibility of*

---

and Prospectus. Nelson Brooks, Charles F. Hockett, and Everett V. O'Rourke. Sacramento, Calif.: Bulletin of the California Department of Education. XXXII, 4 (November 1963), 21–24.

the most serious kind to arrange for the exchange of such vital information in some form other than the indirect and enigmatic disclosures currently in vogue.

Curriculum content

Having indicated above the outcomes that may be expected at the end of each level, it may be useful now to outline briefly the curriculum content of each one. In Level I, great attention is paid to the sound-system of the new language, that is, the individual vowel and consonant sounds as they occur in meaningful utterances and the intonation patterns or melody of the new language that acts as such an important ingredient in meaning. Much attention is given to types of sentences that are found frequently in face-to-face communication. The student may learn and practice these in terms of dialogues, or of basic sentences, or of narrative, and then learn to adapt their contents to his own thoughts in communicating with those about him. The two basic skills of listening and speaking, the audio-lingual skills, are given greatest attention throughout this level. It is usually wise to begin with a few weeks of purely audio-lingual learning before introducing reading and writing. The last are minimized, however, as is the learning of an extensive vocabulary, the emphasis throughout being upon control of phonology and high-frequency patterns of syntax.

In Level II, all that has characterized Level I is pursued vigorously, but now with the intention of familiarizing the learner with all the commonest types of utterance that are heard as we speak. By this we mean statements, negations, questions, pronoun substitutions, directions, requests, comparisons, conditional sentences, sentences involving relative forms, sentences involving the subjunctive mood, and the like. More attention is paid to the acquiring of vocabulary, and Level II is not ended until the student has had an opportunity to work with and absorb in depth at least a few samples of literary writing.

Now we say the basic course is complete and go on to Level III. Conceiving of the learning of structure in the form of a spiral, we take our way around the grammar circle once more, this time with a concern for those pattern variations that could not be included before and also with a concern for those syntactical patterns that are more likely to be found lying on a printed page than passing through the air between speakers. Much attention is now paid to increasing the student's vocabulary in terms of lexical items and idiomatic expressions, these being learned, of course, *not* in isolation or in prepared lists but in relation to a context already read and discussed. Word study as such is important, although this must not involve a return to the student's mother tongue. Instead, words are defined, put into families, paired with their likes and opposites, or related to each other in free association—all this in the target language. The student learns to write sentences that are similar to a model but that contain different lexical items. He learns to write a paragraph that is first outlined orally and then put into writing or one that is the result of formulating the answers to a list of questions.

Before the end of Level III, the student will have read and worked in this fashion with many pages of text chosen for their cultural content or literary merit. Level IV continues all the activities of Level III. Now reading assignments can be longer and more attention can be paid to writing sentences and paragraphs. In addition, the student is now trained in the writing of compositions. This activity too must be carefully modeled by the teacher. There is lengthy oral exploration of the subject to be written about and of ways in which it can be developed: sample sentences that might be used in it, statements that might be made as a point of departure, ways in which the composition is to follow sequentially from one thing to the next, and how the composition is to be drawn together in a conclusion or summary at the end. But notice this important point: not until this audio-lingual exploration of the composition has been followed through in class is the student directed to *write* the composition, making what he will write his own, yet working within the framework that has been sketched out. Thus at the end of four levels of work the learner arrives at the degree of competence that we recognize as fulfilling the language requirement. Long before the student reaches the end even of Level III it will be apparent both to him and to his teachers that he will have acquired from this kind of curriculum all that ever was acquired in a traditional presentation of a modern foreign language, and in addition he has a control over the language as communication that was forever denied him when the language was talked about in English, translated from and into English, and incessantly related structurally and semantically to English in all its aspects.

What happens in class

Throughout the basic course, the teacher spends the first few minutes of class time talking in the foreign language while the students listen, as a stimulus in activating their internalized language behavior. This "preamble" relates at first to situations similar to but not identical with those in the materials being memorized and therefore contains both what is familiar and what is not. As time goes on, a greater number of references that are quite new may be introduced. In general, there is no formal check on the students' comprehension, the purpose being principally to help them put English aside and begin to "think" in the new language. (A list of topics suitable for such discussions is given in chapter 6, pages 90–95.) This is followed by choral response, questionnaire, discussion, pattern practices, and oral give-and-take between teacher and students and between one student and another, both with old material and with new. Pattern practice that includes drills on new and partly new structural forms and vocabulary is a part of every class, though not continued too long at a time. Oral drills may be followed by written exercises; review of known material is followed by excursions into new areas. Needless to say, all this is in the foreign language, with books and printed matter only occasionally used and as little English spoken as possible. If any part of the class is conducted in English, it is brief and at the *end* of the period. This assures the learner of what is available to him nowhere except in his language class: a sustained period of time in which the target language is the sole means of communication with those about him.

In Level III a good language class proceeds without any English, without translations, with books closed most of the time, with structures constantly used but rarely explained, with all the language skills involved, with events and ideas retold and enlarged upon, and with a great deal of participation on the part of all members of the class. After initial remarks by the teacher there are questionnaires, discussions, dialogues, word study, quizzes, oral résumés, comments, drills, and exercises in all the various types of language behavior that are within the competence of the students. In Level IV, much attention is given to writing as well as to reading and vocabulary study. In this level are added oral reports previously assigned to individual students, followed by comments from the class. Toward the end of Level IV there may also be added a few special exercises in translation, in which the techniques of translation are described and illustrated and passages for translation both into and from the target language are assigned.

Typical class programs

Presented below are outlines of class programs that would be typical of both an earlier and a later part of each of the first four levels. Note that there is a variety of activities in every class. The amount of time appropriate to each is suggested by a proposed number of minutes.

Level I (first quarter)

MINUTES
- 3   A. Preamble by teacher.
- 2   B. Review of material already well learned.
- 10   C. Review and further learning of material only recently presented.
- 10   D. Presentation of new material.
- 10–15   E. Pattern practice of new material using familiar techniques.
- 5   F. Pattern practice using a new technique.
- 5   G. An ABC(D) listening comprehension quiz. (See item type 1, page 217.)

Level I (third quarter)

MINUTES	
3	A. Preamble by teacher.
2	B. Repetition exercise (choral and individual response).
3–5	C. Review of material well known.
7–10	D. New material in process of being learned.
7–10	E. New material presented for the first time.
13–15	F. Pattern practice using familiar techniques.
5	G. Written quiz in form of pattern drill.

Level II (first quarter)

MINUTES	
3	A. Preamble by teacher.
2	B. Repetition exercise based on recently learned material.
10–12	C. Questionnaire and discussion based on reading material.
15	D. Pattern practice: replacement and rejoinder.
5	E. Word study. (See page 218.)
5	F. Reading exercise modeled phrase by phrase by the teacher.
5–8	G. Quiz, dehydrated sentences. (See item type 14, page 219.)

Level II (third quarter)

MINUTES	
3	A. Preamble by teacher.
2	B. Repetition exercise based on outside reading assignment.
10	C. Questionnaire on and discussion of reading assignment.
15	D. Pattern practice: pronoun substitutions and relayed message.
5	E. Word study.
5	F. Reading exercise based on text not previously studied.
10	G. Dictation based on text studied for this purpose.

Level III (first quarter)

MINUTES	
3	A. Repetition exercise based on day's assignment.
2	B. Résumé of previous class discussion.

15	C. Questionnaire and discussion of day's assignment.
5	D. Word study.
10–15	E. Pattern practice: form and position of adjective and idioms with reflexive pronouns.
5	F. Comments on assignment for next time.
5	G. Quiz: fill-ins in a passage selected from day's reading assignment. (See item type 10, pages 218–19.)

Level III (third quarter)

MINUTES
3	A. Preamble by teacher.
15	B. Questionnaire and discussion of day's assignment.
5	C. Word study.
2	D. Pattern practice: tense change in conditional sentences.
3	E. Pattern practice: integration exercise.
10	F. Oral preparation of paragraph to be written in class.
10	G. Writing of paragraph.

Level IV (first quarter)

MINUTES
5	A. Recitation of memory passage.
10	B. Questionnaire and discussion.
5	C. Word study.
10	D. Oral report by student (prepared in advance).
5	E. Comments by class.
10	F. Pattern practice (first oral, then written).
5	G. Discussion of writing to be done as homework.

Level IV (third quarter)

MINUTES
10	A. Oral report by student.
5	B. Comments by class.
10	C. Questionnaire on and discussion of day's reading.
5	D. Word study.
5	E. Discussion of techniques of translation.
10	F. Translation exercise (written).
5	G. Class discussion of translation exercise.

Establishing the ground rules

The "ground rules" of the course must be clearly established as it begins. The student should know what he is expected to do and not to do, and why. A preliminary class (or even two) spent in explanations of this kind will bring rich rewards in the months that follow. It should be made clear to the learner that a class is a drill session in which books are little used, English is inactive, lengthy explanations of grammar are circumvented, and the classroom is filled with the sounds of the new language, modeled by the teacher and repeated by the students until they can talk with the teacher and with each other in speech patterns that are linguistically and culturally authentic. In order to play his role properly, the student must understand at the beginning of Level I (and be so reminded at least once or twice during each succeeding level) *why* he is not allowed to use English, *why* translation is not only pointless but harmful until one has acquired a considerable store of knowledge in the two languages concerned, *why* he should not have constant access to open books as he learns to communicate in the target language, *why* classroom time should not be spent in endless explanations of structure when what is really wanted is a control of structure and practice in it.

The following points may be found helpful in discussing ground rules on the first day in Level I and may well be referred to again at a later time when the learner is more advanced.

1. A foreign language is traditionally studied by relating it and comparing it to English at all times. The learner is mainly concerned with grammar rules and examples, long lists of vocabulary, and the translation of sentences and texts. It is also possible to learn a foreign language in a very different way, even in American classrooms. Through hearing, comprehending, and speaking the new or "target" language from the start, with English used only a little by the teacher, just to make meaning clear, the mother tongue can be made inactive. The student's mind soon learns to

work almost entirely with its small but growing store of the target language without going back to English. The kind of language learned at first is the kind of language used in face-to-face commuciation.

2. The aim of this new kind of course is to learn to do with the target language what is done with it by those who speak it natively. This means listening, understanding, imitating, repeating, speaking, and learning by heart all the elements of language that must come automatically.

3. The students first learn by imitating what is modeled by the teacher (and also, if facilities permit, what is modeled on the tape in the language laboratory and on the take-home disc). Learning from texts and books follows a little later.

4. There are four language skills, all very different: listening, speaking, reading, writing. Listening and speaking go together in face-to-face communication, while reading and writing go together when language appears on paper. But these skills are also paired in another way. Two of them are *receptive:* listening and reading; we use them when language comes to us from a speaker or a writer and we merely receive the message that is sent. The other two are the *productive* skills, speaking and writing, which are used when the individual sends the message and produces language on his own. The receptive skills are the easiest to learn and are the most enduring, whereas the productive skills are more difficult, need constant practice, and tend to diminish rapidly if not used. However, we need to know a far greater amount of language receptively in order to understand the greatest possible number of speakers and writers. Our control of the productive skills need not be so extensive, but it must be stronger and more direct, so that the words and structures we wish to use are the right ones and are quickly available. If not, we make mistakes and are often not even understood.

5. Language in action runs in a double stream of code and meaning. The code is made up of four strands: sound, order, form, and choice. This is quickly seen if we take the simple statement "It's a beautiful day; let's enjoy it" and distort

each of these strands one at a time. In doing so, we might, for example, hear something like this:

(Sound) Eets ay bootiful day; let'z anjoy eet.
(Order) Beautiful day it's a; it enjoy let's.
(Form)   It's a beautiful days; let's enjoys it.
(Choice) It's a frabjous dight; let's adlish it.

Of course there can be code without meaning—any foreign-language broadcast we do not understand proves that. It is quite possible to attach the code of the new language to the meaning of the mother tongue. Yet this is but a very small part of what we wish to do with a foreign language. We wish most of all to know what the new code means to those whose language it is. So we must learn new meanings to go with the new code. This is the purpose of the study of culture, to learn to relate the new language code to the thoughts and habits and lives of its native speakers.

6. The first three strands of code—sound, order, and form—are the grammar. The fourth, choice, is vocabulary. We first learn the grammar by actual use of communication, thinking of rules only after having learned many examples very well. During this time we pay relatively little attention to the building of a large vocabulary. When grammar has been well learned (after two levels of study) the time comes to emphasize the learning of vocabulary and idiom. This is done by selecting and working with a great number of such items as found in the context of sentences in the stories being read.

7. There is little point in asking or explaining "why" grammar and vocabulary are as they are, at least until the grammar and vocabulary in question are familiar through actual use. Comparable questions in nature study would be "Why does a pine have needles?" and "Why does an oak have leaves?" That the one has needles and the other leaves is clear enough, but *why* this is so is a very different matter and if answerable at all had better be left unasked, at least until the learner can tell the two apart.

8. In order to help students put English aside in the foreign-

language class, thus clearing the way for the target language, and in order not to waste time in useless explanations, the rule will be established that students will never use English in class. Nor the teacher either, except occasionally to make meaning clear or to show how certain exercises are to be done. Now and then, the teacher will announce some minutes before the end of the period that the foreign-language class is over—and will then listen to and answer any and all questions in English. This is a welcome relief and gives ample opportunity for such explanations as are vital to success.

9. Since language is primarily what is said between persons and only secondarily what is written or printed, only the spoken language will be learned during the beginning weeks. The printed texts of the early lessons will be introduced when their content has been well learned orally. From then on, all four skills will be fully developed, separately and together, although reading and writing will not be strongly emphasized until the third level.

10. It is in general futile to try to translate from one language into another until one knows a good deal about both. To do so too soon tends to diminish the small stock of the target language that has been gained. This is why translation is postponed until well into the fourth level of study.

11. Before the first class is over, the students should have the opportunity to hear, repeat, and begin to learn the equivalent of a few expressions such as *hello, how are you? please, thank you,* and *good-by*. This gives the satisfaction of having started out on the new linguistic journey.

Some questions about the stream-level plan

What provision is to be made for drop-out in the four-level plan as outlined in the preceding pages? At present this is a grievous waste, since the great majority of young Americans who study a foreign language do so for no more than two years. Desirable though it might be, no one expects *all* students to continue foreign-language study from grades 3 to 12. A dropout may take place as early as grade 5, for the student will have had the language for two years. A valuable result of an early beginning is that, with the accompanying drop-out, those who continue will do so both because they wish to and because they can—known facts that have been arrived at in the most dependable way, by experience. Those who drop out will have equally good grounds for their decision, and will have pursued the subject long enough to have abstracted from it some immediate and permanent gain. In Streams B and C, drop-out should be seriously considered at the end of Level I. It should then be strongly discouraged until the end of Level IV, when a substantial measure of achievement has been gained.

What about the study of more than one language? It is the consensus that any student is far more welcome in college with *one* foreign language, either classical or modern, if it is well learned, than if he presents himself with an inadequate preparation in *two*. However, this plan is adaptable to the needs of the student who will study more than one language before college, though it is most important to remember that a language he is planning to continue in college should be a part of his program in grade 12. A three-, four-, or even six-year sequence in Latin is quite compatible with this plan for the students who wish to take two languages. Two modern languages are likewise possible, with beginnings spaced at least two years apart. The student who has followed Stream A and who can elect only one language per year will have completed Level II at the end of grade 8 after several years of study. This permits him to elect Latin *after* a substantial sequence of learnings in a contemporary language and to have three or even four years of Latin before college.

The fact that achievement at the end of each level can be described in terms that are applicable in all three streams does not mean that the outcomes are identical. There will be a quality of naturalness and of durability in the learnings in Stream A that will not be found in B, and again in Stream B that will not be found in C. This has to do with the language-learning capacity of the young, an ability that tends to diminish steadily as the individual grows older. The competent student who pursues Stream A is assured of an opportunity to do college work in the language of his choice during his final year in secondary school, with a chance of winning the advantage of advanced standing in college. This opportunity is also within the reach of the gifted student in Stream B.

A contemporary study of continuity in foreign-language learning could hardly be terminated better than with the following quotation written more than three centuries ago by John Amos Comenius in his book *The Great Didactic* (1628–32).

> The study of languages, especially in youth, should be joined to that of objects.
>
> Words should not be learned apart from the objects to which they refer.
>
> Complete and detailed knowledge of a language is quite unnecessary.
>
> The intelligence as well as the language of boys should preferably be exercised on matters which appeal to them, what appeals to adults should be left to a later stage.
>
> Each language must be learned separately. First the mother tongue, then the language that may be used in its place, I mean that of the neighboring nation. Then Latin may be learned, and after Latin, Greek, Hebrew, etc. One language should always be learned after, and not at the same time as, another; since otherwise both will be learned confusedly. It is only when they have been thoroughly acquired that it is of use to compare them by means of parallel grammars, dictionaries, etc.
>
> All languages are easier to learn by practice than from rules. But rules assist and strengthen the knowledge derived from practice.
>
> In writing rules for the new language the one already known must be continually kept in mind, so that stress may be laid only on the points in which the languages differ.
>
> The first exercises in a new language must deal with subject matter that is already familiar.
>
> All languages can be learned by this method, that is to say, by practice, combined with rules of a very simple nature that only refer to points of difference with the language already known, and by exercises that refer to some familiar subject.
>
> [As for] accurate translation, it is not probable that there exists any language so poor in words, idioms, and proverbs that it

could not furnish an equivalent for any Latin expression, if judgment were used.

Suggestions for further reading

Andersson, Theodore. *The Teaching of Foreign Languages in the Elementary School.* Boston: Heath, 1953.

Comenius, John A. *The Great Didactic* (1628–32). Tr. by M. W. Keatinge. London: Black, 1907.

Johnston, Marjorie C., ed. *Modern Foreign Languages in the High School.* United States Dept. of Health, Education, and Welfare, Education Office Bulletin 1958, No. 16. Washington, D.C.

National Association of Secondary-School Principals. "Modern Foreign Languages in the Comprehensive Secondary School." *Bulletin,* June 1, 1959.

Parker, William R. *The National Interest and Foreign Languages.* 3rd ed. Washington, D.C.: Government Printing Office, 1962.

METHODS AND MATERIALS

10

The purpose of this chapter is to outline and discuss the principal features of a methodology that is in accord with the objectives that have been described and to indicate why these methods are recommended. Directions for their application are given in the chapters that follow and in Appendix A.

Methods

Since the days of Comenius, and especially in the nineteenth and twentieth centuries, there has been much discussion, and at times controversy, about methods. Much of this debate has been beside the point. By definition, a method is a procedure for arriving at a destination. Almost any method is justifiable if it is humane, is not too costly in time and effort, and remains faithful to the desired objective. In subsequent comments on methods and materials it is understood that the objectives remain those previously set forth.

Now, in choosing methods surely something must be said about the expenditure of time and energy involved, the availability of aids, and the interests and resources of the travelers concerned. As long as methods in language learning do not falsify and betray objectives, they may vary according to the size of the class, its age and ability, its interests, its previous training, the materials available, and many other details that are likely to be peculiar to a given situation. This means that the teacher must make the ultimate decision about methods, for only the teacher working regularly with his class has all the information needed to assure that there will be a maximum of progress for effort expended. In fact, the greatest liberty should be allowed the teacher with regard to the choice of methods, provided objectives are constant.

This responsibility is a serious one, and it cannot be discharged unless the teacher is fully aware of the cardinal points within which his decisions will be valid. He must be sure that the learnings are coordinate and not compound. He must remember that students learn to do what they do and that they do not learn what they do not do. He must adapt the materials at hand to the needs and progress of his students. He must have all available information about the learnings his students have had in the past and are going to have in the future. He must especially be on his guard against the false objectives already enumerated: the pairing of single words in two languages, translation, the analysis of grammar for its own sake, "finishing the book," and coaching for extramural tests.

Choice of materials

Nor can his responsibility be fully discharged unless the teacher is acquainted with a wide variety of procedures and materials from which he may choose as occasion demands. Improperly designed materials have been a millstone about the teacher's neck for many decades. The teacher must now reject such faulty materials entirely or make such partial use of them as fits his concepts of objectives and methods. At the present time, a choice of greatly improved materials is available. Many of these are integrated materials, designed to provide a complete program for work in the classroom, at home, and in the laboratory and including material for quizzes, tests, and examinations. And many are appropriate to the objective "language as communication," which has now gained a high degree of general approval. With them, teachers may expect far greater returns for their efforts, especially if they are more fully informed about methods and more selective in their choice of methods leading to coordinate learnings.

Classroom procedure

The procedures that can most confidently be relied upon to lead to bilingualism are these:

The modeling of all learnings by the teacher.

The subordination of the mother tongue to the second language by rendering English inactive while the new language is being learned.

The early and continued training of the ear and tongue without recourse to graphic symbols.

The learning of structure through the *practice* of patterns of sound, order, and form, rather than by explanation.

The gradual substitution of graphic symbols for sounds after sounds are thoroughly known.

The summarizing of the main principles of structure for the student's use when the structures are already familiar, especially when they differ from those of the mother tongue. (But he is never formally asked to regurgitate these rules.)

The shortening of the time span between a performance and the pronouncement of its rightness or wrongness, without interrupting the response. This enhances the factor of reinforcement in learning.

The minimizing of vocabulary until all common structures have been learned.

The study of vocabulary only in context.

Sustained practice in the use of the language only in the molecular form of speaker-hearer-situation.

Practice in translation only as a literary exercise at an advanced level (not before Level IV).

It is not yet sufficiently well understood that overt language behavior in its most frequent form is neither individual behavior nor group behavior, but rather dyadic or dual behavior. It is communication of this kind that is the student's prime objective. Like partners on the dance floor, speaker and hearer are directly related in a way that makes the reactions of each dependent upon those of the other. The teacher must set up this relationship between himself and the class, then between himself and an individual student, and finally between one student and another. The language class, at early levels, is essentially a drill session, with learnings modeled by the teacher and gradually incorporated by the student into the repertoire of his own behavior patterns. As learnings increase, drill turns into discussion, for the student eventually has a stock of structural patterns and lexical items that enable him to express his own intentions and views without, in desperation, being obliged to invent what he has had no model for. If drills have been sufficiently representative and have been fully practiced, analogy will guide the learner along the right linguistic path, as it does in the mother tongue.

Training in a methodology that will be faithful to the objectives that have been recommended consists in learning how to:

Introduce, sustain, and harmonize the learning of the four skills in this order: hearing, speaking, reading, and writing.
Use—and not use—English in the language classroom.
Model the various types of language behavior that the student is to learn.
Teach spoken language in dialogue form.
Direct choral response by all or parts of the class.
Teach the use of structure through pattern practice.
Guide the student in choosing and learning vocabulary.
Show how words relate to meaning in the target language.
Get the individual student to talk.
Reward trials by the student in such a way that learning is reinforced.
Teach a short story and other literary forms.
Establish and maintain a cultural island.
Formalize on the first day the rules according to which the language class is to be conducted, and enforce them.

Separation of skills

Good language learning is not likely to result from a heterogeneous mixture of the four skills from the start, so different are they physiologically and psychologically. There is a natural affinity between hearing and speaking, for both are partners in the audio-lingual band. There is an equally natural affinity between reading and writing, partners in the graphic-material band. In the first pair, emphasis upon hearing should come first, since the ear is the key organ in all speech; it not only permits the individual to hear what is said but also controls what he says when he acts as speaker. In the nature of things, the learner will always hear much more than he speaks and read much more than he writes. Listening and reading are the receptive skills, and progress in them is easier than in the productive skills, speaking and writing. The ability to hear and to read is more durable than the ability to speak and write. As a speaker and a writer, the learner is essentially a practitioner of *parole;* in hearing and reading, his essential activity is to follow the patterns of *langue* as he receives them.

Of fundamental importance, as pointed out so often in this book, is the separation during the early stages of hearing-speaking from reading-writing in order that the former may not be hampered by the latter. And when the transition is made from audio-lingual and gestural-visual to graphic-material, it must be in terms of areas of meaning with which the student is familiar.

Since these are skills which—like all skills—are subject to a degree of mutual interference when only partially learned and to a weakening through disuse no matter how well they are eventually learned, it is important not only to introduce them in the proper order but to keep them up to pitch and to maintain them in the proper proportion to each other. Once they have been learned, all should play their role in every language class.

It is quite possible, and probably advisable, in most cases to make a limited use of English at the early levels. Again the criterion is the same: to what extent can English be used without defeating the objective of coordinate learning? It can be done if the learner only *hears* English without being permitted to speak it, if English is used not for communication but only for semantic clarification, and if the proportion of English to the foreign language remains less (and preferably much less) than one to ten.

The learning of language involves behavior patterns that the learner cannot create on his own, nor derive from books. They must be modeled for him. Within the limits of a machine, this can under the right circumstances be done mechanically. Yet even with this he still has need of experience in the alternate dual role of speaker and hearer, which is only possible with a living person, with whose language behavior his own becomes involved.

Dialogue

There are many reasons why language in dialogue form is the most rewarding for the learner to work with at the early levels. It involves a natural and exclusive use of the audio-lingual skills. All the elements of the sound-system appear repeatedly, including the suprasegmental phonemes, which are often the most difficult for the learner. All that is learned is meaningful, and what is learned in one part of a dialogue often makes meaning clear in another. From the start the student learns to address people directly and to use the first person singular—items of basic importance in communication. If the materials are appropriate, the learner finds a personal interest in what he is saying and a possible use far beyond the classroom for the expressions which he masters. Time is not wasted in learning isolated words and isolated sentences that may be credited with logical meaning but are devoid of psychological meaning. Rightly constructed, all dialogues have a dramatic potential that can be exploited to advantage in the classroom.

There is an important intermediate step between dialogue and discussion called dialogue adaptation, in which the expressions learned in the dialogue are, with the aid of the teacher, at once made personal by the student and adapted to communication about himself and his interests. Another intermediate step is called re-entry, in which parts of several dialogues already learned are put together to form a new dialogue similar to but not identical with those that have preceded. In this way freedom from the lock step of role learning is gradually attained.

Dialogue learning is greatly facilitated by a special form of out-of-class work called the take-home disc, often included in integrated materials. This is a small 33⅓ rpm disc on which are reproduced the dialogues (and sometimes a selection of pattern practices) that have been prepared for use in the laboratory. It is especially helpful in Level I when there are limits on the time each student can spend in the laboratory, and it provides an ideal type of homework in the early part of the course when the learner is not yet able to work to best advantage with printed materials.

Choral response is also an important method of dialogue learning because it involves participation by all the members of the class, no matter what its size. Beginners pronounce both the segmental and the suprasegmental phonemes better when they speak together, apparently because they are not so inhibited. Difficult areas of sound can be repeated that would be time-consuming and often embarrassing if done individually.

Pattern practice

Pattern practice is a cardinal point in the methodology proposed in this book. Pattern practice (or structure drill, as it is sometimes called), contrary to dialogue, makes no pretense of being communication. It is to communication what playing scales and arpeggios is to music: exercise in structural dexterity undertaken solely for the sake of practice, in order that performance may become habitual and automatic—as it must be when the mind concentrates on the message rather than on the phenomena that convey it. Pattern practice capitalizes on the mind's capacity to perceive identity of structure where there is difference in content and its quickness to learn by analogy. Analysis is important in its proper sphere, but analogy is used the periphery of an individual's command. Frequency lists of lexical items can thus be of great assistance to a teacher in indicating what vocabulary areas are suitable for study by a learner at a given stage.

A quite different comparison is appropriate for the learning of phonology, morphology, and syntax, for these are all finite and well within the range of near-mastery by the learner of a second language, as they are for the five-year-old in the mother tongue. Progress in these matters according to a well-defined plan is better compared to a spiral, in which the total area is encompassed once in a measured period, then again and again, but each successive time with a greater dimension in depth. This permits an early emphasis upon the grammar of talk, which is later matched by emphasis upon the grammar of writing.

The language laboratory is most useful if the program of exercises scheduled for it are fully integrated with work in the classroom. Scripts and tapes should contain practice on the same structural and content materials that are being studied in class. This integration works best when new materials are first presented in the classroom, are then practiced and learned in the laboratory, and are finally reintroduced into the class program, where they can be given the full dimensions of communication.

A most important point in learning theory is that the shorter the time span between the trial of a new response and the knowledge of its rightness or wrongness, the faster and better the learning. This is fully applicable in language learning if we remember that there is a point at which the time span can be shortened so much that it inhibits learning. Students must not be stopped in the middle of a word or an utterance in order to be corrected if communication is to be successfully learned. Another important matter in the rewarding of trials in a way that encourages learning is the fact that, because of the nature of phonemic distinctions, many trials are almost right but still are quite wrong. The learner must know whether or not his trial is acceptable, for if it is not and he is not made aware of it, the wrong response that is almost right is very likely to be learned instead of the right one.

Literature and culture

The teaching of suitable examples of literary forms, especially short stories, short novels, and plays, is important as early as Level II. As a preliminary step in teaching a literary work, dialogues may be extracted from it and learned as separate units. When the student then comes to the entire text, he will have had some preparation for it and be in a better position to appreciate its worth.

A "cultural island" in the language classroom contributes first of all to the development of coordinate learnings, for it results in a suspension of the mother tongue. It contributes to a development of meaning that is appropriate to the new culture and is not the same as meaning in English. It provides the one place in which the student's new learnings are as effective as he is eager for them to be.

Preparation

The success of a course is often conditioned to a marked degree by what is done the first day. What the objectives of the course are and how the teacher proposes to attain them should be made clear. What the student may do—and may not do—should be made equally clear. These classroom rules will have a direct influence upon learning. They will mainly restrict the use of English, of books, of translation, and of explanations of structure. The reasons why these rules will be imposed should be clearly stated, and the teacher may count upon the full cooperation of the students if he enforces them consistently and fairly.

Preparing materials for learning language as communication is an undertaking of vast proportions and profound significance. It can no longer be left to individual authors and their publishers, for it is now recognized that the preparation of materials suitable to the needs of language learners is too complicated and difficult a task to be undertaken by one or two persons, no matter how excellent their training and experience. This fact becomes clear if we remind ourselves of the complex nature of language and language learning and if we grant that materials cannot be called suitable unless they reflect the special contributions that must come from the classroom teacher, the descriptive linguist, the psychologist, the cultural anthropologist, and the literary scholar. In addition, materials as recommended here must reflect the objectives and the methods that have been described and the concept of levels and streams, and they must provide for the inclusion of work in the language laboratory when circumstances permit this adjunct to classroom learning.

In particular, materials must provide for audio-lingual learning by means of dialogues and pattern practices dealing with selected situations, and they must provide for the learning of reading and writing. They must provide for the learning of structure and vocabulary and for the development of cultural insights and literary appreciation through passages of writing that have been appropriately selected. They must be accompanied by scripts for tapes and by writing exercises that are to be used in the language laboratory and that parallel the learnings in the classroom. Appropriate exercises for work outside the classroom and the laboratory must be provided throughout.

The teacher must know how materials are made and he must have helped make them. He cannot, however, be expected to create materials for his courses as he goes along. Teaching is a full-time occupation, and so is the preparation of materials. No one can engage in both simultaneously and do justice to either.

We may end this chapter by suggesting that in order to obtain the maximum results from these methods and materials the teacher should know how to:

Arrange the schedule of assignments for a semester's work.
Prepare a unit.
Prepare a dialogue.
Prepare a questionnaire.
Prepare pattern practices based upon a dialogue or a literary text.
Select words and expressions for vocabulary study.
Seize upon the word or utterance that is of special cultural significance and make its meaning clear.
Prepare scripts for tapes.

Voice a tape.

Make and evaluate tests that involve all the language skills.

These activities are treated in detail in Appendix A.

Suggestions for further reading

Modern Language Association. *Reports of Surveys and Studies in the Teaching of Modern Foreign Languages.* New York: Modern Language Association, 1962.

———. *Selective List of Materials.* Mary J. Ollmann, ed. New York: Modern Language Association, 1962.

Northeast Conference on the Teaching of Foreign Languages. *Reports of the Working Committees.* 1963.

O'Connor, Patricia. *Modern Foreign Languages in the Secondary School: Prereading Instruction.* United States Dept. of Health, Education, and Welfare, Education Office Circular No. 583, June 1959, Washington, D.C.

Politzer, Robert L. *Teaching French: An Introduction to Applied Linguistics.* Boston: Ginn, 1960.

PATTERN PRACTICE

11

In this chapter we give our attention to a kind of learning exercise, both spoken and written, known as pattern practice or structure drill. It is not especially new: Gouin used it in his Series in 1880, and there are excellent examples of it embedded in the Lessons and Exercises of Grandgent and Wilkins' *Italian Grammar*, published in 1915. But its worth has been much more generally recognized as the analysis both of language and of learning behavior has developed during this century. During the past two decades it has been widely applied in many different areas of language learning.

A principal reason for the recent popularity of pattern practice is that analogy and analysis as factors in the acquisition of another language have been reassessed. Instead of relying exclusively upon analysis, as we have been doing for centuries in the study of all foreign languages, we now invoke the aid of analogy, which may be defined for our purposes as hidden sameness. Since as children we learn the mother tongue quite by analogy and not at all by analysis, why should we not try to make analogy work for us in the learning of a second language? This is the secret and the guiding principle of pattern practice or structure drill. Instead of asking the student to learn by working with utterances in which a considerable number of variables, none of which he knows very well, are all varying at once, we ask him rather to work with utterances in which there is either identity or minimal change, often even in the same place in the sentence, so that he may become habituated to what is constant and what varies. This new behavior on his part may reach awareness and be formalized in words, though it does not always need to be, as is evident in the language ability of children the world over.

If the understanding of a language pattern led immediately and directly to automatic control of that pattern, language learning would be far different from what it is. The intellectual perception and verbal statement of the nature and function of language patterns are of course of great interest from the point of view of scientific description. Whether or not this description is an aid to learning is another matter. In point of fact, the formal verbalization—the rule—may be either a hindrance or a help, and manipulation of the interplay between practice and rule is one of the most delicate operations of the language teacher.

Pattern generalization

As materials are at present being developed, the companion of pattern practice is the pattern generalization—a rule, simply stated, that summarizes for the learner in language understandable by him the shapes and changes in sound, form, or order that he has been led to follow repeatedly through his own performance in the new language. At this point, the reader may suspect that under the guise of pattern practice we are really talking about grammar—and indeed we are. In any such discussion, we must recognize that grammar is to language what anatomy is to the human body. Every living body—and even a dead one—is bound to have anatomy. The same is true of language and grammar. To say that grammar can be brushed aside as inconsequential or irrelevant is of course nonsense. The question to ask is rather to what degree must we be aware of the grammar we use, just as we may ask to what extent we must be aware of the anatomy of our bodies as we act and play and think and work. It would be naïve to propose that in formal education we should not provide our students with useful rules of grammar. But such rules should not be very numerous and should be stated in language that makes the matter clear not only to someone who already knows but also to the learner who does not yet know. In general, they should be given to the student after he has had sustained practice in using the structure the rule refers to, and the amount of class time devoted to their consideration should be minimal.

Pattern practices make no pretense of being communication, but they take the learner through the types of behavior that must be automatic when he does communicate. Pattern practices are to language in action what practice exercises in any skill are to meaningful performance in that skill. The pattern practices of languages become meaningful when they take their place in the normal exchange of communication. How far this approach is from being new is illustrated in the remark of John Amos Comenius, who said, 350 years ago in *The Great Didactic:* "All languages are easier to learn by practice than from rules. But rules assist and strengthen the knowledge derived from practice."

Pattern practice can be effectively used in many different ways. It is no less helpful in learning to write than it is in learning to speak. It is highly efficient as a classroom technique with its manifold applications and no less so for exercises in the language laboratory and for questions in tests.

Learning by analogy

From the point of view of psychology, pattern practice is an effective learning tool because it depends upon the reaction to hidden sameness as contrasted with minimal differences when one utterance is compared with another. The full story of learning by analogy is not yet known, but it is recognized that analogy functions liberally in the acquiring of the mother tongue. Pattern practice attempts to exploit the potentialities of analogy in the learning of the second language. For analogy to function to its fullest capacity, the new patterns to be learned must faithfully follow a logic of consistent change. As all will admit, languages are not always logical. Exceptions and irregularities must be dealt with in their own terms. But the fact remains that language structure is to an often amazing extent consistent and logical. As long as this is true, pattern practice provides an ideal learning technique.

This type of learning has a strong appeal to the descriptive linguist because of his special interest in identifying and describing the full inventory of patterns discoverable in the code of a given language. Not only is he aware of them in their totality, he is also aware of the order of their frequency and of their internal relationships. Furthermore, he is well aware of the contrastive nature of the patterns in one language as compared with those of another. He seeks out these areas in which the patterns of two languages may be identical or slightly different or very different. Language behavior is largely a matter of habit. Habits being what they are, the linguist knows that learning problems may well be accentuated at points where two language codes are highly similar or totally unlike. Linguistics has contributed greatly to the successful application of pattern practice through its description of the patterns that are to be found and of similarities and differences when one code is compared with another.

Types of pattern practice

Pattern practices come in a rich variety of shapes and sizes. Although they do not illustrate communication as such, each one starts with an utterance that is or could be a part of interpersonal exchange. It then shows the learner, by having him either hear the utterance and then repeat it or read the utterance and then write it, how a certain segment of it can change in a consistent way.

It is rare that a pattern practice can be effectively invented on the spur of the moment before a class. For the most part they must be carefully prepared ahead of time, and their preparation has become a major task in the construction of integrated materials. To make them well is difficult and time-consuming, and the fact that they are now available in a variety of integrated texts is an invaluable aid to the teacher. But there are times when the teacher will want to prepare such drills for a special purpose. It may be to give further practice in the elements of the sound-system, either the individual vowels or consonants or the intonation patterns. Or it may be to give more practice on changes in form, or changes in word order, or patterns of agreement. The drills may simply be invented for the purpose in view, or they may be selected from a text. Often a suitable item is found in a text and taken as a point of departure, other comparable items being invented to exemplify the same pattern change.

To participate in pattern practice, the student must have two kinds of knowledge: he must know what type of change, if any, is to be made, and he must know how to make the change. The first of these is a matter of technique, the second, of language. If there is confusion about technique, performance in language will of course suffer. Different types of variation should be kept separate until the techniques are thoroughly understood.

Many kinds of pattern practice are useful in classroom and in laboratory, for example:

1. Repetition
2. Inflection
3. Replacement
4. Restatement
5. Completion
6. Transposition
7. Expansion
8. Contraction
9. Transformation
10. Integration
11. Rejoinder
12. Restoration

Two or more of these are sometimes involved in the same pattern change. (It is understood that most of these drills may be done in writing as well as orally.)

Here are comments on each of these types of pattern practice, with examples in English:

1. *Repetition.* The student repeats an utterance aloud as soon as he has heard it. He does this without looking at a printed

156 / LANGUAGE AND LANGUAGE LEARNING

text. The utterance must be brief enough to be retained by the ear. Sound is as important as form and order.

> EXAMPLE
> This is the seventh month. —This is the seventh month.

After a student has repeated an utterance, he may repeat it again and add a few words, then repeat that whole utterance and add more words.

> EXAMPLE
> I used to know him. —I used to know him. I used to know him *years ago*. I used to know him years ago *when we were in school*.

2. *Inflection.* One word in an utterance appears in another form when repeated.

> EXAMPLES
> I bought the *ticket*. —I bought the *tickets*.
> *He* bought the candy. —*She* bought the candy.
> I called the young *man*. —I called the young *men*.
> We *stay* at home. —We *stayed* at home.

Inflection of one word often requires inflection of another.

> EXAMPLES
> She dropped *her* glove. —*He* dropped *his* glove.
> We respect *this* man. —We respect *these men*.

3. *Replacement.* One word in an utterance is replaced by another.

> EXAMPLES
> He bought this *house* cheap. —He bought *it* cheap.
> *Helen* left early. —*She* left early.
> They gave their *boss* a watch. —They gave *him* a watch.

Replacement and inflection are often combined.

> EXAMPLE
> *Mary drops* her glove. —*She dropped* her glove.

There is a progressive form of pattern practice, involving replacement and inflection, that is an excellent class exercise. An utterance is made, then one additional word is given which is then fitted into the first utterance. Another word is given, which is fitted into the utterance last made, and so forth.

EXAMPLE
She dropped her glove. (watch) —She dropped her *watch*.
(he) —*He* dropped *his* watch.
(lost) —He *lost* his watch.
(they) —*They* lost *their watches*.
(hat) —They lost their *hats*.
(I) —*I* lost *my* hat.
(found) —I *found* my hat.
(her) —*She* found *her* hat.

In another useful drill involving progressive change a replacement is made alternately in one of two words (or slots) in the sequence:

EXAMPLE
They find the restaurant.
They *know* the restaurant.
They know the *waiter*.
They *ask* the waiter.
They ask the *price*.
They *pay* the price.
They pay the *bill*.

4. *Restatement.* The student rephrases an utterance and addresses it to someone else, according to instructions.

EXAMPLES
Tell him to wait for you. —Wait for me.
Ask her how old she is. —How old are you?
Ask John when he began. —John, when did you begin?
Tell him you don't believe him.—I don't believe you.
Tell him not to go without you. —Don't go without me.

5. *Completion.* The student hears an utterance that is complete except for one word, then repeats the utterance in completed form.

EXAMPLES
I'll go my way and you go . . . —I'll go my way and you go *yours*.
We all have . . . own troubles. —We all have *our* own troubles.
Her cooking is good, but yours is . . . —Her cooking is good, but yours is *better*.

6. *Transposition.* A change in word order is necessary when a word is added.

> EXAMPLES
> *I'm* hungry. (so) —So *am I.*
> *I'll* never do it again. (neither) —Neither *will I.*

7. *Expansion.* When a word is added it takes a certain place in the sequence.

> EXAMPLES
> I know him. (hardly) —I *hardly* know him.
> I know him. (well) —I know him *well.*

8. *Contraction.* A single word stands for a phrase or clause.

> EXAMPLES
> Put your hand *on the table.* —Put your hand *there.*
> They believe *that the earth is flat.* —They believe *it.*
> I hope *they will remember us.* —I hope *so.*

9. *Transformation.* A sentence is transformed by being made negative or interrogative or through changes in tense, mood, voice, aspect, or modality.

> EXAMPLE
> He knows my address.
> He doesn't know my address.
> Does he know my address?
> He used to know my address.
> If he had known my address.
> My address is known to him.
> He used to know my address.
> He may know my address.

Of course, such exercises are accompanied by a cue that points to the desired transformation.

10. *Integration.* Two separate utterances are integrated into one.

> EXAMPLES
> They must be honest. This is important. —It is important that they be honest.
> I know that man. He's looking for you. —I know the man who is looking for you.
> I saw the girl. You were dancing with her. —I saw the girl you were dancing with.

11. *Rejoinder.* The student makes an appropriate rejoinder to a given utterance. He is told in advance to respond in one of the following ways:

Be polite.
Answer the question.
Agree.
Agree emphatically.
Express surprise.
Express regret.
Disagree.
Disagree emphatically.
Question what is said.
Fail to understand.

Be polite.

EXAMPLES
Thank you. —You're welcome.
May I take one? —Certainly.

Answer the question.

EXAMPLES
What is your name? —My name is Smith.
Where did it happen? —In the middle of the street.

Agree.

EXAMPLES
He's following us. —I think you're right.
This is good coffee. —It's very good.

Agree emphatically.

EXAMPLES
Pretty hot, isn't it? —It's terribly hot!
That was stupid of me. —It certainly was!

Express surprise.

EXAMPLES
I'm leaving tonight. —Not really?
He told the police. —He told the police?

Express regret.

EXAMPLES
He says he can't come. —That's too bad.
We missed the bus. —What a shame!

Disagree.

EXAMPLES
I liked the film. —I didn't like it.
I'm sure he is honest. —I don't think so.

Disagree emphatically.

> **EXAMPLES**
> You're angry. —I'm not angry at all!
> Some day you will like them. —Never!

Question what is said.

> **EXAMPLES**
> She's forty years old. —It's impossible.
> She smokes cigars. —I can't believe it.

Fail to understand.

> **EXAMPLES**
> That's so much hocus-pocus. —What did you say?
> That's one for the book. —I don't understand.

12. *Restoration.* The student is given a sequence of words that have been culled from a sentence, but still bearing its basic meaning. He uses these words with a minimum of changes and additions to restore the sentence to its original form. He may be told whether the time is present, past, or future.

> **EXAMPLES**
> students/wait/bus. —The students are waiting for the bus.
> boys/build/house/tree. —The boys built a house in a tree.
> door/close/after/push/button. —The door will close after you have pushed the button.

By working with a series of sentences that differ, more or less widely, in vocabulary content but that have *an identity of structural logic,* the student gradually gains control of the structural pattern involved. It is to this structural mode that he later refers as he constructs other sentences of the same type. Complete inventories of all the types of sentence that can be identified in a given language are not yet available. But it is not difficult to list a number of such sentence types that appear again and again in the more frequently taught languages.

On the next page is a diagram designed to help the teacher plan class exercises so that over a period of time students will have practice in all common language patterns.

GRAMMAR CIRCLE

This check list of grammatical forms, structural modes, and types of utterances may be useful in the preparation of dialogues and pattern drills to make sure that common structural patterns are not overlooked. Below the circle is an example of each type of utterance.

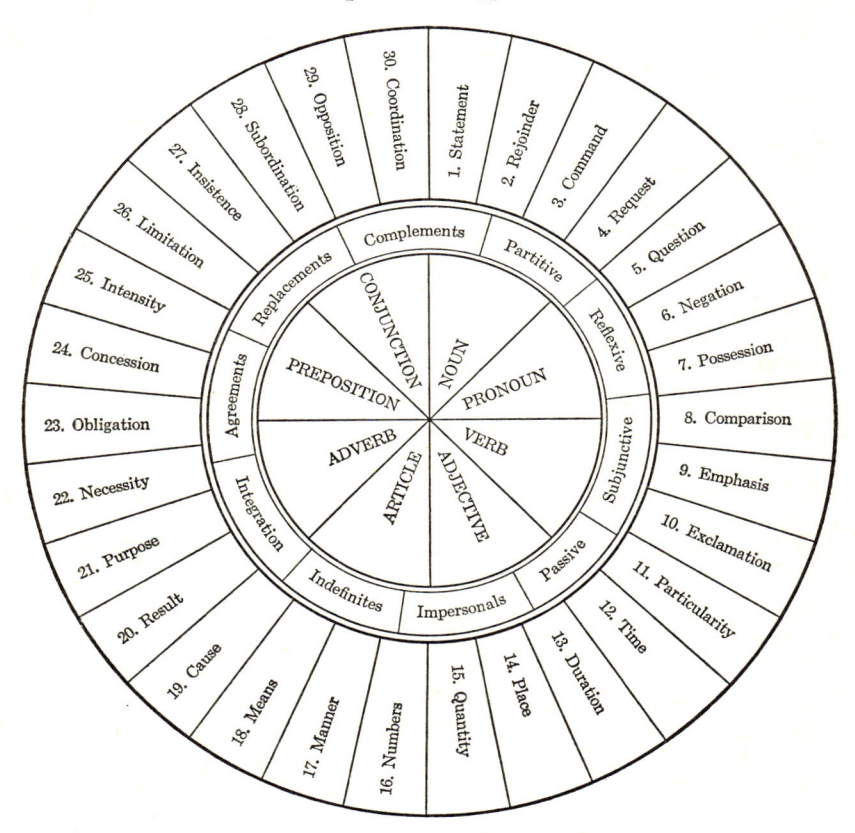

1. The earth is round.
2. Of course.
3. Stand up.
4. Kindly remove your hats.
5. Do you understand?
6. I don't hear anything.
7. The furniture is mine.
8. He is older than I.
9. *I did it.*
10. How she has grown!
11. This man speaks the truth.
12. I'll come at ten o'clock.
13. He has been ill since yesterday.
14. They landed at Provincetown.
15. We made many mistakes.

162 / LANGUAGE AND LANGUAGE LEARNING

16. Three times four is twelve.
17. I accept with pleasure.
18. He came by bicycle.
19. I ran because I was afraid.
20. If you call, I will answer.
21. He cheated in order to win.
22. You must answer the question.
23. We ought to help them.
24. Although he tried, he failed.
25. She seemed quite happy.
26. I have only ten dollars.
27. I like to travel, especially by plane.
28. I believe he is waiting for us.
29. He had neither pen nor paper.
30. We must win or everything is lost.

Suggestions for further reading

Gouin, François. *The Art of Teaching and Studying Languages.* New York: Scribner, 1892.

Gravit, Francis W., and Albert Valdman, eds. "Structural Drill and the Language Laboratory." Report of the Third Language Laboratory Conference held at Indiana University in March 1962. *International Journal of American Linguistics,* April 1963, Part 3.

Moulton, William G. "What Is Structural Drill?" *International Journal of American Linguistics.* XXIX, 2, Part 3 (April 1963), 3–15.

Myers, L. M. "Two Approaches to Languages." *PMLA,* LXXVII, 4, Part 2 (September 1962), 6–10.

Northeast Conference on the Teaching of Foreign Languages. *Reports of the Working Committees.* 1958.

Pimsleur, Paul. "Pattern Drills in French." *French Review,* XXXIII (May 1960), 568–76.

Roberts, Paul. *Patterns of English.* New York: Harcourt, Brace & World, 1956.

Sweet, Waldo E. *Latin, A Structural Approach.* Ann Arbor, Mich.: University of Michigan Press, 1958.

Twaddell, W. Freeman. "Does the Foreign-Language Teacher Have to Teach English Grammar?" *PMLA,* LXXVII, 2, Part 2 (May 1962), 18–22.

READING AND WRITING

12

When a period of training in the audio-lingual skills precedes the introduction to reading and writing, the learner's experience differs decidedly from what it is when all four skills are attempted simultaneously at the start. An advantage to the student is that he has gained—or more precisely regained—the ability to learn audio-lingually, something that was of prime importance to him before he became literate in his mother tongue and that diminished as he became more and more dependent upon words in printed form. It is important not to sacrifice this advantage as the first steps are taken in learning to read and write in the target language.

On the other hand, if the "fit" of speech to writing is not very good—and this is the case in many languages—the student is often dismayed and discouraged when his eyes first fall on the printed forms of the new language sounds with which he has become acquainted. Previous learning is, as always, a vital factor in the learner's success. The new language is very likely to be written in symbols all or nearly all of which are used in his mother tongue. He will long ago have acquired fixed habits of response to these symbols as they appear singly and in clusters or words, but he must now associate these symbols not with the sounds of his mother tongue but with those of the new language, and these are all new and different—and often very different.

Two important points of procedure at this time are these: All that the teacher does and says about reading and writing should make it clear to the student that he is not interpreting the way in which the written symbols are to be pronounced, but that, quite the contrary, he is being presented with the way in which the sounds that he now knows look when they appear on paper. This sound-to-writing direction should be implicit throughout the initial stages of learning to read and write. This recommendation implies the second one, namely, that the student be asked to read and write only that which he has learned to understand when spoken and which he can himself actively produce. If this procedure is not followed, and the learner is suddenly presented with a text he has not already learned, he will obviously tend to pronounce the written symbols as he would pronounce them in his mother tongue. This is sure to damage whatever control of the sound-system of the new language he has gained. Only after at least some months of experience with the written form of what has first been learned through the ear should we expect him to work with new material in printed form and to interpret these letters as sounds.

The question is often asked whether or not reading and writing should be introduced simultaneously or if one should be developed at some length before the other. As is well known, no definitive answers can be given even when such questions are asked about becoming literate in one's mother tongue. It is all the more unlikely that thoroughly dependable answers can be given about the correct procedure with regard to the learning of a second language. The best that can be done is to describe procedures that appear to work successfully, without stating categorically that they are the only or even the best ways of arriving at the desired goal. Research and study programs of great magnitude will have to be designed and followed through before definitive answers can be given.

When a class is presented for the first time with the script of a dialogue or a narrative that has already been thoroughly learned audio-lingually, most students will have little trouble in producing the suitable sounds as their eyes follow the printed words. The situation is in some ways like seeing for the first time in musical notation a song or melody that one already knows by heart. The element of surprise that it should be written "that way" is accompanied by a certain intellectual satisfaction in matching what is known through the ear to what is now being followed by the eye. In so far as the two systems have a one-to-one relationship logically, all goes well. However, sometimes certain sounds are not reproduced in writing (*ch* in *don't you*), or, on the contrary, the writing contains letters that are not reproduced in sound (*k* in *knowledge*). At other times, a single sound appears to be spelled in more than one manner (*see* and *sea*), or the same letter or letters seem to be pronounced in more than one way ("Now *read* what I *read* yesterday"). Then the learner is temporarily at a loss, and the problems of "teaching" reading and writing properly begin.

At this point in our discussion of reading and writing, we are concerned with the meaning of these words as used to designate skills, the possession of which distinguishes the speaker who is literate from one who is not. Later on we shall be dealing with these words in a different way. Then the mere skills that are implied will be taken for granted, and we shall be speaking of reading and writing with our attention fixed upon the content of what is being expressed rather than upon the mechanisms used in the process.

How reading and writing differ

The skills of reading and writing are physiologically and psychologically very different from those of hearing and speaking. Just as the ear is the dominant organ throughout in both listening and speaking, the eye is dominant in both reading and writing. Sensitivity to sound now gives way to sensitivity to light. This distinction is important from the point of view not only of the matter and manner of the new learning but also of the special capacities and limitations which the learner brings to the process. We need to make sure that his sight is normal as he learns to read, as well as to make sure that his hearing is normal as he learns to listen and speak. The factor of inertia must also be taken into account. Just as one can learn to understand without learning to speak, so one can learn to read without learning to write. The extent to which one will speak and write in the new language will be vastly less than the extent to which he will listen and read, yet this makes it all the more necessary to take the learner through the steps required to put him in control of all four language skills.

We may carry the distinction between the skills still further by recalling that the difference between *langue* and *parole* is as valid with regard to reading and writing as it is with regard to listening and speaking. The receptive skill of reading is much more easily acquired and more easily retained than the productive skill of writing. But the learning of reading also has special characteristics that relate to its institutional or *langue* nature. The learner must know how to respond as a reader to writing of many different types, of many different degrees of difficulty, recorded at different times and in different places. Writing, on the contrary, like speaking, is a highly personal affair, in which the learner must respect all the mandatory features of the target language code as it appears when written, while at the same time being permitted and encouraged to exploit the volitional and creative aspects of the new language to the extent that his ability and his experience permit.

There are certain gross differences in the patterns characteristic of writing which need to be pointed out. For one thing, words as they appear in printed books often look quite different from words as they appear in handwriting on the blackboard or in a letter. Individual letters often have one form as they begin a sentence or a word and another form as they appear within words or within sentences. There are punctuation marks that separate one thought or one speaker from another or relate thought to each other. There are diacritical marks that relate to a difference in sound or in meaning. All these gross aspects of the writing system will be more or less involved as the student who is in possession audio-lingually of some elements of the new language proceeds to become literate within the limits of the language he knows.

Spelling

It may be well to deal with spelling, as an end in itself, as a separate issue, if for no other reason than to understand its peculiar characteristics and its special role in becoming literate. Spelling is of relatively minor importance as far as reading is concerned; it becomes a major factor in the productive skill of writing. In many languages there is a high degree of consistency in spelling practices; in others—and English is a prime example—there is not. It is probably fair to say that all spelling is logical up to a point; the trouble starts when illogic sets in. One way of keeping spelling problems at a minimum at the beginning is to concentrate on words in which the fit of sound to symbol is fully satisfactory and consistent.

Sounds and letters

If our student has had some weeks or months of purely audio-lingual training, what questions present themselves as he goes through the process of learning how the sounds he knows appear in print? And what questions may be asked when he eventually takes up an unfamiliar text with the intention of interpreting the printed forms as sound? The student himself need not be directly concerned about these questions or their complete and accurate answers. But the following matters should certainly be in the minds of those who prepare materials for the learner at this stage and of those who direct his activities in the classroom.

FROM SOUND TO LETTER

What different sounds are there in the language?
Which ones are classed as vowels? as consonants? as semi-vowels?
In what positions and combinations do they occur?

What is their order of frequency?
Has the student met all sounds audio-lingually before beginning to read and write?
What sounds (if any) are consistently spelled in only one way?
What sounds are spelled in more than one way (for example, *e*ven, f*ee*t, b*ea*t, c*ei*ling)?
What letters are used in the new language? What punctuation and accent marks?
In what different spellings does each sound appear?

FROM LETTER TO SOUND

What letters or letter combinations (if any) are consistently pronounced the same way?
What letters or letter combinations are pronounced in more than one way (for example, *c*ost, *c*ent; *th*is, *th*ing)?
What is the significance of diacritical marks?
How are words divided into syllables?
Which syllable of a word is stressed?
Are letters pronounced differently when stressed or unstressed?
When are letters not pronounced at all?
What sounds appear or disappear as words or syllables come together?
What guidance as to intonation is given by punctuation?
(Note the special status of personal names and place names, in both pronunciation and meaning.)

There is no sharp limit that marks off the learning of reading and writing as skills from learning to use these skills while concentrating essentially on the content of the message. The following steps suggest how the one may lead into the other:

SEQUENTIAL STEPS IN READING

a. Show how a word (say the equivalent of *boy* or *dog*) looks when written.
b. Ask for other words in which the same sounds occur. Write the appropriate suggestions, which illustrate the way or ways in which a given sound is written.
c. Write out several familiar sentences. Read them and have them read aloud.

d. Distribute printed text of dialogue or narrative (of some length). Read it aloud and have it read aloud.
e. Prepare sentences that are composed of known words put together in a new way. (For example, the student knows: "My father has a new car." "He bought it yesterday." He now reads: "Yesterday my father bought a new car.")

Texts for reading gradually introduce new sequences, new forms, and new words, until what is new makes up a considerable part of the reading exercise.

SEQUENTIAL STEPS FOR WRITING

a. Copy known words and expressions from the board.
b. Copy similar material from printed text.
c. Write dictations of known sentences with some words supplied, some spaces blank.
d. Write whole utterances and sentences (known) from dictation.
e. Copy from familiar text with minimal changes (for example, in person or number).
f. Write new sentences with a model given and the words to be used supplied (for example, "This boy has lost his hat" girls/pay/money).
g. Rewrite a narrative text as a dialogue, and vice versa.

Once reading and writing are well established as skills, that is, in terms of familiarity with the types of marks that the eye will encounter when scanning the printed page, and in terms of what the learner must put on paper in order to be rightly read by a native speaker of the target language, there follows the development of these skills as a means to an end rather than as ends in themselves.

Development of reading

Important for the student now are the factors of speed of reading, newness and difficulty in vocabulary and structure, and the content of what he reads. These factors should be present in such a way as to permit and encourage both learning and performance in the target language, so that comprehension may take place without reference to English. If what is to be read is too difficult in terms either of vocabulary or of structure, the natural tendency of the student will be to recode the target language into English and withhold attempts at comprehension until this recoding has been accomplished.

The damage that is thus done to the internalized processes of language is of course severe. The psychological double-talk that results is characteristic of neither the target language nor the mother tongue. Every effort should be made therefore to aid the student in avoiding this costly side trip into English. The materials used and the coaching done by the teacher should constantly aim at comprehension that is linked directly to the code of the target language.

Often the learner must be told that this is possible and desirable. It should be pointed out to him that meaning relates to an isolated word only when he is reading a dictionary or a vocabulary list. Otherwise, whether in fiction or nonfiction, poetry or anecdote, dialogue or narrative, meaning is no longer related solely to a single word but to clusters of words as they are interrelated in utterances and sentences and paragraphs. The reader may not know the meaning of a single word encountered by itself—indeed, may never have heard or seen it before—but when he comes upon it embedded in an environment of other words that are familiar, the context often endows it with meaning for him. This may not happen at once, that is, the first time the new passage is scanned, but areas that are at first clouded by meaninglessness gradually become clear as the passage is read a second or a third time. It should be pointed out to the student that if by this process of rereading he strengthens his ability to go directly from the target language code to comprehension, he will be accomplishing the most valuable objective in learning to read in the target language. Naturally this will not happen for every new word. When context does not reveal meaning, it must be arrived at in another way. The most appropriate is the footnote or the gloss in the target language that restates meaning in different words already known to the student. Yet this step will not always clarify meaning either. It is at this point that the equivalent in English *not of whole propositions but only of the term or terms in question* is fully desirable. When words are matched in the two languages we are dealing almost entirely with vocabulary alone; when whole utterances or sentences are matched we must deal also with structure, and the imposition of English structure upon that of the target language greatly enhances the latent interference of the mother tongue—producing a result which the learner needs most of all to avoid.

Throughout the basic course, that is, Levels I and II, the student's reading will usually be restricted to passages, both short and long, that have been especially prepared as a part of the total program he is following. Many teachers, however, will not wish to complete Level II without giving the students an opportunity to read some pages that were not especially prepared for use in a classroom. The amount of this material cannot be very great if the development of the control of the language skills is to continue to be the dominant objective, and it should be most carefully chosen and should be presented in such a way that it reinforces the language skills being learned. Above all, it must not lead to the unwonted interference of English. A workable plan is to select the readings that are to be used in the latter part of Level II, then to introduce earlier in this level dialogues, narrative, or exercises extracted from this reading and so familiarize the student with what is to come. In this way both vocabulary and structure can be put at the disposal of the student so that he can eventually read the passage in its entirety with confidence and relative ease.

INTENSIVE READING

The nature and the quantity of reading take on a new dimension of importance in Levels III and IV. The ability to read rapidly and accurately is probably best developed by the two techniques of intensive reading and extensive reading. By intensive reading we mean the careful study and detailed classroom handling of a short assignment of perhaps two to four pages per day. Questionnaire, pattern practice, vocabulary drill, word study, dictation, and general discussion are all a part of the technique of intensive reading. Texts that are fully suitable for this purpose in both form and content are of course difficult to discover. But student success at these levels will be directly related to the quality and appropriateness of the reading selections.

EXTENSIVE READING

In contrast to this, the technique employed in extensive reading should be definitely different. An entire short story, or a chapter or sequence of chapters of a novel, or an entire one-act play should be assigned, read, and briefly reported on as a single unit. The student should understand that in this type of reading his interest is to center upon a total or over-all comprehension of characters and events rather than upon the precise details of either language or story content. Extensive reading is done outside of class, the assignments are given some time in advance of the terminal date, and only a few moments of class time are necessary to check on whether or not the student has understood the main features of the story. A sequence of completion exercises or a list of questions to be answered in a single sentence usually suffices as a check on outside reading. This should of course be done in the target language.

Writing

Learning to write with the emphasis upon content appears to divide itself into three principal phases: subsentence writing, sentence writing, and paragraph writing. In the first of these the learner's problem is simply to complete a sentence when a part of it is given. This is much more than the writing of words or expressions, for we are no longer on the level of terms—lexical items that are merely capable of carrying meaning—but are rather on the level of propositions, in which terms are linked together to produce a far higher level of meaning than is given by a dictionary. In the second, the learner must manipulate all the parts of a proposition and himself put them together in acceptable and meaningful sequence. In paragraph writing he must put propositions together in logical order and with a sense of selection and synthesis that is culturally authentic and in accord with usage. Beyond the paragraph lies an area in which there is added to all the foregoing an increment of composition and stylistics in which concern for creativity and for writing as a fine art begins to assume major proportions.

The first step, then, is to practice completing sentences in which certain words have been deleted. The second step is to practice writing sentences, using material that is suggested and following a model. The third step is to learn to arrange sentences in paragraphs, again following a model for some time so that to correctness of form may be added logic of presentation and aptness of expression.

Up to now, our most grievous errors in training students to write in the foreign language have been:

a. To require the translation of endless sequences of isolated sentences from English into the foreign language, a procedure based upon the premise that the way to learn a second language is to grasp the first language firmly and never relinquish it. The result is to add to the normal difficulties of the second language a further set of difficulties resulting from the lack of identity of the two systems.
b. To require the translation of long passages of specially prepared (and often badly warped) English prose.
c. To require the writing of original compositions too soon and too often, which results in the invention and consequent learning of unacceptable forms.
d. To encourage the notion that it is sinful to imitate an author under study.

Instead of the above the student should do the following:

a. Banish English from the process completely.
b. Become aware of the areas of difference between what is spoken and what is written.
c. Begin by copying representative samples of writing in the foreign language, first from the printed text, then from dictation.

d. Learn to rewrite such passages by making them shorter, or simpler, or changed in point of view, in time, or in style.
e. Learn to write a passage that will parallel a model passage in structure, subject matter, treatment, or style.
f. Learn to retell in his own words what has been read only after the passage has been discussed orally and the form and wording of the retelling have been agreed upon orally.
g. Learn to write critical opinions of what has been read only after oral discussion and an oral statement of what he intends to write.
h. Learn to write the language as it has traditionally been written. In the languages we are dealing with, originality can prosper only when it is firmly rooted in the accepted patterns of writing.

SUBSENTENCE WRITING

A useful exercise in the transition from hearing and speaking to writing is what is sometimes called "spot" dictation. The student is given a sheet of paper on which separate sentences or connected passages are printed, but with certain preselected words or expressions left blank. He then hears the text read in its entirety, being given time to write in the blank spaces the words and expressions he hears but does not see. Later, he completes sentences and passages prepared in this way, without hearing the text read.

SENTENCE WRITING

A useful exercise in sentence writing is to write out a suitable sentence chosen from a known context, then give a list of words that can be used to replace nouns or verbs, adjectives or adverbs in this sentence. Instruct the student to write a new sentence that contains the structure of the original or model, while at the same time using the word replacements that are suggested.

Another good method is to select a suitable sentence from a text and "dehydrate" it, deleting articles, prepositions, and other noncontent words and putting verbs, nouns, and adjectives in their lexical form if they have been inflected; omit as many words as can be left out without making the meaning unclear. Write the remaining words across the page, without punctuation, and separate them by diagonal lines. Instruct the student to rewrite the group of words as a complete sentence, using each word in the order given, changing form when necessary and adding whatever words are required for completion.

EXAMPLE
now/time/all/good/man/come/aid/party

In yet another type of exercise, a sentence is quoted from a text and is followed by a word or expression in parentheses that can be used as a paraphrase for a part of it. The instructions are to rewrite, using what is in parentheses as a substitute.

EXAMPLE
The pamphlets were distributed without cost. (to give away free) —The pamphlets were given away free.

When the student has developed competence in sentence writing, single-sentence answers to separate questions are often useful; the effectiveness of this exercise will notably increase if the directions are stated thus: Answer each of these questions in a single sentence (in the target language), making your answer in each case at least as long as the question.

PARAGRAPH WRITING

Suppose we are at Level III and wish to model the writing of an acceptable paragraph. We assume that there have been reading assignments and that the content of the reading is to be used in writing. Here is a suggested plan of procedure. Select a subject relating to pages recently read and write a paragraph of perhaps seven to ten sentences about it. Do this in terms of the language of the text and of the student's ability to use this language as a model. In class, allow twenty or thirty minutes for the following exercise in writing. First, distribute a blank sheet of paper to each student. Then read aloud the first sentence of your paragraph (in parts if necessary) and have it repeated aloud by one of the students. Have it repeated aloud again by one or two other students. Then direct the class to write this sentence on their papers. When everyone has finished, write your sentence on the board, so that the students may compare and correct their sentences if they have made any mistakes. Then proceed in the same way with the second sentence, having it repeated aloud several times before the class commits it to paper. As the class finishes each sentence, write it on the board for comparison and correction. After a while the entire paragraph will appear on the board and on the paper of each student. Now erase the paragraph that is on the board and instruct the students to turn their papers over and write the paragraph again on the blank side. Before they begin, write on the board, one after another, a two- or three-word nucleus extracted from each sentence. This will help the students to remember ideas and to arrange them in the proper order. When they have finished writing, they have only to turn their papers over to find a complete model for correction. This learning device is also useful as a point of reference for future quizzes and tests. What the student has written, to be sure, is not his paragraph but yours. Yet by following a model a number of times—a little less closely on each occasion as will be indicated below—the student becomes able to write paragraphs of his own, still staying within the limits that the correctness of language and the nature of a paragraph require.

Here is another suggestion for teaching the writing of a paragraph. Suppose the students are at Level III and are reading a play in which one of the principal characters is a doctor. During the class discussion, with books closed and no printed or written words in sight, the students are directed to answer a series of questions as if each was the doctor. Ten questions are asked and answered orally in the first person singular: "What is your profession?" "What is your age?" "Where did you get your degree?" "How long have you been in this city?" "Do you have many patients?" etc. When the questionnaire is finished, the students are given a blank sheet of paper, the questions are repeated, and the answers are written, as follows: After time for each student to write an answer, the teacher writes a suitable one on the blackboard, according to which the students accept or modify their own. When the ten answers have been written and corrected, the students are instructed to turn the sheet of paper over and are told: "You are Doctor X. Write about yourself. Do not look back at what you have just written." This time the student has written sentences similar to but not necessarily identical with the spoken and written models.

A series of further exercises in paragraph writing in which the student gradually proceeds more and more on his own may be set up as follows. First, compose a sequence of sentences that form a paragraph and "dehydrate" them, giving them in appropriate sequence. Ask the student to reconstruct the original paragraph, directing him to retain as much as possible of the original form and meaning. Second, compose or select a suitable paragraph, then prepare a series of questions in logical order, the answer to each one being a sentence of the paragraph. Give the student these questions and instruct him to answer each one in order, then to arrange his sequence of answers as a complete paragraph. Third, select a suitable paragraph from a text and present the first half of it in writing with blank lines immediately following. Instruct the student to recall the events of the story and to continue the quoted passage until he has doubled its length.

LENGTH OF WRITING ASSIGNMENTS

In the writing of sentences or paragraphs or compositions, it is difficult to brush aside the consideration of how much is to be written. Whether directions can be suitably complied with in two words or ten, in a hundred words or a thousand, is a matter of prime importance to the one who must do the writing. Wherever possible, precise instructions as to length should be given. Superficially, this would seem to encourage the mere fulfilling of requirements, with the student busily counting words to that end. Yet at a deeper level, one must admit that a knowledge of the length of the statement to be made has much to do with the treatment of ideas and with the language and style that are employed.

Another element of prime importance in successful writing is an awareness of the person or persons to whom the writing is addressed. Is the student writing for his teacher, as in the standard classroom theme? Is he writing to a person of his own age, as in a personal letter? Is he writing to himself, as in a diary? Is he writing for the general public, as in an article written for the school or college paper or magazine? Is he writing to show a sample of his writing ability to the dean of admissions of a college or a graduate school or to a prospective employer? Wherever possible, an indication of the reader or readers to whom writing is to be addressed should be given, for this too is a factor that is bound to have an effect upon the content and the manner of what is written.

The terse advice of Harold Nicholson is valuable even at the beginning of the writing experience: "Decide what you wish to say and to whom you wish to say it. Then write."

Suggestions for further reading

Brown, Rollo W. *How the French Boy Learns to Write.* Cambridge, Mass.: Harvard University Press, 1915.

Mallinson, Vernon. *Teaching a Modern Language.* London: Heinemann, 1953.

Mirrielees, Lucia B. *Teaching Composition and Literature.* New York: Harcourt, Brace & World, 1952.

Northeast Conference on the Teaching of Foreign Languages. *Reports of the Working Committees.* 1963.

Tomkins, Calvin. "The Last Skill Acquired." *New Yorker,* September 14, 1963, pp. 127–57.

VOCABULARY

13

Of the four strands of language, sound, form, order, and choice, the last—that is, vocabulary—is the least characteristic. This is why vocabulary items are so easily borrowed by one language from another, but sound-patterns or syntax patterns are not. The learner's first task is to deal with sound, order, and form, using only a minimum of vocabulary. Once he is at home with these three, the enlarging of vocabulary may proceed without hindrance. Eventually the problems connected with sound, order, and form are exhausted, but the learning of vocabulary is endless. The attempt to evaluate progress at the early levels of language learning in terms of quantity of vocabulary items is as misleading as it is useless. It seems to say that the purpose of this learning is to master a section of lexicography, yet surely nothing could be further from the truth. The learner's early progress is to be measured by the number of situations in which he can communicate as a hearer and a speaker and by the structural patterns he has at his disposal. The question "How many words do you know?" is in fact without meaning, for there is no agreement as to what is signified in this question by either *words* or *know*.

When vocabulary is emphasized

The special emphasis placed upon the learning of structure in Levels I and II, and the consequent de-emphasis upon the learning of vocabulary, implies that in Levels III and IV there will be a compensatingly greater concern for building up the student's stockpile of words and expressions for use in all the skills. In this chapter we are concerned with the ways in which this can best be done.

As we have seen, language in action proceeds in a dual channel or stream, one of code and one of meaning. Of the four strands of code, it is the fourth, vocabulary, that is the principal medium for interconnecting these two channels. There is, of course, a type of meaning that attaches to structure whether or not the semantic or vocabulary meaning of individual words is understood. The structural meaning is constantly active as language proceeds, yet its role is a relatively minor one as compared to that of semantic meaning, which depends upon the message borne by each individual word. Lewis Carroll's "Jabberwocky" is a good example of language that has structural meaning but little semantic meaning.

For the present, our concern is with vocabulary as the principal bearer of meaning. The isolated word of the lexicographer bears a potential for meaning that is quite generally agreed upon, so much so that it can be formally stated and considered as relatively fixed. We tend to have a respect for and a faith in lexicography. The answer to the question "What does the dictionary say?" settles many an argument. But unless we exercise caution, this attitude can lead to the assumption that meaning belongs to or is a quality of a given word. It seems natural to assume that there is something about the sound and shape of the word *stone,* for example, that relates it intrinsically to the block of mineral matter with which we build a wall. Meaning, according to this way of thinking, is to be sought through a closer and closer scrutiny of the term or word as we intend to use it in the vocabulary strand of code. But meanings shift and vary as terms are used in propositions, that is, as words are used in utterances and sentences. Vocabulary items often take on a wholly new character with the passage of time, or when they are put side by side in a new or unexpected way. The intonation pattern of an utterance (for example, in satire or irony) often gives to a word a meaning that is the exact opposite of what is usually intended. For these reasons, meaning is best thought of not as a quality but as a function; what a word means depends upon how it is used. This is the basic reason why vocabulary should be studied in context.

Types of words and expressions

In general, words may be divided into three types for aid in learning. There are the "little" or "empty" words that have little meaning in themselves but serve to particularize items in an utterance and to relate them to each other as well as to change and guide the direction of the thought. Such words are *an, these, but, although,* and the like. Secondly, there are "content" words that tell their own story, such as *salt, ugly,* or *holiday.* Thirdly, there are "clusters" of words, such as verbs that convey special concepts when used with given pronouns or prepositions (for example, *call it off* and *go without*). These last present special difficulties for the learner, for in them vocabulary and structure are intimately combined.

It is useful also to distinguish between what may be called a vocabulary item and an idiom. The simplest distinction is to say that the vocabulary item contains a single word, while the idiom contains more than one word. A stricter analysis would say that an idiom is composed of a group of words having a meaning not immediately discernible in any of its constituent parts. Typical English idioms are *to have a bone to pick with someone, to be comfortably off,* and *to splice the main brace.* We may distinguish further between lexical items and idioms by noting that in the former the syntactic or grammatical factor is minimal, whereas in the latter there may be extensive changes in form and order as the item appears in different contexts. For example, the vocabulary entry *to go away* may well appear in context as *away she went.*

It is customary to say that the learner's vocabulary is divided into two main areas, *active* and *passive*. The first of these is a small, central area of items subject to *recall*, with boundaries that are fairly sharp and clear. This is implanted upon a far greater area of items subject to *recognition*, the boundaries of which are vague and variable. Our recognition knowledge of an individual word may be quite uncertain when it is considered by itself but become much more certain when the word appears in context. At bottom, the difference between these two areas of vocabulary is related to the *parole* and *langue* aspects of language. Although the words *active* and *passive* are useful to describe these differences, a more accurate set of terms is *receptive* and *productive*, chiefly because *passive* suggests a cessation of activity, and alert listening or reading involves anything but that.

Vocabulary and reading

It is frequently assumed that the student should not attempt to read a passage until he has a recognition knowledge of all the words it contains or unless he stops to "look up" the meaning of each word new to him as he encounters it. Otherwise he is "just guessing" at meaning. This view results from a misunderstanding of the nature of guessing and the nature of reading. A pure guess at the meaning of a word, say of seven letters, would be to assign to it the meaning of any other seven-letter word in the language selected at random. This, of course, is absurd. The student is doing much more than making a guess when meaning is read into an unfamiliar word appearing in a context that is otherwise understood. What we often term a guess is rather a choice. This fact is related to the phenomenon noted by Roman Jakobson and Morris Halle in their statement that "all phonemes denote nothing but mere otherness." [1] We can apply this by saying that a segment of language means what it does because all other possible meanings are rejected through the processes of comparison and elimination.

---

[1] Roman Jakobson, *Selected Writings* ('s Gravenhage: Mouton, 1962), p. 470.

Only one possible message could have been intended, and this is the one that is understood. This analysis agrees in a singular way with the theory of essences as proposed by George Santayana in *The Realm of Essence*.[2] He states that essences are the data of the mind and sees each essence as different from every other and as equal to or identical with nothing but itself. Yet there may be countless instances of the same essence. An essence is recognized through the immediate rejection of the possibility of its being anything but itself. That this is a continuing central process in language communication seems most likely. The advice to the student to read a new passage over several times is the best that can be given; he will often be surprised to find how meaning and comprehension build up upon successive readings, without reference to English.

Literal translation

In the establishing of meaning in the target language, some use of the meaning stream of the mother tongue, which is so well known, undoubtedly should be made. Does this involve translation, and if so of what type and to what extent? One language may be compared with another in terms of their vocabularies, item by item, and this is precisely the role of the bilingual dictionary. But when a message or statement or sequence of utterances has been coded in one language and is then to be recoded in another, the recoding cannot adequately take place at the level of terms. Rather, it must be done at the level of propositions. We have already seen how frequently and how widely meaning may differ at these two levels. The literal or analytical translation—the word-by-word matching of two language codes—by its very nature not only conveys far less adequate meaning than restatement at the level of propositions but in addition gives a distorted notion of the way in which people in the "other" language communicate. The jerky, twisted, and inept syntax and morphology of the literal translation suggest that all this awkwardness of thought and expres-

---

[2] (New York: Scribner, 1927.)

sion is characteristic of those who speak the original language. The true nature of expression in the original language is thus quite misjudged. For our purposes it is probably better to avoid the use of the word *translation* unless we mean the thorough and complete restatement of the message that fully respects the norms of both languages in question.

It is quite possible to use English to identify the meaning of single, isolated words, without involving translation at the proposition level at all. The reason for this is that the transfer of meaning at the word level is essentially a matter of lexical meaning only, while the matching of whole utterances always involves structural patterns as well, and these often interfere with and are harmful to the internalized behavior patterns of the student in the target language.

Vocabulary aids

Various types of apparatus designed to help the learner with problems of vocabulary are currently in use, such as interlarded or marginal equivalents (in either the target language or the mother tongue or both), footnotes, facing translations, glosses and notes (separate from the text), and cumulative vocabulary (at end of section or end of book). The cumulative vocabulary may be in the target language only, or it may be bilingual. In some textbooks vocabulary items are first treated in the target language and then, if it is considered advisable, in English. This last procedure is a dependable aid to comprehension and permits extensive use of word studies in class that can thus be carried on without reference to English.

There is some usefulness in all these vocabulary techniques, yet they are not all equally valuable to the learner, and some of them may hinder more than help. The effect upon internalized language behavior of presenting two languages so that the eye can embrace both of them at the same time has not yet been precisely determined. There is a likelihood, however, that this may be harmful to the learner. It is mandatory that meaning be made clear, but there are many ways of doing this without simultaneously presenting the two languages. In presenting whole sentences in facing translation for the purpose of making meaning clear, it should be remembered that the need for English in such an exercise is not a constant, as a full translation suggests. More than half of the English words are not needed at all. Yet if presented they tend to detract from what the student has already learned of the target language. How can we help the learner reinforce the target language rather than English, yet make meaning clear at those points where he needs help? One suggestion is that facing translations be presented in opposite columns, with the target language on the right. In the left-hand column give the sentence translated not in its entirety but with blanks for the words it is assumed that the student knows and English equivalents only for words and expressions that are new. This format can make meaning clear without the intrusion of English structure and without heightening the interference that is caused by reinforcing the English equivalent of what is already beginning to be known in the target language.

Word lists

The growth of the receptive vocabulary is related to the amount of reading done and to its character and difficulty. How can the student at the same time most effectively increase the size, range, and readiness of the vocabulary used in the productive skills? A practical way is for him to single out and make his own certain words and expressions that have already been encountered in recent reading and have played a part in class exercises. But he needs guidance in the choice of items to be chosen for this kind of learning. Whatever the type of reading he has recently been engaged in, there will be on every page a number of words that he should make a special effort to learn. What is already known may be passed over, and words that are too unusual should not claim his attention for this purpose either, for they are too difficult to learn and are less immediately valuable. He should concentrate on the items that fall near the growing edge of his own vocabulary, words and expressions of high frequency that do not yet come easily and quickly to him when he wishes to speak and to write. The teacher who understands the learner's needs in these terms can easily identify from ten to twenty learning items on almost any page of reading text. These should include examples of both vocabulary and idiom as explained above. To give the student long lists of isolated words or expressions to learn in order to increase his vocabulary is likely to yield a low return with respect to language control. If, however, the student prepares his own lists of words and expressions, made up of items called to his attention in contexts that he is now in the process of learning, these taking the form of restatement in the target language (plus the English equivalent if desirable), a much higher yield in learning may be expected. This is because such a list actually reflects the progress being made by each individual student.

Referring now to pages of text read and commented on in class some days before, how is the list of selections that have been made by the teacher to be communicated to the students without loss of valuable class time? One way is to provide a duplicated list of such expressions indicating the page and line where they occur. Or, if the students can have access to a library or study-hall shelf on which the teacher has placed a copy of the text in which words and expressions have been underscored, the student can transfer these underscores to his own text in a very brief time. A third way is to prepare a vocabulary tape in which sentences and partial sentences taken from the text and containing the items to be learned are first listened to and repeated, then written on a self-correcting laboratory sheet prepared to accompany this tape, this sheet being kept for reference by the student. It is understood that all these vocabulary items are worked with in context, and not only the context of an isolated sentence but one that refers to the characters and the events of a story currently being read.

Word study

From the latter part of Level I on, word study can be a useful part of any class exercise. Different types of words lend themselves to different kinds of treatment, but all can be carried on in the target language, with English resorted to only in an emergency. Words may be defined in the usual lexical fashion, words with similar meanings can be given as synonyms for each other, and those with opposite meanings as antonyms. Free associations of the type exemplified in *crime–guilty, forgive–forget, storm–thunder, drum–dance* are endlessly intriguing and are a clear indication of meaning comprehension, without reference to another language. Words often appear in different categories in somewhat different forms, as *know–knowledge–knowledgeable,* or *comfort–comfortable–comfortably,* or *sing–singer–song–sing-song.* It is always interesting and profitable for the learner to compare and contrast words that are similar in sound, such as *sleep* and *slip, hallow* and *hollow, weather* and *whether,* and *cuff* and *cough,* or similar in meaning, such as *city* and *suburb, theater* and *movies, story* and *novel, star* and *planet,* and *holiday* and *vacation.* Of course, such exercises are done entirely in the target language.

Suggestions for further reading

Fries, Charles C. *Teaching and Learning English as a Foreign Language.* Ann Arbor, Mich.: University of Michigan Press, 1945.

Morris, Charles W. *Signs, Language and Behavior.* New York: Prentice-Hall, 1946.

Osgood, Charles E., G. Suci, and P. Tannenbaum. *The Measurement of Meaning.* Urbana, Ill.: University of Illinois Press, 1957.

Skinner, B. F. *Verbal Behavior.* New York: Appleton-Century-Crofts, 1957.

THE LANGUAGE LABORATORY

14

The language laboratory can be effective in learning, not in terms of the dual nature of authentic language behavior—a friendly chat with a machine is still quite a distance in the future —but rather in terms of the repetition and overlearning of behavior patterns that are to become habitual. The advantage of the machine over the living person for purposes of sustained repetition is obvious: the machine can repeat in identical fashion what was said before, and it can do so without fatigue or irritation. The machine can also record the student's response, which he may judge more critically when replayed than he can as he hears himself speak. He can also compare his response with the original, often perceiving what was not clear to him while he listened and replied.

Essential components

The essential components of a laboratory are these: tape recorders, earphones, microphones, and positions at which the students may work. (Sometimes provision is made for viewing pictures which serve as substitutes for situations.) These may be combined in many more or less complicated ways, with many more or less complicated controls and interconnections, but the basic functions are these: provision for the student to listen to a "master" voice, to repeat what he hears, and at times to record his response for review and correction. Language laboratories can be simple and inexpensive as well as luxurious and costly. Regardless of the investment, the return depends essentially on the integration of work in the classroom with activity in the laboratory. At best, laboratory work can be only peripheral to authentic talk. Its virtue is to provide the repetitions for overlearning that are absolutely essential to the student but tedious and taxing to the teacher. The teacher can thus reserve his energies for speaker-hearer exchange in which the student can hope to meet him halfway.

It is often asked whether a language laboratory is indispensable in the successful learning of language as communication. The answer appears to be definitely in the negative. It is probably best to plan for the successive levels of learning as if the language laboratory did not exist, then to decide at what points and in what ways the machine can best assist both learner and teacher. Provision can then be made for the use of electro-mechanical aids in terms of the space, the funds, and the staff available.

When a proposal to install a language laboratory is under consideration, those who must make the decisions have before them a problem that involves not only the usual matters of budget, salary, and purchase that accompany all such expenditures, but also the following topics that concern language learning in particular:

Equipment	Laboratory program
Installation	What the student hears
Upkeep and repairs	Length of tapes
Schedule	Voicing and timing of tapes
Supervision	Written exercises to accompany tapes
Length of laboratory period	Culture in the laboratory
Language-learning materials	Literature in the laboratory
	Tests in the laboratory

In the following paragraphs we enumerate the major points that these topics involve.

Mechanical equipment

The tape recorder is the essential piece of equipment that will quicken the learner's progress in the mastery of communication by language. Although recorders of many types and at many prices are now available, not many types of equipment especially designed to aid the language learner are on the market at the present time. This means that those who make the choice for purchase must be thoroughly acquainted with the learner's needs and must know whether the machines considered meet these needs. The essential criterion is a very simple one: the sound that reaches the student's ears must be of appropriate frequency range and must be undistorted. Ideally, a tape recorder should add no sounds of any kind to those issuing from the lips of the speaker who made the tape, and should reproduce all the speech accurately in the earphones of the listener. It is well within the capacity of a tape recorder rightly designed and installed to do this. If something less than perfection is all that can be afforded, the ideal still remains as a standard for comparison.

The decision to select one piece of equipment rather than another cannot be made merely on the basis of an advertised range of response. This rating may be accurate enough for what is being picked up at the playback head in the machine, but there are many steps between this and the impact made upon the student's eardrums and many points at which this rated response may be seriously reduced, especially in the earphones themselves. Since no sound in the new language is technically identical with those of the mother tongue, and since many of them are very different, the learner must hear them all with complete clarity if he is to reproduce them. It goes without saying that only a critical ear trained to hear the sounds of the new language accurately is competent to pass judgment on the capacity of the equipment to perform this essential task. This can only be done if the equipment is heard in action.

Physical installation

Once the fidelity of reproduction is assured, the next problem is to make the equipment available to the number of students who are to use it. In most schools or colleges the working unit is the class, and even though provision is often made for individual work in the language laboratory, we may say that in general an installation should provide for the largest number of students a class is likely to contain. When the laboratory is used for testing more than one class at a time, it must, of course, be able to accommodate the total number of students in these classes.

A laboratory is best installed in a room by itself. It may also occupy part of a regular classroom; at times all the necessary equipment is made portable and is wheeled from one room to another. At the position at which the student works there are earphones with which he listens to the master voice, a volume control so that he may adjust the loudness of what he hears, often a selector switch if the same position is designed to serve learners at different levels or in different courses, and a place for books and papers so that the student may write. In addition there is usually a microphone into which he speaks his response. If the earphones are "activated" he hears himself through them, and if provision is made for him to record, he can subsequently play back what he has said. Each position is often surrounded with sound-absorbent material, thus reducing the background noise that may interfere with hearing and that may be too distracting when picked up and recorded through the microphone into which he speaks. The "booth," as it is called, is not an unmixed blessing. It presents a problem with regard to the supervision of those at work in the laboratory, and its cost is usually all out of proportion to its worth. The earphones provide the best means for "isolating" the student, and the money saved by dispensing with elaborate and largely unnecessary booths is better spent on good-quality earphones, often the least satisfactory piece of equipment in the installation.

Sometimes the installation is designed to serve a dual purpose: The students in this case proceed in a usual learner-teacher relationship for a part of the class time and then, without changing their places, turn to the equipment of a normal laboratory and continue their work with earphones, microphone, and tape. This is called an electronic classroom.

When the laboratory is in operation, a tape is played so that a number of students can hear it simultaneously; in a more expensive installation, each student has a master tape at his own position and may stop and start the master as he wishes, thus advancing at his own rate. With adequate wiring and a sufficient number of positions the laboratory is able to accommodate students who are working on different tapes or at different levels in different languages. This is accomplished by providing a bank of tape decks and by supplying each position with a selector switch that enables the student to choose one of a number of different "programs" which his earphones can receive.

Tape recorders are subject to the unpredictable failures, great and small, that characterize all machines. Most of them will give many hours of satisfactory service without any difficulty. But tapes will sometimes spill and break, earphones will refuse to work, tubes will occasionally burn out, and other mechanical defects may bring an interruption in service. All recorders occasionally need an overhaul and cleaning, and provision for upkeep and repair must be made. The more machines are used as aids in teaching, the greater becomes the need to have all equipment in good working order at all times. A program of preventive maintenance provided at regular intervals is essential for best results. Educational institutions usually have on their staff and in their student body a considerable pool of amateur enthusiasts whose services may be invited when minor adjustments are called for; of course, professional repairmen must be appealed to when matters are serious.

Scheduling and supervision

The student should have a laboratory period at least twice a week, more often if possible. Part of the time already allotted for class periods may be spent in the laboratory with noticeable gain. The laboratory period need not be very long—it is often half the time of a regular class period—for fatigue in repetition must be reckoned with. It is of the greatest importance to provide the student not only with exercises in listening and speaking, but also with an exercise in writing (as soon as he is sufficiently advanced), dealing with the same material he has been hearing and repeating.

A laboratory should be constantly supervised by a responsible person who can keep a watchful eye on the activities of both learners and machines. The scheduling of laboratory periods is of course largely conditioned by local circumstances. But some general recommendations can be made as a result of experience and observation in many different institutions of learning. Much more time should be spent in listening and repeating than in recording and playback, the proportion being perhaps four or five times as much of the former as the latter. Important as it is for the student to hear his mistakes and correct them, it is far more important for him to spend his time listening to the master as his model, and not to himself.

Content of tapes

What the student hears on the master tape must be closely related to what is expected of him in the classroom if work in the laboratory is to win his full cooperation. Unrelated material presented on tape is of limited value. He must know that what he does in the laboratory will prepare him for what he is expected to do in class and that if he does not participate fully in laboratory exercises he will be at an obvious and constant disadvantage in the classroom. What this means in terms of the preparation of material is a task that must be resolutely faced. Without this integration between laboratory and classroom, the investment in equipment is largely wasted. This new need has been recognized in the preparation of integrated materials in which there is a laboratory equivalent of the dialogues, the pattern practices, the reading selections, the vocabulary and idiom study, and the quizzes and tests which are a part of regular classwork.

The scripts of such materials are voiced in such a way that the modeling is authentic, well timed, and interesting. They include laboratory exercises that involve the use of all the language skills in appropriate sequence and with appropriate emphasis. When the student comes to the laboratory he should, at early levels, hear materials that have first been presented in class. At Level I he should hear the materials of dialogues said in such a way that he can listen to all the sounds over and over and have an opportunity to repeat them himself. If the installation permits, he may record his repetition after the master voice, utterance by utterance, then play both back and compare.

Preparation of tapes

Pattern practice lends itself well to laboratory exercise, and there are many ways in which the student may be coached to repeat, to complete partial utterances, to change one utterance to another, and then to hear the correct response given immediately after his attempt. As soon as the student is sufficiently advanced, tapes can be prepared that provide drill in the learning of structure and vocabulary, the material for such exercises coming from the reading selections that are being studied in class. If words, expressions, and utterances have been chosen from pages of reading recently studied in class, students can deal with materials that have a psychological meaning, for the situations to which they refer are still fresh in their minds.

Tapes should not be very long, not more than fifteen minutes and often less. It is better to present a unit of material in this length of time, then to have the entire tape played again, rather than to prepare tapes of longer duration. The fatigue element must be reckoned with, for there is a limit to the time one can participate in pseudo-communication with a machine.

On a typical tape for Level I, the student hears (without seeing the text) a dialogue that has been presented in class. There is usually no need for any English on this tape, for meaning will have been made clear at the first presentation. Since it is a dialogue in which two or more persons are speaking, it is desirable to have a different voice for each part, feminine voices when they are appropriate. The dialogue is spoken in a number of different ways, all calculated to transfer the patterns of speech from the tape to the student with all the details of sound, intonation pattern, tempo, and meaning. First, the dialogue is spoken from beginning to end as it would normally be said in the situation. For the moment, the student just listens. Second, each utterance of the dialogue is broken up into short sequences of syllables, never more than five at a time and often less. Each utterance is treated as follows: A sequence is spoken, then a pause ensues, giving the student just time to say these few syllables; then the following sequence is spoken, followed by a similar pause, and so on until the utterance is complete. Next the utterance is repeated two more times, each time divided into sequences in the same way. After this, the whole utterance is presented as in normal speech, and time is given for the student to repeat it all at once. Then on to the next utterance. The script for such an exercise looks like this, the student's responses being in parentheses:

A. Can you tell me where to mail a letter?
B. There's a box across the street at the next corner.
A. Can you tell me (Can you tell me) where to mail (where to mail) a letter? (a letter?)
Can you tell me (Can you tell me) where to mail (where to mail) a letter? (a letter?)
Can you tell me (Can you tell me) where to mail (where to mail) a letter? (a letter?)
Can you tell me where to mail a letter? (Can you tell me where to mail a letter?)
B. There's a box (There's a box) across the street (across the street) at the next (at the next) corner. (corner.)
There's a box (There's a box) across the street (across the street) at the next (at the next) corner. (corner.)
There's a box (There's a box) across the street (across the street) at the next (at the next) corner. (corner.)
There's a box across the street at the next corner. (There's a box across the street at the next corner.)
A. Can you tell me where to mail a letter? (Can you tell me where to mail a letter?)
B. There's a box across the street at the next corner. (There's a box across the street at the next corner.)

This cutting of the stream of talk into small segments that are repeatedly presented gives the student the opportunity to hear and to repeat all the fine details of articulation, then to reproduce them in meaningful utterances as they are used in communication. Dialogues are usually presented in sections, all dealing with the same speakers and the same situation, but with only four or five utterances in each section. A tape may present only one section or an entire dialogue.

The voicing and the timing of tapes are of great importance. The first can bring the naturalness of communication to the learner, making the needed repetition more appealing. In timing, the master voice must not come in too soon after a pause or the learner does not have time to repeat; it must not wait too long or a dead space ensues that leads quickly to inattention and boredom.

A typical tape at Level III may be described as follows. Assume that a story is being read in class and that this tape deals with the vocabulary of six or eight pages of that story. From these pages a series of utterances is selected, each containing a word or expression chosen for study. These utterances should not be long and need not be complete sentences; only enough to put the item in context. On the tape the student hears these utterances presented in this sequence: First an English word (never spoken more than once) identifies the semantic area of the key word or expression. Then the utterance is said in the foreign language with special emphasis upon the target word. Time is given for the student to repeat. This is done again, and again there is time for him to repeat. On the third repetition the utterance is given in normal fashion, without emphasis on the key item. This the student repeats. Thus the meaning has been made clear, the vocabulary word has been identified in context, and it has been repeated in a natural way.

After the series of items has been completed, the tape tells the student to take the sheet on which a laboratory exercise has been prepared. He then hears these expressions read again and finds them written—all but the key items—on this sheet. As they are read, he fills in the missing forms. When the list is finished he is told to turn the sheet over. He finds a list of the forms he has been asked to write and may thus check for correctness what he has written. He also has a printed list of items that are now additions to his vocabulary.

Tapes must always be voiced from a prepared script. The making of the script is the time-consuming task that alone will guarantee the success of a language laboratory. If the script is well made and relates the laboratory work to that of the classroom, the student may be counted on to cooperate fully in this learning experience.

Other uses of the language laboratory

At higher levels the laboratory provides opportunities for presenting to the ears of the student selections of many kinds that have cultural and literary value. Often these can be recordings made in the foreign country; they thus have an authenticity of the highest order.

The language laboratory can also play a valuable role in testing. If suitably installed and equipped, the laboratory is an ideal place for biweekly tests, for the student even when working with an entire class can then demonstrate his achievement in all four skills.

Suggestions for further reading

Eddy, Frederick D. "1959 Revisited." *Audiovisual Instruction*, VII, 9 (November 1962), 602–23.

Hayes, Alfred S. *Language Laboratory Facilities*. United States Dept. of Health, Education, and Welfare. Education Office Bulletin 1963, No. 37, Washington, D.C.

Hutchinson, Joseph C. *Modern Foreign Languages in the High School: The Language Laboratory*. United States Dept. of Health, Education, and Welfare. Bulletin 1961, No. 23, Washington, D.C.

Iodice, Don. *Guidelines to Language Teaching in Classrooms and Laboratory*. Washington, D.C.: Electronic Teaching Laboratories, 1961.

Najam, Edward W., ed. "Materials and Techniques for the Language Laboratory." Report of the Language Laboratory Conference held at Purdue University, 1961. *International Journal of American Linguistics,* XXVIII, Part 2 (January 1962).

TESTS AND MEASUREMENTS

15

The word *test* as used by Chaucer referred to a process of verifying the purity of precious metals by the application of heat. A glance at a roomful of present-day students hard at work at a test points up the aptness of metaphor in our current use of the word.

There are those who would have us dispense with tests in the academic world. This attitude often results from the observation of badly made tests or of tests that employ techniques harmful to learning. When it does result from such observation, it is quite justifiable. But when a test or a test program is free from such negative factors and gives clear evidence of being a positive stimulus to learning, welcomed by teacher and learner alike as well as by those who observe at close range, it encourages a more positive attitude. This chapter is addressed to those who believe that tests of the right kind and quality are a desirable if not indispensable adjunct to formal learning.

Since the beginning of the present century, there has been an increasing need for a thorough and systematic program of tests designed to measure success in many subject areas. The nature of the tests used in modern foreign languages has been greatly modified during the succeeding decades. Until the mid 1930's, the traditional grammar-translation-composition exercise was the rule, with the student writing out his answers in full. Then came the gradual introduction of fixed-response tests, which were widely adopted in the early 1940's because of their apparent superiority with regard to brevity, economy, and efficiency—at least in assigning a rank order to each candidate in a large test population. As for the role of the different skills, the earlier tests had involved reading and writing only, while the fixed-response tests involved reading alone. It was not until the mid 1950's that widely used tests began to be concerned with anything more than pencil-and-paper activity. With the introduction of the listening comprehension test, the ear was brought into play. Finally, at the beginning of the present decade, the development of speaking tests increased the number of skills involved to four.

Why, it may well be asked, is such an elaborate program of measurement necessary? Can we not choose what is easiest to measure and let that be an index of over-all accomplishment? Such a plan may indeed be workable if there has been appropriate and sustained emphasis upon each of the four skills from the beginning of the learner's classroom experience. But it is quite possible to develop one of the skills to a considerable degree while paying little or no attention to the others, a fact that is especially true of listening comprehension. In addition, it is becoming more and more apparent, as we teach and measure the two audio-lingual skills separately and together, that they are in their nature very different from reading and writing and that there is often a marked difference in the pattern of achievement in the former two as compared with the latter. We must also recognize, rather regretfully, that the effect of testing upon teaching being what it is, teachers have tended to put major stress upon what they are sure will be measured. For these reasons, extrapolation from any one skill to total accomplishment has not proved dependable in practice. There seems to be no recommendable plan except to measure all the skills.

In such a comprehensive program, the distinctive nature of each language skill must be respected and all four measured one at a time and in various combinations. The special characteristics of the receptive and the productive skills must be considered in selecting item types and in deciding upon the nature and difficulty of their meaning content. In all language behavior there are some factors that are mandatory and others that are volitional. These should be incorporated in varying proportions into the sequence of tests designed for different levels of advancement. Tests should permit the learner to demonstrate progress not only in control of language code and in knowledge of meaning, but also in awareness of patterns of culture—for example, the various equivalents of the pronoun *you* and how they are used—and in acquaintance with and appreciation of literature.

Although there is as yet no systematic program for the study of culture in the anthropologist's sense, the fact remains that a language plays a central role in the culture in which it is spoken and often reflects certain characteristic and highly important factors in a very direct way. This is to be observed especially in the ways in which people address each other in speaking. There are usually cultural patterns that are learned very early in life, and are well beneath the threshold of awareness in the thoughts of the native speaker. But the second-language learner must learn these cultural usages, just as he must learn the "deep" grammar of the new language—a kind of learning that plays no part in formal education in the target culture because it has already been so thoroughly learned. Therefore we must devise tests that illustrate the direct impact of cultural patterns upon the language itself and that measure the learner's developing sensitivity to the modes of thought and action that are typical of those whose language he is learning.

The program we are describing will inevitably be complicated, time-consuming, and costly. And in order to justify its existence, the program should make it possible for us to answer such questions as these:

a. How can we predict before the student begins what degree of success he is likely to have during his first years of second-language learning?

b. How can we use tests to provide a steady index of the learner's progress as he makes his way through one level after another?
c. How can tests aid us in identifying areas of strength and weakness in what is being gained by the student and what is being offered by the program?
d. As the learner moves from one institution to another, how can the test program give an accurate evaluation of what he brings from the one and indicate where he should be placed to his best advantage in the other?
e. How can the test program review whole areas of language learning, of cultural and literary studies, and give assurance that the student has reached a satisfactory degree of achievement and is therefore qualified, if he so desires, to go on to more advanced work?
f. Above all, how can it be shown that the program of measurement is in no way a hindrance to either teacher or learner, but that it has, on the contrary, at all times a positive effect upon learning?

In summary, we may distinguish between a number of different kinds of tests needed to give different kinds of information. The *prognostic* test should tell us how well the student is likely to succeed before he begins. The *progress* test should tell us how well he has mastered the contents of a specific program. The *achievement* test should give an index of his growth without being directly related to any single learning program. And the *proficiency* test should show how complete a mastery has been acquired when a well-rounded course involving language competence, cultural insight, and literary acquaintance has been completed.

Prognostic tests

It appears evident that a prognostic test must have an audio-lingual phase as well as a visual-graphic phase and that the second should not be administered until the learner can understand and say a few valid expressions in the target language.

The forecast of success in hearing and speaking should not risk being blurred by whatever special abilities or limitations the learner may demonstrate in the visual-graphic area before a degree of audio-lingual control has been established. He should have familiar sounds that he has heard and spoken to refer to as he reads and writes.

The main features of a prognostic test that will foretell success in audio-lingual learning are these:

How accurately can the student repeat meaningful utterances in the new language immediately after hearing them?

How quickly does he grasp the nature of structural variations that he hears when analogy is his only guide?

To measure the first of these we may, for example, ask a speaker of Russian who knows no English to repeat the following phrases from Lincoln's Gettysburg Address (he is told the Russian equivalent before each phrase, and merely repeats the English as soon as he has heard it):

years ago	created equal
of that field	a great civil war
will little note	increased devotion
who fought here	so nobly advanced

Each of these phrases contains one or more sounds which the subject is not familiar with in his native tongue.

As a test of awareness of structural changes, the subject is asked to repeat a series of utterances in which the same change is consistently made, then to make such a change himself. For example, after being told the meaning of *a* through *e* in the groups below, he hears and repeats them one at a time. He must then supply on his own what *f* should be in each case.

a. Wait!
b. I'm waiting.
c. Go!
d. I'm going.
e. Look!
f. (I'm looking.)

a. He gave an order.
b. He gave orders.
c. He wrote a letter.
d. He wrote letters.
e. He made an error.
f. (He made errors.)

a. She knocks at the door.
b. She knocked at the door.

a. The name of my father.
b. My father's name.

c. She looks at her watch.
d. She looked at her watch.
e. She walks away.
f. (She walked away.)

c. The friend of my sister.
d. My sister's friend.
e. The home of my brother.
f. (My brother's home.)

When the subject has been given some training in audio-lingual activities *without* reading and writing (at least for a few days), he may be asked to show his ability in manipulating the written symbols of the new language by dealing with what he has learned as it appears on paper. Of course, the degree to which he is likely to master the visual-graphic skills and the vocabulary of a new language can be inferred fairly well from his performance in similar activities in the mother tongue. But in fairness to him and in deference to accuracy, it seems wise to postpone the prognosis in these skills until he has had a chance to gain a measure of confidence and control in listening and speaking.

There seems to be no quick and easy way around the problem of a prognostic test. A single, brief screening may select most of the good learners but may still not tell us how many other good learners in the group have not been identified because the normal sequence in the development of the skills has not been followed.

Progress tests

When learning is viewed from the tester's angle, the intimate relationship of measurement to objectives, materials, and classroom procedure becomes most apparent. This intimacy is closest, of course, at the earlier levels, the time when progress tests are most appropriate. A progress test is less difficult to prepare than most tests because the tester has precise knowledge of the segments of code and meaning that the student is in the process of learning. A great many of the techniques of classroom learning and drill can be readily adapted for use as item types in such tests. In so doing, one must distinguish between *what* the learner is to show that he knows and *how* he is to show it. For example, a knowledge of endings of verbs or adjectives can be demonstrated in a number of ways; the student should know that he will be tested only by being asked to work with complete utterances in the target language, used as they occur in communication. Before the test, he should become familiar with all the techniques that the test will employ.

The progress test can be used not only to measure individual success in comparison with peers, but also to show in detail what areas must be better mastered by the learner and more effectively taught. The unhappy practice of requiring the learner to produce linguistic forms for which he has had no adequate model (thus forcing him into error) can be successfully avoided if progress tests are carefully made.

Achievement tests

In contrast with the progress test, the achievement test should measure learning that has been acquired, with reference not to any specific course of study but to a great number of such courses. This means that such tests cannot become reliable until the latter part of Level II, when the student can be expected to have at his disposal models of all the commonest forms of language used in speech, whatever may be the course of study he is following. Despite the widely varying content in the language curriculums of our schools and colleges, reliable achievement tests employing all the skills are now becoming available for use from the second half of Level II onward. There appears to be an increasing tendency for such tests to reflect the content of the succeeding levels as we have described them.

Proficiency tests

The proficiency test is prepared without regard for specific current or previous learnings and is based rather upon uses to which the new language is customarily put. Although these tests cannot fairly estimate the performance of a student in a given course or sequence of courses, they have a legitimate use when the student presents himself for placement in a new institution or when he resumes his study of a language after an interruption of a year or more. Such tests should include measurement of all four skills, structure (including vocabulary), and cultural awareness. The types and variety of items used in a proficiency test will not differ from those used in an achievement test; the difference is rather in the source material and in the anticipated standards according to which the tests are constructed. Whereas achievement tests can in all fairness relate only to the learnings that a given curriculum provides, proficiency tests seek rather a set of competencies and a store of information in the candidate but do not adhere solely to the materials which every candidate has had an opportunity to study. Both achievement and proficiency tests will be measurably improved if the difference between them is recognized and reflected in their construction.

What is an objective test?

Anyone who has addressed himself to the task of evaluating the answers given by a hundred students to the same question soon becomes aware that there is not only a pattern of similarity in the answers that can be called right but that there are also distinct patterns of similarity to be observed in those that must be called wrong. If it happens that the number of students to be measured runs into many hundreds or even thousands, efficiency suggests that the same discrimination may be made between those who know and those who do not by presenting each student with a typically right answer and several typically wrong answers, asking him merely to indicate which is right. If the number of students to be measured is large, we are very likely to accept the shorter, more economical procedure, provided we have confidence that the students really are being measured with the same degree of accuracy in both cases.

If we give a group of students a written test and an objective test, each containing the same questions presented in these different ways, and find that they align themselves in the same rank order in both tests, we may safely conclude that the one is doing the same job as the other. There are certain notable differences between the two types of test. The construction of the objective test is much the more time-consuming, yet the time required for scoring it is very much shorter than that required for the written test. Likewise, the time needed for administering the objective test is considerably briefer.

Before deciding in favor of the objective test, one may have some further reservations. Such tests involve only recognition; is this really an index of what the student can recall and actively use? And if a single, carefully made objective test measures as well as a performance test, does this mean that all tests in which the objective technique is used will do likewise? The answer to the first question relates to the learning program the student has followed. If all four skills have been appropriately learned, the reply is an unqualified yes: recognition will always be much greater in quantity than recall, but the correlation between the two will be high. The answer to the second question is, of course, no. In order that the objective test may perform properly, not only must the right answers be wholly right and the wrong ones wholly wrong, all must truly reflect the working of a student's mind and present the same degree of plausibility even when the reply is incorrect.

As the student proceeds through a number of years of language study, he is likely to encounter tests made in three different ways. The first is the homemade test, constructed by his own teacher or the department in which he studies. The second may be called the ready-made test, printed in quantity and coming to his school from some outside agency or organization. The third is the standardized test, also coming from outside his school but with a history of preparation very different from that of the ready-made test.

What is a standardized test?

Since the meaning of this term is often only partially understood, it may be useful to list the steps that must be taken in order that a test may be so described. We should note that in formal testing, the basic unit is the *item*, that is, the test question or problem that counts as one unit in the final score. The selection of item types to be used and the writing of items appropriate to the learning to be measured are of supreme importance at every point. A single test may have only forty or fifty items or as many as several hundred.

PRELIMINARY AGREEMENT ON SPECIFICATIONS

Before any items are written, those who teach subject matter and those whose field is the science of measurement must agree on the types of items to be used, their quantity and arrangement, and the directions for procedure that will be given to the candidate.

ITEM WRITING

The writing of test items is a highly specialized activity that is in part a personal gift and in part a learnable technique. It is a truism that not all those who know have the gift of teaching well; it is equally true that not all those who teach well have the gift of preparing suitable tests of what they teach. It is for this reason that item writing must proceed under supervision and is, in fact, best done by those who possess this special gift and have had ample opportunity to develop it. But all who teach should be encouraged, through collaboration, to improve their effectiveness in the preparation of test items.

EDITING OF ITEMS

Once the proposed items are down on paper, they must be edited by competent representatives of classroom teaching and of scientific measurement. This joint editorial process attempts to foresee as well as possible what the student's reactions will be as he faces the given problem and to make sure that both the form and the content of the problem relate directly to the learner's control of subject matter. A teacher's first attempts at test writing are likely to result in items that measure best what he himself knows. This is often followed by a phase in which he prepares tests for what he assumes his fellow teachers know. Eventually he learns to make tests that measure what is taking place at the growing edge of the student's knowledge—and this is often very different in both form and content from what the mature professional person knows about the subject in question,

INTEGRATING OF ITEMS

A test must of course be more than a simple sequence of items, even if each one of them is fully valid in itself. Items of the same type should be grouped together and presented under a single set of directions. Usually they are arranged in order of difficulty, with the easiest first. Repetition must be avoided in order not to waste time testing the same thing twice. There should be enough variety in the types of items presented to sample effectively the various areas of the subject matter in question. The student taking the test is entitled to feel that it has an organic unity and that it permits him to display he knowledge he has.

PRETESTING

Up to this point the test is at best a shrewd estimate on the part of a group of professional adults as to the most satisfactory way in which a group of adolescent amateurs can manifest their knowledge—or lack of it—in a given subject area. But not until the test has been given to a group of students who are typical of the entire population that will eventually take the test can it be known precisely how it will work in practice. This is the purpose of the pretest. The size of the pretest group is usually two hundred or more and the test itself is somewhat longer than it will eventually be. It is common practice to pretest three items for every two that will appear in the final test.

OFFICIAL SCORING OF PRETESTS

The scoring of a pretest may be done in three different ways. In a fixed-response test, in which choices have been indicated on a special answer sheet prepared in advance, the scoring may be done electronically. This is accomplished through the use of an electric eye that scans the answer sheet and quickly tells how many black marks have been inscribed in the right places. The scoring of such a test may also be done "by hand," that is, by using a stencil or masking sheet with holes so punched that the black marks on the answer sheet show through if correct choices have been made. Thirdly, if the test involves overt performance, evaluation must be made by a person who has special competence in the subject matter and who has been trained in scoring.

In measuring the language skills, it has been found possible to prepare very satisfactory tests of reading comprehension and listening comprehension by the use of fixed-response items. The active skills of speaking and writing, however, are another matter. If the candidate is to speak or to write, his performance must be written or recorded and later evaluated by a knowledgeable scorer. The official scoring of such tests requires the collaboration of a group of scorers who first of all familiarize themselves with the full range of responses that have been made. They then agree on the way in which the various responses are to be evaluated and proceed to score the entire set of pretests, adhering as closely as possible to the quality scale that has been set up.

STATISTICAL ANALYSIS OF PRETEST ITEMS

The analysis, item by item, of the scores made on the same test by several hundred students yields information of various kinds. Of first importance are two questions about each item: (a) How difficult is it? and (b) How well does it perform individually when compared with the entire test as a means of discriminating between those who have learned and those who have not? The answer to the first question is simple: If most of the students get a given item right, it is easy; if most of them get it wrong, it is difficult. But this needs to be checked by the second question: How many of those who do well on the test as a whole get this item right, and how many of them get it wrong? Not infrequently an item is so presented that the poorer students tend to get it right and the better ones fail to do so. The result of item analysis is to give an accurate indication of the difficulty of every item and of its ability to discriminate in the desired way. In addition, if the test is composed of fixed-response items, analysis shows how many students chose each individual wrong answer or "distractor" in each item. A distractor that is found to be of little or no interest to the test population is not performing its function and must be replaced.

FINAL EDITING

A final editorial revision is now made in the light of the results of pretesting, scoring, and item analysis. Only the best items are kept for the final forms. Those that have not performed well are revised and improved if possible; otherwise they are discarded. In the final editing, careful attention is paid to any comments or suggestions offered by those who administered the pretest and by those who scored the productive skills. Such comments are often of great value in making final decisions concerning the content and form of items, the wording of instructions, and the over-all proportions of the test.

NORMING

It is to be expected that a given school or college will wish to compare the performance of its students with that of others in similar institutions. For this reason the final forms are first given in a selection of typical schools with recognized differences in respect to size, composition and ability of the student body, type of instruction offered, the general nature of the curriculum content in the subject in question, and the character of physical equipment available for student use. Separate sets of figures are then prepared that show the results of the test in each one of a variety of typical institutions. Any school can then compare the results achieved by its students with the data reported from the school most like itself.

EQUATING OF FORMS

Once a student has been measured by a given standard, it is very desirable to measure him again at a later time by the same standard in order to know the exact degree of growth. If the same test were used a second time, memory might be a strong enough factor to discredit the result. But if the second test is exactly the same in difficulty though different in content, a just comparison can be made. This is accomplished by preparing different forms of the same test and giving these in separate sections to the same test population. Since the population is the same, it is known that the different forms are measuring with the same accuracy.

As may be surmised from the foregoing summary, the teacher of any subject who has never submitted a test of his for editing by colleagues and for statistical analysis of results very likely has some surprises in store for him if and when he does so. By the same token, it is apparent that ready-made tests that have not been standardized must inevitably retain a considerable degree of inaccuracy in measurement.

Homemade tests

Those who construct homemade tests are no less eager than those who make standardized tests that the measurement process shall be accurate, representative, and fair. We continue with a list of practical suggestions for the preparation of homemade tests, largely inspired by the procedures followed in standardization.

1. Make the assignment for study and review as specific as possible. The student usually puts his best learning effort into review for a test; he will learn more if he knows upon what the effort is to be expended.
2. Make the directions clear. Many directions that are clear to the giver are not clear to the receiver. Try them out ahead of time upon another person.
3. Acquaint the student with all the techniques before the test. The point at issue is the nature and extent of the student's knowledge, not the manner in which he is to demonstrate it. Examples should precede all questions requiring techniques with which the student may not be familiar.
4. Test one thing at a time. The responses we ask for are often very complicated; accuracy of measurement will be directly related to our success in holding all the variables constant save one and carefully noting its performance. When two or more factors are unavoidably or deliberately involved in a single item—for example, responses that require reading in a *listening comprehension* test—make every effort to minimize the difficulty of what is not being tested.

5. Test vocabulary only in a context of normal speech or by pairing naturally associated words and expressions in the foreign language.
6. Give the student ample opportunity to show what he can do by preparing a sufficient number of questions that are different from each other and of the right degree of difficulty.
7. Test everything you announce you are going to test. Fairness demands this; besides, it will directly affect the student's effort on the next test.
8. Present normal problems. Associating words with each other, completing a form, a thought, or a description, answering a reasonable question or giving a reasonable rejoinder, identifying or recalling forms that satisfy both sense and syntax, writing or saying what is likely to be written or said—such things can be called normal problems. An example of an *ab*normal problem is asking the student to operate on that ubiquitous half-breed of the grammar books, the bilingual sentence, part of which is in the mother tongue and part in the target language.
9. Use material that comes from the normal modes of speech. Do not "invent" paragraphs specifically for a test. Not only is the student entitled to deal with authentic language, but measurement will be more accurate if he does so.
10. Put the student at ease at once. Begin with problems he can attack promptly and confidently.
11. Maintain a pattern of difficulty. Present the material in each part of the test so that the questions gradually increase in difficulty.
12. Prescribe the length of the answer. Particularly when writing is called for, always specify within narrow limits how many words are to be written. The length of the piece is in every case an important factor in successful writing. When the student is to answer questions, a useful formula is: "Make your answer at least as long as the question."
13. Organize the test by putting together what goes together. If you borrow from other tests or texts, abridge fearlessly and adapt the borrowed material to the limits and purposes

of your test and to the capacities of the group being measured.
14. Make up more questions than you will need and let second thought weed out those that are least appropriate. This always improves the quality of the finished product.
15. Keep the test in the foreign language. Use English only for directions.
16. Invite the collaboration of an editor. Have every test read over and if possible tried out by a disinterested third party.
17. Avoid the use of anecdotes, misspellings, and incorrect forms. Anecdotes depend too often upon the understanding of a single "punch" line. The use of misspellings and incorrect forms presents problems that are false and gratuitous for many learners. Such items may be suitable in tests for teachers, but they have no place in tests for students.

Item types

The learning of language as communication implies the use of many more types of activity than have traditionally been employed in language testing. This new field is now being explored with notable success. For example, in the past decade it has been discovered that listening comprehension is a factor in language behavior that lends itself remarkably well to measurement, and such tests are now coming into general use. They usually include these types of item: phonemic discrimination, the completion of utterances, answers to questions, rejoinders that fit into a conversation, and long passages on a single subject; all these are heard but not seen. The success of such tests has been due chiefly to the fact that they approach a normal use of language, such as catching a name over the telephone, understanding a question that is casually asked in conversation, and comprehending what is said in a lecture hall or over the radio. These tests contain no English, no dictation, no anecdotes, and no incorrect forms. The stimulus is directed exclusively to the ear. The response is the choice of a picture or a printed statement that correctly matches what is said.

Among the types of test item that are familiar to everyone, there are many that do not violate the basic principles noted earlier in this chapter, and most of them are to be recommended. Without attempting to review all of these types of item, our purpose now is to suggest a number of kinds of test questions that are not in wide use at the present time.

The distinction between *langue* and *parole* permits an insight into many new possibilities for the construction of test items. The distinction between the sign and symbol uses of language and between verbal and nonverbal behavior is likewise most fruitful in this regard. Under *langue* appear the elements of phonology, syntax, morphology, and meaning that can readily be presented to the student in test form. Under *parole* appear the types of response that the student can make to indicate his reactions to a verbal or nonverbal stimulus. It is possible for a nonverbal stimulus to elicit a verbal response and for a verbal stimulus to elicit a nonverbal response. This usually involves a sign use of language rather than a symbolic use, but the sign use is an important step in the mastery of language per se.

The principal elements in language behavior that may be singled out for separate measurement (and with which nonverbal behavior may at times be combined) are these:

Listening comprehension	Control of structure
Audio-lingual integration	Knowledge of meaning
Speaking	Appreciation of content
Writing	and style

The types of stimulus that may be used, alone or in combinations, are these:

Actual situations	Pictures
Spoken words	Writing

The types of response that may be elicited, alone or in combination, are these:

Hearing	Arrangement
Reading	Retention
Speaking	Discrimination
Writing	Recall

Body motion
Selection
Association
Completion

Restatement
Commentary
Appreciation
Invention

Of special interest among such test items is the body-motion test. The student may be told to perform acts such as the following, or, much more difficult, he may see them performed and be asked to describe what he observes:

Hold out your right hand.
Clap your hands.
Look at the ceiling.
Point to the clock.
Throw a ball.
Knock on a door.
Take a sip of hot coffee.
Comb your hair.
Act as though you had a headache.
Read a letter.
Act as though you had a toothache.
Look at your wristwatch.
Blink your eyes.
Stifle a yawn.
Fold your arms.
Walk backward a few steps.

Take off your glasses; put them back on.
Peel a potato.
Dial a telephone number.
Deal cards from a deck.
Beat an egg.
Dry your hands on a towel.
Drive a car.
Thread a needle.
Type on a typewriter.
Play a violin.
Unscrew the top of a bottle.
Walk with a limp.
Count the change in your pocket.
Shield your eyes from the bright sunlight.

A remarkably accurate measure of a student's progress in a new language is possible through the use of completion tests that leave out occasional words in a connected passage, the context indicating what the missing forms should be. If the passage is new to the student, deletions can be made only of "little" or "noncontent" words such as articles, prepositions, auxiliaries, and the like. When the student has recently studied the passage, content words may be deleted which he then restores according to his knowledge of the language and the passage in question.

A wide variety of new test items may be constructed once it is recognized that language behavior covers a much greater area than that which is circumscribed by a pencil and a piece of paper, and that it is quite possible to test all areas of the new language without recourse to the mother tongue.

Following is a list of examples of item types that have been found satisfactory and useful in practice. In some cases the stimulus may be spoken, in others written. The responses (found on pages 222–24) may involve mere selection of possible answers, or they may require the writing of words, sentences, or paragraphs.

1. Choose the one word that will correctly complete the sentence.

    EXAMPLE   Won't you come and have dinner at my _____?
    ( ) family
    ( ) evening
    ( ) home
    ( ) lunch

2. A statement is followed by several suggested rejoinders, only one of which is appropriate. Select the rejoinder that a speaker would use after hearing the statement.

    EXAMPLE   Hurry or we'll be late.   ( ) So do I.
    ( ) I'm coming.
    ( ) Don't mention it.
    ( ) No more, thanks.

3. Answer these questions, substituting a pronoun for the noun in the question.

    EXAMPLES   a. Have you any postcards?
    b. Did you find your hat?

4. Rewrite the following sentence, incorporating the additional words.

    EXAMPLE   He bought a great many paintings.   old   fine

5. Restate the following sentences in the negative.

    EXAMPLES   a. You find paperbound books everywhere.
    b. Everybody was late this morning.

TESTS AND MEASUREMENTS / 217

6. Rewrite the sentence, substituting pronouns for all nouns.

    EXAMPLE   The messenger handed the letter to the clerk.

7. Complete the passage by writing in each of the blank spaces a word selected from the list in the column at the right. Select words that will make the meaning clear and change form where necessary. Do not use a word more than once.

    EXAMPLE

    Early the _____ morning, he went to the borough Commissioner's. But it _____ out that he was still asleep. He _____ at ten and again was _____ he was asleep. He _____ back at eleven and was told that the Commissioner was not _____. He tried again during the dinner hour but the secretaries in the reception room would not let him _____ and wanted to know what _____ had brought him.

    before
    business
    come
    go
    home
    in
    next
    return
    sleep
    tell
    turn

8. Imagine that you are talking on the telephone to a friend.

    EXAMPLES   a. Ask your friend if he can be ready at six o'clock.
    b. Tell him to come and meet us at your house.

9. In the following passage some words and expressions are left blank. You will *hear* the passage *read in full,* including the words and expressions you do not see. As you hear the passage read, write in all the missing words in their proper form.

    EXAMPLE

    If Mrs. Smith's handwriting gives no _____ to her charm and _____, this is a _____ she shares with millions of fellow Americans. We _____ a nation of scrawlers and _____. Each day brings a _____ of horrible examples to the _____ in post offices.

10. Complete the following sentence by writing in the remainder of the missing word, the first letter of which is given.

218 / LANGUAGE AND LANGUAGE LEARNING

EXAMPLES a. This paper is a standard q_____, ensuring a good writing surface.
b. We went out into the garden to get some f_____ air.

11. Write a question that pertains to the underscored word in the following sentence.

    MODEL Henry found a <u>dollar</u> on the floor of the station.
    What did Henry find on the floor of the station?

    EXAMPLE This author has already published <u>four</u> novels.

12. Use the verb in the sentence a second time, writing it in its appropriate form.

    EXAMPLES a. If you were going out, I _____ out with you.
    b. If she _____, I should have accepted also.

13. A complete sentence is given as a model, followed by a list of separate words. You are to write a new sentence that has the same structure as the model. Use all the words in the list, in the order given, changing form when necessary, and adding what is required for completion.

    EXAMPLE Let him continue his trip on his bicycle.
    them/finish/homework/room

14. The following series of words is to be written as a complete sentence. Use all the words, in the order given, changing form when necessary and adding whatever is required for completion.

    EXAMPLE we/now/well/into/second /year/this/program/and/ able/report/that/on/schedule

15. Complete the sentence by using the words below the line. Change forms as required and add what is necessary for completion.

    EXAMPLE If I had more money I _____.
    go/Europe/summer

16. Write in the blank space the one word needed to complete the sentence.

EXAMPLES a. The door was locked and Henry began fumbling in his pocket for the _____.
b. High in the sky the hawks hung immobile on their outspread _____.

17. Rewrite each of the following two utterances as a single sentence.

EXAMPLES a. There's the girl from Texas. She just won a prize.
b. Joe and Bill went fishing. When?

18. Rewrite the following sentences, making the changes that are made in the model.

MODEL Whenever he hears his name, he stands up.
Whenever he heard his name, he stood up.

EXAMPLES a. Whenever the telephone rings, she answers.
b. Whenever there is danger, he runs away.

19. You will hear a series of quotations [1] read, each one with a number. Identify the speaker by writing the *number* of the quotation after the *name* of the person speaking.

EXAMPLE (on answer sheet) Benjamin Franklin ( ) ( )
Thomas Carlyle ( ) ( )
Horace Greeley ( ) ( )
Abraham Lincoln ( ) ( )
Nathan Hale ( ) ( )
Horatio Nelson ( ) ( )
Woodrow Wilson ( ) ( )

(heard but not seen)
1. My only regret is that I have but one life to give for my country.
2. England expects every man to do his duty.
3. Turn your face to the great West.
4. With malice toward none; with charity for all.
5. A war to end war.

---

[1] These quotations would come from the texts being read. The quotes should be vital ones, easily attributable to the person speaking by virtue of their style and content. There is often more than one quote by the same person.

20. A statement is given, followed by four others. Select the one sentence that is a logical continuation of the statement given.

   EXAMPLE   I intend to give the delivery boy a gift at Christmas.

   ( ) He sets my nerves on edge.
   ( ) He's always obliging.
   ( ) He hasn't been here for years.
   ( ) We need some new decorations.

21. Listen to (or read) the following paragraph, then by the appropriate choice below, indicate what it is about.

   "I have not permitted myself, gentlemen, to conclude that I am the best man in the country; but I am reminded in this connection of a story of an old Dutch farmer, who remarked to a companion that it was not best to swap horses when crossing a stream."

   ( ) a wedding
   ( ) an election
   ( ) farming
   ( ) a flood

22. Restore the following passage to its original form by writing in the blanks the letters and syllables that have been deleted.

   EXAMPLE   If we re-experience sensations that we once felt in the past—such as the taste of a cake dip_____ in tea—we _____live all the experienc_____ asso- ciat_____ with them. The past come_____ back to us vivid_____, as it real_____ was; the flight of time has stop_____, we feel oursel_____ to be _____mortal.

23. Rewrite the following sentence, substituting other words for those that are underlined, but keeping the structure of the original.

   EXAMPLES   a. Tell your brother to wait for us.
   b. That's more than I had expected.
   c. At last we saw the house in which the lawyer lived.

TESTS AND MEASUREMENTS / 221

24. The following questions all relate to an event in a passage recently read. Think out a suitable answer to each question, then write these answers in such a way as to form a complete paragraph.

> EXAMPLE With whom did Joseph speak in front of the village church?
> What did the old man tell him? On what condition?
> Why had the old man gone to Italy years before?
> Whom had he met in Rome? What did this person become for him?
> Why did he want to introduce this person to his parents?

25. Write a paragraph of forty to sixty words in which you tell who is speaking in the following quotation, to whom, where, when, about whom or what, and why.

> EXAMPLE "Friends, Romans, countrymen, lend me your ears. I come to bury Caesar, not to praise him."

ANSWERS

1. No. 3

2. No. 2

3. a. Yes, I have some.
   b. No, I didn't find it.

4. He bought a great many fine old paintings.

5. a. You don't find paperbound books anywhere.
   b. Nobody was late this morning.

6. He handed it to him.

7. next
   turned
   returned
   told
   went
   home
   in
   business

222 / LANGUAGE AND LANGUAGE LEARNING

8. a. Can you be ready at six o'clock?
   b. Come and meet us at my house.

9. If Mrs. Smith's handwriting gives no *clue* to her charm and *ability*, this is a *failing* she shares with millions of fellow Americans. We *are becoming* a nation of scrawlers and *scratchers*. Each day brings a *spate* of horrible examples to the *dead-letter collections* in post offices.

10. a. quality
    b. fresh

11. How many novels has this author already published?

12. a. If you were going out, I would go out with you.
    b. If she had accepted, I should have accepted also.

13. Let them finish their homework in their room.

14. We are now well into the second year of this program and **are** able to report that we are on schedule.

15. If I had more money I would go to Europe this summer.

16. a. key
    b. wings

17. a. There's the girl from Texas who just won a prize.
    b. When did Joe and Bill go fishing?

18. a. Whenever the telephone rang, she answered.
    b. Whenever there was danger, he ran away.

19. 1. Hale
    2. Nelson
    3. Greeley
    4. Lincoln
    5. Wilson

20. No. 2

21. No. 2

22. If we re-experience sensations that we once felt in the past—such as the taste of a cake dip*ped* in tea—we *re*live all the ex*periences* associat*ed* with them. The past comes back to us

vivid*ly*, as it real*ly* was; the flight of time has stop*ped*, we feel our*selves* to be *im*mortal.

23. Possible answers:
    a. Ask your sister to look for us.
    b. That's less than I had ordered.
    c. First of all we saw the laboratory in which the chemist worked.

24. When Joseph came out of the little village church, he spoke with the old man he had noticed inside. The old man told Joseph his story, on condition that it should never be repeated to anyone else. Years before, in his youth, he had gone to Italy to regain his health. In Rome he had met a charming young girl who had become the love of his life. He wanted to introduce her to his parents and to marry her.

25. (Original paragraph by the student.)

Typical classroom tests

The following outlines indicate the types of question that could appear in a sequence of biweekly tests given in Levels I through IV. The tests suggested here would occur near the midpoint of each level. For details concerning each question or item type, see the item types listed immediately above and corresponding to the numbers in parentheses.

Level I

A. Spot dictation. (9)
B. Pattern practice: Augmentation. (4)
                    Pronoun substitution. (6)
                    Fill-ins. (10)
C. Rewriting of a passage of some length, changing from first to third person.

Level II

A. Dictation.
B. Listening comprehension: completion of sentences, to be written. (16)

C. Pattern practice: Restatement. (8)
    Tense change. (18)
D. Vocabulary fill-ins, with lexical list provided. (7)
E. Sentence writing, with model and word list given. (13)

Level III

A. Dictation.
B. Listening comprehension: identification of speakers in story. (19)
C. Dehydrated sentences. (14)
D. Fill-ins: relatives and demonstratives.
E. Paragraph writing, replying to list of questions. (24)

Level IV

A. Dictation (from text not previously studied).
B. Listening comprehension: logical sequence. (20)
C. Sentence rewriting, using structure of model but substituting new vocabulary items. (23)
D. Fill-ins: conditional sentences or subjunctive forms.
E. Paragraph writing on a quoted passage, indicating who is speaking, to whom, about what, what has just happened, what is about to happen, what is significant. (25)

Suggestions for further reading

Buros, Oscar K. *Mental Measurements Yearbook.* Highland Park, N.J.: Gryphon Press, 1938, 1941, 1949, 1953, 1959.

Lado, Robert. *Language Testing.* London: Longmans, Green, 1961.

Lindquist, Everet F. *Educational Measurement.* Washington, D.C.: American Council on Education, 1951.

Northeast Conference on the Teaching of Foreign Languages. *Reports of the Working Committees.* 1954–57.

Pimsleur, Paul. "A French Speaking Proficiency Test." *French Review,* XXXIV (April 1961), 470–79.

Starr, Wilmarth H. "MLA Foreign Language Proficiency Tests for Teachers and Advanced Students." *PMLA,* September 1962, Part 2, 31–37.

BUILDING A PROFESSION

16

It is man's essential task to be both contemplative and practical. He must meditate in order to sharpen the intellect which is his hound's nose and his eagle's eye; he must act in order to inherit the place which is his birthright on the surface of our planet. This book attempts to be both theoretical and practical on the subject which is its title—a subject that invites treatment at a dual level, for though language is an intimate possession of every living person, it is at the same time one of the most potent and mysterious creations of man's mind.

Having made a brief analysis of language and language learning and having offered some suggestions about the practice of this learning in the classrooms of America, we consider now a final and important question: Under whose aegis are the new efforts we have made a case for to be marshaled and led forward?

Aspects of language reviewed

We must be realistic about the outcomes that may reasonably be expected from the learning we have recommended. Our learners already have a mother tongue, and they are not within the cultural field of the community that speaks the language they are studying; therefore their mastery of the new language can only be that of an outsider. What we may confidently expect is clearly outlined by Edward Sapir in "The Case for a Constructed International Language,"[1] as follows:

> It is quite a mistake to suppose that an English speaking person's command of French or German is psychologically in the least equivalent to a Frenchman's or a German's command of his native language. All that is managed, in the majority of cases, is a fairly adequate control of the external features of the foreign language. This incomplete control has, however, the immense advantage of putting the native speaker and the foreigner on a footing of approximate mutual understanding, which is sufficient for the purpose desired.

In stressing language as communication, we do not overlook the fact that language is much more than this. To the businessman and the soldier, whose thinking dominates our culture at the present time, language is essentially communication, indispensable to the vast networks of production, transfer, and exchange which they organize and direct. But as we are reminded by René Wellek and Austin Warren in *Theory of Literature*, page 13, "It would be false to limit [language] merely to communication. A child's talking for hours without a listener and an adult's almost meaningless social chatter show that there are many uses of language which are not strictly, or even primarily, communicative."

To see language only in its utilitarian function, to consider it only as a tool, a response to a need or a means to an end, is a mistake. Language is rather a product of the incessant symbolization processes with which the mind occupies itself, whether for some practical purpose or not. Once this basic fact about language has been recognized, we at once reaffirm the significance of language as communication, especially from person to person, for which today's world has the greatest need

---

[1] From *Propositions, Deuxième Congrès International de Linguistes*, August 1931, pages 42–44, as quoted by Charles C. Fries, *Teaching and Learning English as a Foreign Language*, page 6.

and which has largely been neglected in our language programs. At the same time, though we have stressed the importance of the audio-lingual aspects of language learning, we by no means disparage the importance of the gestures and body motions that accompany talk. Indeed, gestures can have a semantic of their own, quite independent of talk; it must be noted, however, that as a "language" and apart from talk, gesture is incomparably more limited and imprecise. We likewise recognize the profound importance to the individual and to society of speech in graphic form, and of the role of reading and writing in communication, in learning, in human relationships, and in fine art.

Where does language belong?

Because of the complexity of language and language learning, it is not easy to say under whose official patronage the activities we are discussing belong. Are those who are responsible for language learning to look to science and technology for a new home and new leadership? Are they to remain under the surveillance of literary scholarship that has, up to now, been ultimately responsible for the programing of language courses? These are pointed and disturbing questions, yet we must summon the courage to ask them and attempt to answer them. They cannot be answered without a frank survey of the capacity and the limitations of both science and literature as they affect the development of the field of language learning.

Language and science

The philosophy of science requires that it progress along a path paved only with cold, hard facts. There is a nobleness about this austerity that commands respect and for which the world can be very grateful. It grew out of a determination on the part of the men of the Renaissance to have done with a tremendous burden of obvious nonsense in various fields of study; it began in the discipline of physics and is still in progress in psychology in the twentieth century. This severity has led the scientist, at times, to a foreshortened and truncated view of what lies about him. A case in point is the work of Charles W. Morris, *Signs, Language, and Behavior*. This book has all those qualities of satisfying clarity and precision that a behavioral analysis of human conduct can provide. It also has all the limitations of such an analysis: what cannot be weighed or measured or recorded on scales or graphs is not allowed to count. Even such a penetrating and sympathetic writer as Morris betrays his vulnerability to the occupational hazard of the scientist: the tendency to regard the world as a marble cake of science and folly, and to reject as nonsense any statement that cannot be publicly verified by anyone, at any time, anywhere. Yet even the pure sciences do not attain to what may be called absolute truth. Susanne K. Langer reminds the scientists that for all their insistence upon palpable public proof, they would get nowhere without mathematics, which is the most unreal, the most intangible symbolic edifice that the human mind has ever constructed. It happens in the pure sciences that mathematics and reality coincide remarkably well, *but not absolutely*. A margin for error must be allowed in every case. Erwin Schrödinger tells us in *What Is Life?* page 16, "The laws of physics and physical chemistry are inaccurate within a probable relative error of the order of one over the square root of n, where n is the number of molecules that cooperate to bring about that law." In the sciences that are closest to language learning—linguistics and psychology—there has not been agreement so far on the nature of language behavior. John B. Carroll in his book *The Study of Language*, page 88, asks why, and continues:

> A part of the answer is surely rooted in semantic difficulties. . . . People have not agreed upon what they mean by such terms as speech, language, and thought. The very utterance of a term like "thought" or "idea" or "meaning" is anathema to many behavioristic psychologists, and taboo among many linguists.

The scientist feels that he must, in the nature of his discipline, rule out and cast aside the moral and aesthetic considerations that the language teacher cannot ignore, even if he would. We can only conclude that, although science and technology can in many ways offer much needed help to language teaching, the value system and the limited field of scientific interest preclude the possibility of centering the activities of the discipline under discussion within the area bounded by science.

Language and literature

But if science has its limitations as the guardian of and sponsor for language learning, so has literature, and it is only fair to review these also. The liberating effect of the knowledge of another language is never lost upon the literary scholar. The Committee on the Objectives of a General Education in a Free Society, in *General Education in a Free Society,* page 120, states this as follows:

> To learn that other languages have words with meanings which no English word carries, that they sort meanings in other ways and link them up in other patterns, can be a Copernican step, one of the most liberating, the most exciting, and the most sobering opportunities for reflection that the humanities can offer.

Despite this, literature remains essentially interested in the effectiveness, the accuracy, and the excellence of language in its graphic form and raised to the level of fine art. The man of letters grows restive and impatient, not to say sardonic, when asked to trudge along at the speed of the apprentice and repeatedly to correct the wrong responses that are the inevitable concomitant of the elementary learning process. His interest lies in imagination and individuality, in ideas and the expression of ideas, while the language learner must slowly and patiently acquire the tools and techniques with which an idea is expressed. The literary scholar's knowledge of and interest in methods of language learning, in the preparation of materials for this learning, and in the training of language teachers is, for the most obvious and understandable reasons, meager. Language as audio-lingual communication is only an incidental concern of the scholar and the critic. He is interested in the different language skills only so far as they are appropriate to literary analysis and appreciation. This attitude cannot be that of the language teacher, who must see that all the skills are learned and kept active. The relating of one language to another appears in a different light to the literary scholar and to the language teacher, who must exercise extreme caution in this regard if he is to inculcate a coordinate system in the learner. Finally, we must be blunt enough to say that literary scholarship, *through no inherent quality of its own,* takes precedence over good teaching in the academic value system. Competence and good intent are not lacking in the young college instructor; quite the contrary. But good teaching is hard work, and the realization soon comes that there is not a one-to-one relationship between success in the classroom and promotion in the academic hierarchy. College instructors are under pressure to get a degree and to publish; they are in no sense to be criticized if they concede that this is the only likely way of survival and act accordingly.

In sum, for different but no less cogent reasons in each case, neither literary scholarship nor science is in a position to direct the activities of those engaged in language teaching in such a way that they may best accomplish their task. The former lacks a full understanding of the problems involved and finds them peripheral to its principal interests until the student's apprenticeship is all but accomplished; the latter operates in a sphere of interest that does not extend far enough to include a major part of what language learning is responsible for.

A new site must be chosen from which one may see language steady and see it whole; a new discipline must be established that is independent yet in clear and effective relationship with those neighboring disciplines that have heretofore tended to absorb it. An appropriate dwelling must be designed to house the disparate concepts of symbolism, meaning, analysis, behavior, learning, artifact, and art that reflection on the nature of language finds it to contain. A new field of professional practice—already existent in fact—must be recognized and granted autonomy.

This new field of activity—once it is clearly marked out and acknowledged—will need to be identified by a new name. We propose to call it *linguistics* and to call the person who is trained in this field a *linguist*.

The province of *linguistics*—whatever the term by which it may finally be known—is the theory and practice of language and language learning. We may scan the perspective embraced by this new discipline by recapitulating the principal themes that have been touched upon in the earlier chapters of this book.

Viewed in one way, language is behavior, an activity engaged in by all, involving skills that are receptive, listening and reading, and skills that are productive, speaking and writing. Language is a complex of these interrelated skills, and the ways in which we learn and perform in these skills are rightly the concern of the behavioral science we call *psychology*.

Now if we move close to the speaker as he speaks, noting carefully the flow of ever changing sounds as they issue from his lips, we are rather surprised to find that this apparently continuous and variegated pattern is in fact highly systematic. The message that is borne by the sound-sequence is related at every point to a code whose elements are nested one within the other in a way reminiscent of a Russian Easter egg. The key to this systematic complexity was clearly foreshadowed in the first alphabetic writing, and the way in which a message lies on a page today, divided up into sentences, phrases, words, syllables and letters, reflects the way in which the elements of the code are integrated. In recent times, and especially in recent decades, a more rigorous analysis of speech in its spoken form has revealed that it is even more systematic than we had supposed. These discoveries are the result of work done by scientists called *descriptive linguists*, and we are deeply indebted to them for the enlightenment they have brought to our understanding of the nature of language and the way in which it works.

Again, we may imagine that we are able to tune in on a whole community as it uses a single language, whether it be a small one comprising a few hundred or a few thousand speakers, such as that of an American Indian language, or a large one, containing millions of people, to all of whom a single language is mutually intelligible, such as English or Spanish or Russian. A small percentage of those in this community are not able either to speak or to understand their mother tongue. These are the children, not yet a year old. Time soon takes care of this, however, and when these same children are five or six, they are in complete command of their mother tongue in its spoken form—and they all sound very much like native speakers. Of the ties that bind together the members of a common culture, certainly none is more central than their language, for it permeates the inner life of every individual and is the medium of communication that makes the total cultural life possible. The study of language as it relates to the belief and behavior patterns of a total community or culture falls within the realm of the *cultural anthropologist*. The meaning of the language code used in the culture is in fact the total way of life that the anthropologist seeks to identify and describe.

If we change the direction of our scrutiny once more and speculate upon the manner in which the sound waves that we utter come to stand for the reality that we perceive about us and within ourselves, our attention shifts to the ways in which the meaning of words alters and varies and carries less or greater emphasis as these words fit together into utterances and sentences and especially upon the way in which language permits us to communicate with each other about that which is totally absent from the situation in which we are. As we do this, we must turn to the *philosopher,* who helps us understand language as a symbolic transformation of existence and reality, one of a number of such systems, others being music, mathematics, myth, and ritual. The mind is constantly relating the reality of speech to the nonreality of thought, and the philosopher must be appealed to for a plausible explanation of this crucial process.

So far we have spoken of language only as it is at the present time. But, as we view it in still another way, we are reminded that everything in language has a history, indeed one of the oldest histories of human events, for we can probably not say that we were human before we had language. Language in written form appeared only a few thousand years ago, but as we all know, this innovation produced radical changes in the human picture. The history of language in written form, the establishing and interpretation of texts, and the comparison of texts in one language with texts in another are all in the special province of the *philologist.* He traces the history and the nature of changes in the meaning of words, their forms, and the syntactical patterns by means of which they fit together. In our day-by-day use of language we give scarcely a thought to the history of the code we are using or to meanings that the words once had in the past. Yet such a history is a scholarly pursuit of first importance.

Viewing it now in a sixth and final way, we consider language not merely in its functional use in the mundane thoughts and acts of daily life but as the raw material from which the artist of words—the novelist, the playwright, or the poet—selects and assembles, with many a rejection and substitution and rearrangement, just those words and phrases that match the creative urge, the vision of form and beauty, he feels bound to express. As this takes place, the art of words is transformed into the fine art of *literature,* and literature of course ranks with music and architecture and painting as a way of expressing the artist's personal preference and his concept of the aesthetic best.

As we have been listing these various aspects of language, we have referred to six areas of knowledge, each of which may be called a discipline. In each of them one can take a Ph.D. degree and also become a full professor—this is how we recognize them as disciplines. Three of these we class without hesitation as sciences—psychology, descriptive linguistics, and cultural anthropology. The other three—philosophy, philology, and literature—we quite as readily classify as humanities. What makes it so easy for us to separate them into two groups in this way? In order to answer this we must decide what we mean by science and what we mean by humanism.

The word *science* has not always meant what it now does, nor has the word *humanism.* Science as we know it today is chiefly concerned with observation, measurement, experimentation, verification, objectivity, explanation, prediction, accuracy, and completeness. It deals with what is true and what can be proved to be true by anyone, anywhere, any time. Science makes no value judgments other than that of truth. As science it is not concerned with ethics, nor with aesthetics. The model science is physics. It deals with what is real and has little patience with what is not real. The other sciences do their best to be as scientific as physics.

Humanism, on the other hand, while it has no less respect for truth than has science, is also concerned with what is just, what is honest, what is appealing, what is beautiful. It gladly embraces what is nonreal as well as what is real. Its vocabulary willingly includes such words as *mind*, and *soul* and *spirit*, which have been rigorously outlawed by science of the present day.

Our purpose in pointing up these differences, perhaps too sharply, is merely this: to show that those who teach languages occupy a central position with regard to these disciplines and to indicate what their relationship should be to each and all of them. The teaching of language in American schools and colleges is rapidly changing. A new orientation and a new set of objectives are clearly to be discerned by noting what is taking place at the most critical point of our entire activity—the language classroom. The new orientation is toward language *as* communication and *for* communication. Let us note that by communication we mean not only the high-frequency small talk of everyday living but also the communication of ideals and values as it takes place between peoples of different cultures and the communication of and the perception of character and of poetic insight as it takes place between the artist of words and those for whom he writes. Whereas some years ago we talked only of one objective, reading, we now talk about three, the control of all the language skills in the language being studied, awareness and understanding of the culture in which the new language is spoken, and an acquaintance as broad and deep as possible with the literature of the target culture. Needless to say, the realization of these new objectives cannot come about unless there are many changes in the materials with which our students work, in the procedures followed in language classrooms, and in the role played by the teacher as learning takes place.

As we embark upon these more ambitious objectives and assume the far greater obligations that they entail, we shall of course need all the help we can get from the disciplines we have referred to. To know more about the nature of language code and how it operates, we cannot do without the linguist. To know how a language is learned and above all to find out how a second language is learned when a first one has already been established, we must of course turn to the psychologist. To know the full meaning of the code of the new language for those who speak it natively, we must turn to the cultural anthropologist, for the true meaning of a language can only be its meaning to those who speak it as a mother tongue. At the same time we must remember that our teaching takes place not under the aegis of the army or the navy or the diplomatic corps. Our task is not the same as that of preparing the businessman or the traveler for a series of brief encounters with the ticket agent or the waiter or the salesman in a foreign country, important as these aims may be. Our assignment is far more general and far more difficult. The learning that we are responsible for takes place in the academic world, one in which the full range of humanistic values cannot be denied or avoided at any point, nor would we wish to do so. We must look to philosophy to help us understand what language means when it is internalized as thought. We must look to philology for reminders of what we so easily forget—how deeply language of the present is rooted in the past. And we must look to literature and to literary history, to literary criticism and to the appreciation of literature, in order to provide our students with some of the greatest rewards that the study of language can offer them.

Those who teach languages have recently been given a new importance, a new opportunity, a new responsibility. The creation of the FL Program by the Modern Language Association in 1952 under the direction of William R. Parker and the passing of the National Defense Education Act in 1958 were events of the first magnitude for the language-teaching profession—or what is, unhappily, less a profession than what should be and could be one. In order rightly to call language teaching a profession, language teachers must establish the discipline they profess. Comparable developments have taken place, for example, under the name of comparative literature in the humanities or, in the sciences, under the name of biophysics. Linguistics must be recognized as holding a mid-position between the sciences and the humanities, especially those fields that we have specified, and be established strongly and firmly not as an adjunct to or a dependent of any of these, but as a partner and colleague upon an equal footing with any and all of them. If there is to be a graduate school program leading to an advanced degree in the central area that we have outlined, many changes must come about at both the college and the graduate level. Above all, there must be an admission of the value of what language teachers do and an admission of the fact that they can accomplish the goals they have set for themselves. There can be little hope of this unless we see ourselves related in an appropriate way, not to any single one of our neighboring disciplines, but to all of them at once.

If we are to have *linguistics* we must also have *linguists*. How shall we characterize and define a linguist? It would be easy to make of him a superscholar, an expert in all six disciplines we have described and a specialist in a seventh that relates to all the others. We do not need to think of a linguist in these terms. Rather, a linguist is one who first of all possesses an advanced degree in either literature or philology or linguistics and who is quite at home in all three. He also knows in detail what there is in these fields that has a direct bearing on classroom learning. He must be thoroughly at home in at least one language other than his mother tongue and know its culture and its literature well. He must have in all the skills in this language an acceptable competence that he knows how to inculcate in his students. He must understand the nature of language and the interrelationship of methods, materials, and measurements in language learning. He must have a deep sense of professional responsibility for establishing and maintaining this new discipline in the central position it merits among academic studies.

The reader may well find himself asking this question: As an individual teacher in my school or my college or university, what can I do to help bring about these desired ends? The answer to this very reasonable question is this: If one's interests are primarily scientific, for example, linguistic or grammatical, he should remember that as a language teacher there are at least *five other* disciplines that must also claim his attention as he plans his courses, chooses texts and readings, and prepares for and teaches his language classes day by day. By the same token, if one's interests are primarily of a literary nature, in which case one is inevitably drawn to philology and philosophy, he should remember that the science of language, the science of learning, the science of culture, have many secrets to reveal to the teacher whose task it is to bring the students up to the point of accomplishment we call the language requirement. If all language teachers, irrespective of immediate personal interests, can keep this broad perspective, can keep all these aspects of language clearly in view at all times, they will be able not only to deal more justly with the students who come to them for instruction, but also to aid in the most direct and effective way in establishing this new discipline in the position of importance that it is now clearly invited to assume.

We may look ahead with confidence to the great changes in foreign-language teaching which the emergence of this new field implies.[2] Linguistics will be at once old and new: it will respect tradition but it will break new paths through territory as yet unexplored. It will interest itself in learning and performance alike. Linguistics will continue to find in words the present state and past history of their form and meaning, and in language the manner in which it operates and changes. It will interest itself in the accuracy of written texts and in comparisons of the forms

---

[2] An outline of the study required for training in this new field was first suggested in a paper by the present author that appeared under the title "Preservice Training for Language Teachers" in *Modern Foreign Languages in the High School*, edited by Marjorie C. Johnston. This paper was prepared for a conference held in Washington in May 1957, to consider how modern-foreign-language programs in the high school may be redesigned to serve better the national need.

of one language with those of another. But in addition to these considerations, and indeed before them, it will necessarily be concerned with the point of origin of all language: the mouths and ears and inner prompting of living speakers. It will find in the sounds of the human voice, however they may be heard or recorded or refined, symbol system more revealing and compelling than an[y]thin[g] that man can use to express and understand the s[ame] the culture of his origin and wherever else he outer w[orld]
may

[Sugg]estions for further reading

[An]dersson, Theodore. "The Teacher of Modern Foreign Languages," in Ernest Stabler, ed., *The Education of the Secondary School Teacher.* Middletown, Conn.: Wesleyan University Press, 1962.

Birkmaier, Emma M. "Modern Languages: Vehicle for the Humanities." *Educational Leadership,* January 1963, pp. 238–42.

College Entrance Examination Board. *Curricular Changes in the Foreign Languages.* Princeton, N.J.: College Entrance Examination Board, 1963.

Committee on the Objectives of a General Education in a Free Society. *General Education in a Free Society.* Cambridge, Mass.: Harvard University Press, 1945.

Heisenberg, Werner. *Physics and Philosophy.* New York: Harper, 1958.

Mildenberger, Kenneth W. "Recent Developments in Foreign Language Teaching in American Schools and Colleges." *International Review of Education,* VII, 4 (1962), 402–11.

Parker, William R. *The National Interest and Foreign Languages.* 3rd ed. Washington, D.C.: Government Printing Office, 1962.

United States Office of Education. *The Language Development Program.* Washington, D.C.: United States Government Printing Office, 1963. Brochure on Title VI.

APPENDIX A
HOW TO...

In keeping with the general purpose of this book, which is to consider both the theory and the practice of language and language learning, we present in the following pages a series of suggestions and recommendations that are directly related to procedure in the classroom. They are arranged in alphabetical order according to the key word in the subject being discussed.

Assignments, how to arrange in sequence

The year or semester is divided into biweekly periods, the work for each period constituting a unit. In general each unit contains assignments in dialogue or reading, structure, and vocabulary, and ends with a test that summarizes the work of the entire unit. In Levels III and IV a certain amount of text is assigned for each day; one or several problems of structure are assigned for the entire unit and are dealt with as they occur in the material of the assignment and in class. Several dozen vocabulary items—words and idioms—are selected from the pages being read for each unit. These vocabulary items, together with the pattern practice items that involve structure, become a part of each class program, of the tapes that are prepared for laboratory work during the two-week period, and of the test at the end. Class discussions are frequently followed by short writing exercises in the classroom; writing in similar form is then asked for on the test.

At the start of Level I situations are chosen and dialogues developed with regard to what is authentic in spoken language as well as to what appears important in a representative and systematic presentation of structure. The priority of situational authenticity may continue during the first series of topics in the situation inventory. Then, little by little, concern for structure as such enters more directly into the selection and modification of the utterances to be used in dialogues. The need to present in Levels I and II a comprehensive sampling of very common structural patterns is taken into account in devising and selecting what is said between speakers, provided this does not make the communication exchange unnatural.

The situation inventory of Level I should begin with the immediate environment of the students: the classroom. It should continue with circumstances of daily living that are to be found everywhere: greetings and leave taking, family ties, homes, eating, clothes, occupations, amusements, sickness, climate, visits, travel—matters of interest and importance to the Eskimo and the African Bushman as well as to the American student. Interspersed with situations such as these there should be others that are peculiar to the culture being studied—and therefore new to the learner. A suitable beginning point of this kind is the preparation for a holiday that is unfamiliar to the students or celebrated in a different way in the United States. The latter part of the basic course should include situations selected from a text that is subsequently to be read, each selection being learned as an entity in itself. A series of such exercises may then be followed by the reading of the complete text, in which the learner will find himself to a gratifying extent quite at home.

Choral response, how to conduct

A repetition by the entire class of what has just been said by the teacher may be improved by following these suggestions: Do not repeat *with* the students; make them wait until your utterance is finished. Use your hands to indicate when they are to perform. Do not let a response drag in tempo; a whole class can repeat an utterance at the same speed as a single person. The number of syllables that can be retained by the ear is small. Therefore separate utterances into short sequences for repetition; once learned, they can be joined to make a full statement. Do not accept a mere monotone in the response. Insist that all the details of intonation, loudness, pause, and change of pitch be observed.

Cultural islands, how to establish

As in the culture itself, activities and items in the cultural island separate into the linguistic and the nonlinguistic. In the linguistic area, the teacher is the focal point, and by using language authentically he demonstrates not only the sounds that are used in the target culture but the manner of their use and the meaning that they convey. Success depends wholly upon what the teacher feels and thinks and says and does. It is by no means required that the teacher be a native speaker in order to be effective as the center of a cultural island. Many important facets of cultural behavior are so deeply engrained that the person who has grown up in a culture is unaware of their existence or their importance to the foreigner. If these are accurately and sympathetically presented by the non-native, they are no less useful to the learner.

In addition to demonstrating and talking about culture, the teacher will of course discuss and display such nonlinguistic elements of culture as pictures (printed and projected), books, newspapers and periodicals, coins, clothing, jewelry, tools, and other *realia*. Selected recordings, made in the foreign country on either tape or disc, can be of great value to any teacher in presenting a wide variety of sounds, both linguistic and nonlinguistic, that are authentic.

Dialogues, how to prepare

A dialogue is an exchange of conversation between two or more persons about a given situation or topic. It reflects the commonest mode of language use and is therefore of prime importance to the language learner. Until he can participate in such use of the target language the learner has not passed the entrance gate to the new culture.

In its simplest form, a dialogue is constructed as follows: utterances are brief, not more than a half-dozen words; a change of speaker follows each utterance; if a dialogue goes on for more than half a dozen utterances it is broken up into parts, each unified and containing not more than four or five utterances; these parts are learned separately.

Dialogues that are to be used by the learner may be written as original compositions or they may be developed out of scenes in novels and plays. If the first, they must be looked upon as creative writing in which cultural and linguistic authenticity is rigorously demanded; if the second, they are achieved by rewriting that involves abridgment but not substitution and that preserves the author's original intent.

English, how to use

The role of English in the language class is like that of an aside in a play. The aside is neither a part of the interchange of communication taking place between the players, nor a return to normal conversation between them—which would instantly demolish the dramatic reality they are striving to create. It is rather a device that reveals the purpose of the players without returning to the real world that vanished when the curtain went up. In the language class students must understand that English is not available to them for purposes of communication and that although the teacher may occasionally use a word or phrase in English to make a semantic area clear, he does not use English for communicating with them. Unless English is thus reduced to an inactive state, the student is denied the experience of relying on the new language exclusively, as its native speakers do.

It is of the utmost importance that the teacher say nothing in English at the beginning of the class, for nothing destroys so quickly the illusion of the cultural island. It is frequently advisable to end the language class a few minutes before the period is over and to return to English for communication during the remaining time. When the foreign language is dropped in favor of English, it should not be resumed until the next day.

Above all, two languages should never be scrambled word by word and sentence by sentence, as they are, unfortunately, in many textbooks.

When students are being tested, it is only fair that they be given every opportunity to understand the directions fully. If there is the least doubt about comprehension of directions given in the target language, they should be stated in English; limitations in the student's ability to understand the technical terms of directions should not be allowed to obscure his ability to use the new language as directed.

Grades, how to give

Since the total pattern of testable language behavior divides itself into two major areas, the audio-lingual and the graphic-material, which differ in so many respects, we may expect unequal rates of learning in these areas on the part of each student. In practice this means that separate grades should be given for what is usually termed "oral" work (including of course both hearing and speaking) and "written" work (including both reading and writing). The bookkeeping aspects of this proposal are not so formidable as they might seem. An official grade, instead of being, let us say, an A—, becomes A/B, meaning A in audio-lingual and B in graphic-material skills. Or a 75 becomes 72/78, meaning that the student has done better in writing than in hearing and speaking. This dual scoring is already being used in some schools, and it has been adopted for rating some of the tests of the Advanced Placement Program of the College Entrance Examination Board.

Homework, how to give

The all-important matter of homework may be dealt with as follows: During the first class session, say that homework in this course will be of a different kind, especially during the early weeks of Level I, in that it will not at first involve reading and writing in the new language. Instead, the student will be asked to practice repeating what he has learned in class, either in the language laboratory, at home while listening to a specially prepared record, or as best he can from memory. Not until some time later, when he is beginning to read and write, will he have homework that involves reading and writing in the foreign language. However, during the early part of the course, homework may include reading in English about the new language and about the people who speak it; time will be found in class to speak briefly in English about these readings and to check on how well the student has done this type of homework.

Laboratory and classroom, how to integrate

The basic problem in connection with a language laboratory is not the choice of equipment nor the installation nor the scheduling. It is rather the long and arduous task of integrating, day by day and week by week, the work done in the classroom with what is done in the laboratory. This is accomplished by first arranging in detail the content of the assignments for the classroom, then preparing tapes for the laboratory that are based upon the dialogues, readings, and vocabulary or structural exercises that form a part of the classroom work.

The main function of the laboratory is to provide an opportunity for the student to overlearn what he has begun to assimilate while working in the classroom with the teacher. This means that the form and content of what he hears in the laboratory must have a direct relationship to what he hears and says and writes in class. In turn, this means that what the student is asked to do in class cannot be left to chance or to the inspiration of the moment. Unless the materials encountered in the laboratory are similar to the work of the classroom, no advantage can be taken of the opportunity for overlearning offered by the laboratory and its principal worth will remain unrealized. The laboratory is not the place for attempting to answer questions requiring original answers. Rather, it is where the models that have already been presented can be heard again and again and imitated again and again, until the student gains the degree of automatic response that is the principal characteristic of language in action.

Questionnaires, how to prepare

The making of questionnaires is best done by each teacher for his own class; a list of such questions is in general useful only to the one who frames them. Questions that lead to communication are framed with the listener constantly in mind, and knowledge of the listener is the unique province of the individual teacher.

From the pages of the assigned reading the teacher prepares a series of fifteen or twenty questions that review the events of the story in the order in which they occur. These questions are brief, are not more difficult in style than the text itself, and are not answerable by the monosyllabic "yes" or "no." They are phrased in such a way that the answer may easily include the wording of the text and at first are *not* an analysis of character or motives or criticism of writing, but involve merely a restatement of what the text says. The student's comprehension and critical insight are usually far in advance of his ability to express himself in the new language, and the patient and detailed reworking of the author's words provides the best means of training the student in his general use of language (one of *his* prime objectives in the course) as well as preparing him for the more mature literary writing he will eventually undertake. Reading between the lines is encouraged by insisting upon a preliminary acquaintance, accurate and detailed, with the lines themselves.

Once the class has rehearsed the events of the story as the author tells them, questions of another kind are in order, involving what is implied but not stated. Where is the story located? To what social group do the characters belong? What is the attitude of the author toward his characters? What are the emotions of those whose actions are described? Is the author more interested in character, atmosphere, or action? How does he use the elements of suspense and surprise? What point is he trying to prove? Does the reader agree with the author?

To such general questions that apply to most stories may be added many others of the same type that apply to one story in particular. The questionnaire should be much more than a mere series of questions. Other forms of communication that questionnaires can include are suggested on pages 253–54.

Scripts for tapes, how to prepare

The script for a tape is prepared by collecting and arranging items that drill principally on one of the strands of discourse (sound, order, form, vocabulary). These items come from dialogues and readings with which the student is currently working, so that a brief utterance recalls a situation with which he is familiar. The material should be so arranged that such explanations and directions as are necessary are given in English, while the materials that are being modeled and imitated are given in the target language. Most tapes are divided into two parts, the audio-lingual and the audio-visual-graphic. That part of the tape which the student is only to hear and repeat is given first; it is followed at the end by items which involve writing on the sheets provided for the laboratory exercise. Enough material should be assembled to occupy about fifteen minutes when taped, including the time for the written exercise. These points are of special importance in writing the script:

All that is to be said on the tape should be in the script; ad-libbing is not recommended.
Some explanation, especially when learning structure, is useful, but it must be simple and kept to a minimum; essentially it is a brief restatement of what the learner has already studied.
All the items must first be prepared exclusively for reception by the ear. This means that each utterance must be short, not more than five syllables when material is relatively new and not more than ten or twelve syllables when it is better known.
Models must be presented at least three times over; it is the third repetition that helps the learner most.
It is often useful to give special stress to a word or expression

in an item being learned; this can safely be done if in the third repetition normal stress is resumed.

A typical script for a vocabulary tape for Level III might contain the following information:

a. Name of course.
b. Number of tape.
c. Date.
d. Seventy-five to one hundred words in English stating the subject of the tape and describing how each section of it is to be done, with one or two examples.
e. Twenty vocabulary items, each presented as follows: first a single English word, then an utterance in the target language containing the equivalent of this word, to be spoken the first time with special stress on this word, repeated in the same way, then given a third time with normal stress throughout the utterance. Time is allowed for the student to repeat each utterance as he hears it.
f. Directions in English to take the copy of the laboratory exercise that accompanies this tape and to write in missing forms as heard.
g. Reading of the items in this exercise, with time for the student to write the words or expressions that he hears but does not see.
h. Directions to compare what he has written with the key printed on the back of his exercise sheet.
i. "End of tape number —."

Short stories, how to teach

DIVISION INTO ASSIGNMENTS

The assignments are never very long, not more than three or four pages, and the first one is often shorter. This allows the student to adjust to a new author, a new situation, and a new style and vocabulary. Each assignment ends at a point where the story breaks naturally. At the end of the class prior to the one in which a new story begins, some indication of what it is about is given by the teacher. As the story continues, a part of the new assignment is read aloud by the teacher while the students listen without looking at the text.

PREPARATION BY THE TEACHER

This includes the selection of material for the oral questionnaire, for pattern practice, for vocabulary study, and, if desired, for a written quiz. Questions are prepared so that they bring out first what is said and secondly what is understood or implied in the text. For pattern practice the teacher selects portions of the text that involve details of structure that are currently being emphasized and prepares a list of these for oral, and perhaps written, exercise in class. For vocabulary study, words and expressions are selected from the reading assignment or from the pages that immediately precede. The selection is based upon what has previously been chosen and what is most appropriate for immediate study. Because the student will be expected to keep his books closed during the class exercise, the teacher puts his notes, questions, expressions for pattern practice, and items for word study on a single sheet of paper and works from this in class, thus freeing himself as well as his students from the bondage of the book. Communication will be much more natural if he too is so familiar with the contents of the text that he does not need to look at it.

PREPARATION BY THE STUDENT

During the period of outside preparation the student first reads the assignment through without stopping and of course without reference, overt or internal, to English. Comprehension may be patchy and dim at first, but, on a second reading in the same way, places, people, and events begin to emerge and take shape in a manner that surprises those who may have been quite baffled at the start. A third reading isolates the words or passages still not understood, and for these the student is now entitled to the aid of a glossary in the language of the text, fortified, if need be, by English equivalents of the most difficult words and expressions. If English is used in such reading helps, they must not appear on the same page with the text; otherwise the first two steps in the preparation are impossible. Nor should these helps be translations of the text into English; what is wanted in each case is merely a lexical item that fills in the missing semantic area with the aid of English, which cannot be abandoned too soon once this is done. With the text before him the student next formulates and writes out, using for the most part the author's words, a series of brief statements that resume the contents of each page. This sharpens his perception of what the text says and prepares him in the best possible way for the oral and written exercises he will participate in during the class.

WHAT THE TEACHER DOES IN CLASS

After the usual prelude in the foreign language by the teacher, which may or may not be related to the day's assignment, the class program begins. The teacher presents the questions and pattern practices, previously prepared separately or in whatever combination seems best, but always following the sequence of events as they are told in the story. Questions and comments by the students and digressions on matters (other than grammar) which the text suggests and in which the students participate actively are of course encouraged. Remarks on words, expressions, and references that are culturally significant color and enliven this oral give-and-take between teacher and class which has many of the characteristics of true communication, provided books are closed and the blackboard plays only a minor role—say that of the tablecloth during a discussion at the dinner table. Questions and comments at the "retelling" level are followed by queries of an interpretative nature, phrased in such a way that the student is led to use the language within his grasp to express the insights and opinions he is likely to have. This part of the class program—usually by far the longest—is succeeded by a few minutes on word study. Use is now made of the items previously selected by the teacher, who avoids all use of English except perhaps for an occasional word employed in the interests of efficiency, to establish a semantic connection that would otherwise be uncertain or time-consuming. However, *communication* in English is rigorously avoided. The final portion of class time may be used in a number of ways: to prepare for and write a dictation, a quiz, an exercise in the construction of a sentence, an exchange of dialogue, or a paragraph. Instead of or in addition to the above, some time is used to preview the coming assignment, either by reading a portion of it aloud or by some reference to the events that are to follow.

WHAT THE STUDENT DOES IN CLASS

The student from the beginning makes every effort to subdue the mother tongue and reduce it to an inactive role, just as he would forget his tennis game when playing hockey, or his boxing technique when in the swimming pool. He listens sharply, answers with full voice in choral activity, formulates rejoinders, and replies at the coded level to all that is presented, even though it is not his turn to speak aloud. His gain from the class depends on his participation as a hearer and speaker in practicing familiar linguistic forms and imitating and repeating new ones. His contribution is determined by the initiative he takes and the rejoinders, comments, and questions he offers beyond those the teacher demands of him.

Speaking skill, how to evaluate

In evaluating the speaking skill of the student, the teacher listens principally for these five factors:

a. Are the individual sounds (vowels, consonants) correctly pronounced?
b. Are the intonation patterns, the ups and downs and the syllabic stress, satisfactory?
c. Does the promptness of utterance reveal that the student is speaking without internal reference to English?
d. Do the spoken words fall easily into place in the right form and order?
e. How "natural" or "native-speaker" is the general impression given by the student as he speaks?

A 3, 2, 1 scale is usually found satisfactory in scoring each of these factors, 3 meaning good, 2 meaning acceptable, and 1 meaning unacceptable. Most teachers will want to acquaint their students with the techniques of the formal speaking test, in which the learner repeats a series of expressions as he hears them, reads aloud from a printed passage, and talks about some line drawings and pictures, putting all his responses on tape for later evaluation. But this process is too elaborate for very frequent use. Usually, in the few moments following a class period, the teacher can quickly evaluate the speaking ability of each student according to the above scale. Of course, not every student needs to be so graded every day.

Talk by the student, how to elicit

To help the teacher get the student to talk we may cite a variety of types of oral behavior in which the learner may engage in the new language; these are, in order of difficulty: repetition, rejoinder, restatement, question, statement, comment, and criticism. In order to talk, the student must have a model to follow and something to say. He can invent the message but he cannot invent the code by which it is communicated. Silence on his part usually results less from the lack of something to say and more from the lack of the ability to say it. Getting him to talk therefore consists mainly in providing him with the models to which he can refer as he speaks. This is the direct value of dialogue learning, which, with the aid of analogy, helps him find the forms for his message. A limitation in most questionnaires is that the student's answer is usually in the third person. He thus gets little practice in the use of the first person singular, often his greatest need in communication. This is not to say that question and answer are without value, but to point out that there are many possible variations on this theme that are not commonly in use.

Here are some ways of eliciting responses from the student other than the overworked question and answer that merely speak "about."

> The teacher says to the class: "Everyone is to speak as if he were the character X in this story." Then he asks: "X, why

did you steal that money?" "X, why did you remain alone in your room?"

The teacher says to the class: "Student A is now to become character X. I will direct other members of the class to ask questions of A, who will answer as if he were X." The teacher then says to student B: "Ask A why he stole that money." To student C: "Ask A why he remained alone in his room."

The student playing the role of X is coached to make statements in the first person singular by being reminded of events in the second person plural: "You knocked at the door and then you. . . ." The student replies: "I knocked at the door and then I waited several minutes in the rain."

The teacher makes a statement that relates to an incident in the text but he does not complete it. The student repeats what he has heard, adding the missing information. For example, the teacher says: "One night after work X brought home. . . ." The student replies: "One night after work X brought home an invitation." Or again: "X was arrested because he had stolen. . . ." "X was arrested because he had stolen some money."

If the text contains a dialogue, the teacher may quote what is said by one of the characters and elicit from a student what was said by another character in rejoinder.

Before the discussion the teacher writes on the board a series of ten or fifteen words or expressions that are important in the events of the story, listing them in the order in which they occur. These are discussed in turn; their presence on the board will help many students to think ahead and formulate what they wish to say with greater care and success than they could muster on the spur of the moment.

Getting the student to talk is very important in getting him to write. An orientation can be given to what is said that will lead to the more formal language of writing. In another direction, the student, well supplied with the necessary models, may be encouraged to talk on subjects suggested by the text or "on his own," provided he uses the language he knows. Topics that are likely to produce the best performances from him are himself, his home, his friends, animals, and what he likes and does not like.

Translate, how to

Translation, meaning restating in code B what has already been stated in code A, has no place in the early levels of language learning. Two languages are neither thought nor spoken simultaneously, and the process of matching one with another is in fact destructive to the control of both. The virtues of translation and the needs for it are many, but they are not central to the process of gaining control of a new language. In so far as the learner must have adequate awareness of meaning in the new code, reference to meaning by the use of words and utterances in his mother tongue is of course useful. But for this to have a positive rather than a negative effect upon his progress, such reference must be done *for* him and not *by* him, and it must *precede* internal and external behavior in the target code and not come after it. A basic aim in second-language learning is to make the mother tongue inactive while control and freedom in the new code are slowly achieved. To permit (and all the more so to encourage or demand) constant reference to the mother tongue while this control is being built up is to cripple and defeat the avowed objective at every step. These statements should not be taken to deny the worth as an ultimate objective of the ability to move readily and easily from one language to another. After four or five levels of learning have been achieved, the learner may well be coached in this useful skill. But to ask him to do this before he is thoroughly at home in the new code is like asking the musician to play the same piece, phrase by phrase, first on an instrument that he knows well and then on one he is only beginning to learn.

No translation is worthy of the name so long as it bears the slightest trace of the language from which it comes. Those who ask students to translate should recall that the student never writes his mother tongue so badly as when he is translating into it from another language. It is likely that the admonition "translate literally" or "translate in such a way that you show your understanding of the structure of the foreign language" is more responsible than any other influence for the execrable English that is written in the name of translation at all levels of learning. The principal mistake is to attempt to translate at the level of words, whereas an acceptable translation can only be made at the preverbal level, where meaning has not yet clothed itself in words. A further mistake, almost universal, is to ask students to translate before they have the capacity to do so, for a considerable fund of cultural knowledge in the target language is required in addition to that of the mother tongue before what may be called genuine translation can take place. True translation refers the coded message to the situation in the culture that gives rise to the words that are used; this situation is then matched with its nearest equivalent in the other culture, and from this springs the coded message in the other language. For example, translation at the word level would make the French *bonjour* equivalent to the American *good day*. No translation could be worse, for a situation in which a Frenchman says, *Bonjour*, is equivalent to a situation in which an American says, "Hello," "How are you," or, "How do you do," but not, "Good day," which is no longer said by anyone.

As an example of translation in its best sense we may cite the title of the first part of Proust's novel *À la recherche du temps perdu*. In French it is "Du côté de chez Swann." This is translated by Scott Moncrieff as "Swann's Way." At the word level, there is little about *du côté de chez* to suggest *'s way*. Yet when one recalls the situation in which the French words were used —the direction taken by Proust and his family as they set out for a walk on a Sunday afternoon—the English "Swann's Way" is fully appropriate. The translation was not made at the level of coded words, but at the preverbal level of the concepts words stand for.

The unit of longer writing is the paragraph, and when students are sufficiently advanced, usually at Level IV, they may be asked to translate whole paragraphs in the following way: A paragraph is read and reread a number of times until all its significance has been absorbed and is clearly held in mind. Then the original is put aside and the paragraph is written in the other language. Once this is done, a comparison may be made for the clarification or addition of details.

There is a use of the mother tongue in second-language learning that is easily confused with translation but which is in reality no more than a technique for identification. When English has been used to identify the meaning of utterances belonging to a larger context and these have been thoroughly learned in the target language, English is sometimes again referred to in subsequent pattern practices and used as a stimulus to call forth the target utterances as they are desired. This process says: "Of the expressions you now know, this is the one wanted." Psychologically, this bears no resemblance at all to the type of translation problem with which the student is ordinarily presented, in which he takes sentences and paragraphs he has not worked with before and attempts to render them into another language. But in this identification procedure one should go from the mother tongue to the target language, and never the reverse, or the true objectives of coordinate learning are completely betrayed. The name "translation drill" is sometimes used for such an exercise, but this is a misnomer. It should be called what it is: an "English cue" drill. Neither translation nor English cue drills should be used in early-level tests, which should measure command of the target language itself, without benefit of any other.

Up to par, how to keep

The following questions are proposed to help teachers estimate the amount of language learning that takes place in their classrooms.

1. Do you explain at the first meeting of the class what the objectives of the course are and how you propose to attain them?
2. In the training of each student do you distinguish between the *hearer* and the *speaker?*
3. Do you distinguish between *learning* and *performance?*
4. When you give a new type of assignment, do you then demonstrate fully how it is to be carried out?
5. Do you give your class models of what you ask for, or do you let them *guess* what is right? or *vote* on what is right?

6. Does your class period always contain some review of *old* material and ample demonstration of new material?
7. Are the assignments you give busy work? paper work? language learning?
8. Do you give assignments as the students are leaving the classroom? at the beginning of the class? orally? written on the board? printed on slips of paper?
9. Do you put yourself in the position of maintaining that language is logical?
10. When a student performs correctly do you ask him *why* he said what he said the way he said it?
11. Do you emphasize the analysis of structure or the formation of habits for using it?
12. While teaching phonology, morphology, and syntax, do you add the burden of vocabulary problems, too?
13. Do you permit your students to think that one word means another word?
14. Do you ask your students to memorize isolated vocabulary words or lists of equivalents in the foreign language and English—that is, lexicography?
15. If you use English in your classes, do you allow your *students* to speak English?
16. When you say something to your class in the foreign language, do you habitually repeat it in English in the same breath?
17. Have you ever in your professional career banished English entirely from your classroom for four weeks in succession?
18. Do you correct a student as he speaks? after he speaks? just after he has written? a week from the following Thursday?
19. In your classes are books open *all* the time? some of the time? none of the time?
20. Do you make your students "really learn" the language by concentrating on uncommon irregular verb forms?
21. Do you judge a student's knowledge and control of a foreign language by the way he spells it on a piece of paper?
22. Do your students keep a notebook record of important matters as they come up in class?

23. Do you hold your students up to the standard of *your* possible performance or *their* possible performance?
24. Is your class schedule unchanged by, interrupted by, or distorted by, review for extramural tests and examinations?
25. Are your students forced into making mistakes by not having at their disposal adequate patterns of language to which they can refer?
26. Are written compositions always done *orally* first?
27. When you give a reading assignment, is all or part of it *heard* by the students first?
28. Do you spend any, some, or all of your class time translating from the foreign language into English?
29. Do you spend the first five minutes of your class period talking in the foreign language on a subject not previously announced?
30. Do you focus attention only on what the student does with pencil and paper or do you treat as equally important what he can do in the foreign language with his eyes closed?
31. Do you try to set up in your students' heads a second-language system independent of the mother tongue, or does your teaching tend to unite the two systems, rendering them permanently inseparable?

Vocabulary drill, how to prepare

In one type of drill the student hears a series of definitions and repeats each one aloud, twice. Then he hears a series of questions, the appropriate answer to each one being a definition he has just repeated. He hears the question, gives his definition, then hears the original definition again to reinforce or to correct what he has said.

In a second type of drill he hears an English word or expression, then hears its equivalent used in a complete utterance in the target language, with emphasis placed upon the vocabulary item in question, so that he may be certain of meaning. Without further reference to English, he hears and repeats the target sentence twice with emphasis, then a third time in normal intonation.

In a third type of drill the student hears a sentence in the target language, then is given an expression that is to replace or paraphrase a part of the sentence. He gives the sentence with this replacement, then hears it redone for reinforcement or correction.

Voice the script of a tape, how to

The voicing of a tape should be done where there is a minimum of background noise and where those who function as engineer, director, English voice, and native speakers can see each other and work together harmoniously. The engineer manipulates all mechanisms, seats each speaker at the proper distance from the microphone, matches the volume of the voices with each other, and starts and stops the tape at the appropriate times. The director is in charge of timing, especially the length of time for the student's responses, and indicates to each speaker when he is to read his part from the script. Since the use of the same microphone by two persons is usually awkward, there should be a different microphone for each speaker. Voices should be chosen critically, with a concern not only for linguistic authenticity but for student interest and good learning. Not everyone has a good voice for taping, just as not everyone is photogenic; the quality of the voice cannot be judged when heard "live" but only when heard on tape. As a script is read, voices should alternate with each other, a man's voice with a woman's if possible. Voices should be coached to sound as if they were speaking rather than reading, for these involve behavior patterns that are different in many ways. The amount of time allowed for the student to make his response is extremely important. If too little time is allowed, he is cut off before he has finished; if too much, the "dead" space that follows his response leads immediately to inattention and boredom. When minor mistakes are made in the reading of the script it is usually better merely to repeat the word or phrase correctly without stopping the tape. When mistakes are serious or misleading, the tape should be stopped and returned to a point before the error.

APPENDIX B
GLOSSARY OF TERMS

Throughout this book we have used a variety of terms and expressions that may profit from further explanation and amplification. These are treated in the pages that follow, some briefly, some at length, along with a number of other subjects that refer to language and language learning. All are arranged in one alphabetical sequence.

ABCD TEST

This is a listening comprehension test that involves no reading or writing on the student's part. The answer sheet can be prepared by him in a short time. It is especially useful during the audio-lingual period at the beginning of a course. The student is told to list numbers in a vertical column (one for each item of the test) and to write after each number the letters A, B, C, and D. The teacher then presents the items in the following way: A sentence is read that is complete except for the last word or expression. Four ways of finishing the sentence are suggested orally. The student draws a circle around either A, B, C, or D according to whether the right completion has been read in the first, second, third, or fourth position. The items may be read once or twice, depending on how difficult the teacher wishes the test to be. Here are sample items in English:

1. Helen walked back to her chair and sat: up/upon/down/on.
2. Of two evils choose the: less/lesser/lest/least.
3. In this report all aspects of the question are: considering/consider/considerable/considered.
4. Therefore the answer must be either yes: if no/but no/or no/why no.

5. The clergyman walked down the church aisle clasping in his left hand a leather-bound: missal/missive/muscle/muzzle.

ALLOPHONE

An allophone is one of the group or class of sounds that go to make up a phoneme. All the allophones of a given phoneme must be enough alike to pass for one another, and all must be different enough from the allophones of all other phonemes. The allophone is the smallest unit of sound arrived at by the analysis of meaningful forms; a more refined analysis might call the allophone a bundle of distinctive features, with each segment of an utterance containing a different bundle.

ANALOGY

It appears that the claim for transfer of learning, found invalid in many long-cherished items of the curriculum, can in fact be made for analogy. Consider the following statement by Susanne K. Langer in *An Introduction to Symbolic Logic*, page 33:

> The great value of analogy is that by it, and it alone, we are led to seeing a single "logical form" in things which may be entirely discrepant as to content. The power of recognizing similar forms in widely various exemplifications, i.e., the power of discovering analogies, is logical intuition. Some people have it by nature; others must develop it (and I believe all normal minds can develop it), and certainly all may sharpen the precision of their understanding, by a systematic study of the principles of structure.

We proceed in the use of language not by analysis but by analogy. Because in English the word *block* changes in the past to *blocked*, *look* to *looked*, and *ask* to *asked*, then, by analogy, *hoodwink* becomes *hoodwinked*, without rule or further ado. By the same token, if the expression "He draws a picture" changes to "He draws pictures," "I see a cloud" to "I see clouds," and "She made a pie" to "She made pies," then the expression "They designed a cyclotron" becomes "They designed cyclotrons" without further thought about the presence or absence of the article in the different statements. It is thus that we learn our mother tongue and thus that we can make the best progress in a new language. But for this to happen we must work with the commonest and most typical patterns of the new tongue, have them adequately modeled for us, and repeat them until they become automatic. Methods for accomplishing this have been devised in the form of *pattern practice*, which see.

ANALYSIS

It was formerly held that the ability to analyze was one of the most important outcomes of language learning. Closer scrutiny revealed that the ability to analyze language did not guarantee the ability to analyze everything or even anything else. Also, it became clear that while students were learning to analyze language they were not learning to *use* it. This does not in any way make language analysis less important per se, but it does make it less important to those whose goal is to learn to use language, not to analyze it. Language analysis is a difficult kind of learning, equally difficult to forget. Yet if it is learned in connection with a second language, it must be forgotten, that is, made automatic and not conscious, before language behavior can proceed on its normal course.

AUDIO-LINGUAL

Since the words *aural* and *oral* cannot be dependably distinguished in spoken English, the term *audio-lingual* is proposed instead when they must be used together.

AUDIO-VISUAL

A term that needs re-examination when applied to language learning, since *audio* refers to what is central in language, while *visual* does not. It will help language teachers to think in terms of *audio-lingual*, that is, hearing-speaking activities, on the one hand, and *gestural-visual* and *graphic-material*, that is, reading-writing activities, on the other. Strictly speaking, communication by language cannot be discussed in terms of *audio* and *visual*, for communication is a two-way process calling for both the sending and the receiving of a message. Though messages can be *received* in terms of *audio* and *visual*, they cannot be transmitted through either one, for the ear cannot emit sound nor can the eye emit light. The inadequacy of *audio-visual* from the point of view of the foreign-language learner is apparent from the start. Unlike the firefly, the human being cannot send out light, though he can receive it. On the other hand, he can both emit and receive sound. This universal fact is the basis for the development of the sound-symbolism of language. The essence of language is that it is a communication system entirely independent of a source of light. We must recognize, therefore, that the word *audio-visual* introduced a concept (light) that is peripheral to language and at the same time leaves out half of the communication process, the sending of the message—the half that is more important for the learner of a second language.

Much unnecessary confusion comes from the identification of a *printed* word with the spoken phenomenon. The sounds of a spoken word that symbolizes an object and the letters of a written word representing those sounds are on very different levels of symbolic transformation. For the foreign-language learner and for those who direct his work, this distinction cannot be too often or too strongly emphasized. Printed words are not pictures of things; they represent sounds that in turn represent things. Spoken words are thus once removed from the reality they symbolize; written words (pictures of sounds) are in fact twice removed from reality. One symbolic system can eventually replace another, as every reader knows, but the indiscriminate mixing of the two at the start is most unfortunate and perplexing for the learner.

The different services performed by the eye and the ear as receptor organs should be carefully distinguished and the distinctions reflected in the learning techniques that are employed. The visual often accompanies language and the graphic often substitutes for it, yet language can always proceed quite well without either gesture or writing; if this were not true we could not talk by telephone. It is training in the ability to talk without visual and graphic aids that the foreign-language learner both desires and needs, and which he is quite generally denied in the language classes of our schools and colleges. Not only is this ability valuable for its own sake, it is unquestionably the soundest basis for all cultural and literary studies that may follow.

Confusion in the relationship between *audio-visual* and second-language learning is likely to continue until we take the decisive step of defining our terms.

The contribution of visual aids to the learning of a second language is essentially in the form of drawings and pictures that present situations about which talk can center and photographs that represent authentic details of the target culture. A carefully planned program of materials should include wherever possible a use of visual aids that develops the situational and cultural elements as only pictures can and that does not interfere with the audio-lingual skills nor with the use of language as symbol as well as sign.

BILINGUALISM

Bilingualism is a term subject to many definitions. For our purposes we may say that it describes the language behavior of an individual who possesses a mother tongue and also another language, in whole or in part, the two being coordinated but not compounded. This implies that bilingualism is not necessarily a state eventually arrived at after long experience in a second language. Rather, it is a cumulative process built up gradually as one language is held in abeyance while the other functions. As soon as an individual can play his part authentically in a situation involving the new language (this means of course without reference to the mother tongue) he is to that extent bilingual. Bilingualism can therefore begin at Level I and continue throughout the learner's experience. Total bilingualism involves far more than can be accomplished in a language class. The classroom objective is a limited bilingualism that is valuable as far as it goes.

BOOK

A book can neither hear nor speak; for this reason no book can ever play a part in talk except through the substitution of light waves for sound waves. The fact that the human mind can accommodate itself so well to this substitution should not blind us to the nature of the process or the manner in which the process is learned. Sound and sight eventually become so marvelously mixed in language behavior that it is all too easy to overlook their fundamental uniqueness. "What do you mean, you can't write it?" thunders the schoolmaster. "You heard me, didn't you?" This lack of insight is directly related to colossal failure in language teaching. Many teachers make a practice, especially at early levels, of postponing the distribution of textbooks until some weeks (or even months) after the beginning of the course, in order to give full importance to the audio-lingual skills. As an intermediary stage between the period without any printed material and the day books are first distributed, reading and writing can be practiced with materials that have been learned orally and may be duplicated on separate sheets and handed out to the students day by day. This makes it possible for the teacher to control the material the student sees, and above all, to avoid the pairing of two languages in print, a practice that is so characteristic of available textbooks and so destructive to early coordinate learnings. When books are eventually put into the student's hands, rules must be firmly imposed about their use in the classroom. They should be closed and out of reach for a part of the time in every class and for most of the time in most classes. This is to enable the ear and the tongue to continue the training they must have and cannot have if the eye is allowed access to written symbols at all times. There is a great need for psychological studies of the optimum collaboration of ear, tongue, and eye in the early levels of second-language learning.

COGNATES

It is a mistake to tell beginning students that certain words are the same in the target language as in the mother tongue. It is better to say that there are no cognates for the ear, for sounds are not identical in two different languages; that there are no cognates in meaning, for no semantic areas are identical in two cultures. Cognates, then, exist only on the printed page. Words may look alike when written, but the sounds they represent are not the same, nor are the things they stand for. Their similarity in print will be obvious enough to the student; his need is to be shown where the similarity ends.

COMPLETION EXERCISE

A test in which a statement is given with a missing word or expression which the student can supply by studying the rest of the sentence (for example, "Everyone is to bring . . . own lunch"). When variants are possible—and they often are—they must be accepted. It is a most effective exercise, both spoken and written, and it can be used for learning, drill, and measurement.

COMPOUND

A term used to describe the circumstance in which certain features of a second language, especially items of vocabulary or grammar, are added to a learner's mother tongue but are not separated from it. No area of the target language is sufficiently mastered to permit it to function as a system of communication independent of the learner's native language.

COORDINATE

A term used to describe the relationship of two language systems in a person who is truly bilingual. Such a speaker uses one system or the other but *not both simultaneously*. The systems operate independently with only minor or incidental effects upon each other.

CORRECTION

Correction and correctness are traditional concerns of the classroom. But correctness does not necessarily imply correction. Many attempts at performance in imitation of a model are right the first time and continue to be so. When model and performance do not match, correction becomes necessary if the student is to learn the model. The learner may perceive the error himself and on repetition make the necessary correction. He may perceive the error and still not be able to make the correction. He may not perceive the error and will need to be made aware of it. Or he may not be given a repetition of the model and so remain uninformed as to whether or not his performance has been correct. In any case, the shorter the time lapse between performance and knowledge of rightness and wrongness, the better the learning. There appears to be, by immediate feedback, a reinforcement of the right response if it is immediately known to be right. There is, however, a lower limit to the effectiveness of this principle. If correction comes so soon that it interferes with performance (for example, stopping a student in the middle of a sentence) it will defeat its own purpose. We may say that whole units of performance must be allowed to run their course before correction, and that if correction is necessary, the sooner it follows, the better, provided it does not inhibit performance.

CULTURE

It may mean personal refinement, or the products of artistic endeavor, or the total belief and behavior patterns of a language community. With all due respect for the first two of these, it is the third that merits most of the attention in a language class, for the language is itself one of the most important elements in this sense. What do people think about? What do they value most? How do they esteem each other and the activities in which they engage? It is the reflection of these things in the new language that is of most interest and value to the student.

DICTATION

Though it is a useful class exercise, dictation has important limitations, especially when used as a test. It is complicated and specialized, and it involves a kind of skill that is of little use outside the classroom. A dictation makes demands, at the same time, upon listening comprehension, phonemic discrimination, and knowledge of morphology, to say nothing of spelling, punctuation, arrangement, and other details of prime importance to a printer. The writing of a dictation has nothing at all to do with speaking and requires a special kind of listening in which the factors of slowness of speech and repetition are exaggerated far beyond the limits of normal communication. More important still, in a dictation the student is led along a linguistic path chosen by someone else; this is far from being an accurate indication of how well he can do when he may follow a path of his own choosing. At best, a dictation will tell us how well a student can write from dictation, a behavior pattern that is unusual outside of the learning situation, and certainly an uncommon mode of communication.

The worth of dictation as a learning exercise lies principally in the fact that once the ear has been trained to perceive and the tongue to reproduce the audio-lingual features of a language, the transition to an accurate control of the graphic representation of these sound features must be made. The difficulty of this learning is directly related to the fidelity and consistency with which writing depicts sound. Many languages are reasonably dependable in this regard; others, such as English and French, present many inconsistencies and irregularities. Since the conventions of spelling and punctuation, however erratic, must be adhered to, dictation is a most useful exercise in learning the written forms of a new language. The mistake is to look upon ability to take dictation as an accurate index of mastery in all the language skills, which of course it can never be.

DIRECT METHOD

The definition in *Webster's New International Dictionary* is as follows:

> A method of teaching a foreign language, especially a modern language, through conversation, discussion, and reading in the language itself without the use of the pupil's language, without translation, and without the study of formal grammar. The first words are taught by pointing to objects or pictures, or by performing actions.

At no point in this book is the direct method recommended, although a tolerant attitude is taken toward those who wish to adopt its principles, which are unquestionably workable under ideal conditions. Under such conditions, the most serious criticism that can be made of it is that it is somewhat unrealistic (after all, the student does know his mother tongue) and at times inefficient, when reference can be made to lexical items in the mother tongue to establish meaning without interfering with communication in the target language.

DROP-OUT

Questions are often asked about the pre-selection of students for and their drop-out from foreign-language courses. Are such courses to be recommended for everyone? And if not, how are those who are to become foreign-language learners to be chosen? If the course has been begun, how long should it continue in order that the learner may have accomplished enough to be of significant value to him? Up to now, the best and indeed the only safe criterion for the selection of language learners in formal education appears to be participation by the student through Level I of such a course, or at least through the better part of it. The total complex of language behavior is such a delicate interweaving of varied component parts that nothing short of a valid attempt at complete and normal language behavior appears to give reliable information as to the degree of success a learner may expect as he proceeds to more advanced levels. For these reasons, drop-out should be seriously considered at two critical points. The first is during or at the end of Level I when the question of whether or not the learner is to continue should be frankly faced. In most cases, an accurate prediction about future success can be made at this time. The next point at which drop-outs can be seriously considered in terms of value to the student is at the end of Level IV. By this time, his acquaintance with language, culture, and literature is both broad and deep enough for him to feel that a solid and respectable advance in learning has taken place. A point at which drop-out should not be encouraged or even permitted is at the end of Level II when the student has completed the basic course. The value of what he has done so far is chiefly in terms of the application he can make of what he has learned as he proceeds with Levels III and IV. As is well known, the greatest number of drop-outs in language courses now occurs at the end of Level II. It is of extreme importance that this practice be changed. Schools and colleges should be sharply aware of their obligation to provide for continuity through Levels III and IV for full or part time for all students who wish to continue.

DYADIC

Consisting of two. This term is of special importance in both the learning and the performance of language behavior. The speaker speaks as he does because of the way the hearer listens, and vice versa. The interrelation of their respective behavior patterns in communication stands greatly in need of further study.

EXPOSITION

Learning proceeds much faster if the nature of the problem is first made clear. Exposition, which usually needs only a few words and a few seconds of time, sets the framework within which new learnings are to be acquired.

FREQUENCY

An important concept in the preparation and presentation of material, especially during the beginning levels. The words and structural patterns in common use are clearly those that should be learned first. Frequency lists have been prepared for both words and structures in many languages; unfortunately they have been based for the most part on what is written rather than what is said, and, as everyone knows, there is not a one-to-one relationship between these two. It is important to learn what is frequent in the audio-lingual area as well as the visual-graphic and to learn the former first.

GOUIN SERIES

In 1880 François Gouin introduced a type of exercise in which the learner repeats a series of sentences describing an action in which he is engaged (for example, opening a letter or looking for a book). The procedure closely parallels the autistic or monologue speech of the young child as he learns the mother tongue, in which the presence or absence of a hearer is relatively unimportant.

A Gouin Series, in which words are accompanied by appropriate actions, offers the teacher an excellent opportunity for modeling language in a way that makes meaning clear with little or no need for reference to the mother tongue. There is a logic in the sequence of the actions described that is a welcome aid in learning.

Here is an example of such a series:

Opening a door
I'm going to open the door.
I walk toward the door.
I put my hand on the knob.
I turn the knob.
The door doesn't open.
It's locked.
I look for the key.
I find it in my pocket.
I put the key in the lock.
I turn the key.
I push the door.
Now it opens.

Other suggestions for subjects of a Gouin Series are these:

Mailing a letter   Getting ready to go out
Setting a watch   Dialing a telephone number
Drinking a cup of coffee   Selecting a book
Playing a record   Feeding a dog

INTEGRATION EXERCISE

Many important structural patterns are the result of putting together two brief and independent utterances. The exercise consists in giving the two independent statements, which the student must join. Consider this example of the subjunctive in English: "They must be ripe. This is important." Put together, the utterance becomes: "It is important that they be ripe."

LANGUE

A term proposed by Ferdinand de Saussure to describe that part of language which is a passively accumulated repository in relation to which each person is a hearer, not a speaker. *Langue* is not simply a pile of words with their meanings, but also the patterns according to which words go together. It is the institutional element in language and pertains to the entire speech community; no individual can know all of *langue*.

In contrast with *parole* (the individual and active element in language), *langue* is easier to learn and is longer retained. Progress in the learning of *langue* lends itself well to measurement, especially because large groups of hearers can be measured simultaneously. The behavior patterns involved in the use of *langue* are very different from those of *parole,* and students need thorough training in both.

LEARNING

It is important to distinguish between learning and performance. Learning involves an expedition into new territory. Within the new organism new connections are made in the nervous tissue from which result new patterns of behavior and of thought. The newness, naturally, involves work, and brings with it the satisfaction of work accomplished. If what is to be learned seems too easy, the learner soon becomes bored. On the other hand, it may be so difficult that he becomes frustrated, and again bored. Ideally, learning takes place well within these two limits. In contrast to this, performance refers to the retreading of well-worn paths that have long since become familiar. In this process one cannot say that learning is taking place at all. The interest in performance is in the purpose of the act and its results, rather than in the learning of the act itself. In addition, there is an important relationship between performance and learning due to the fact that what is learned may be forgotten. Performance is often an important deterrent to forgetting. In language, the receptive skills are far less subject to the erosion of forgetting than are the productive skills. Performance, then, especially in speaking and writing, contributes greatly to the retention of what has been learned.

MEANING

Words do not "mean" words; they mean, almost always, nonwords. The student should not be given the impression that meaning is merely the equating of different language symbols, either in the same language or in two different languages, but rather that meaning lies in the realm of the things, qualities, or relationships, that words "stand for." A grasp of this insight into the nature of language symbolism is one of the greatest rewards the study of language can offer.

MORPHEME

A unit of discourse that is greater than a phoneme because it can bear meaning, while a phoneme only distinguishes between meanings without adding to or changing them. For example, in the words *dig* and *dog* there is a contrast in sounds by which we distinguish one from the other; however, the sounds that we go by to make this distinction do not in themselves carry a meaning. But if we contrast *dog* and *dogs* we find that the sound that we have added causes a change in meaning. Units of sound that can do this are called morphemes. They can contain one phoneme or several.

A morpheme is often an entire word, but may be less than a word. A prefix, a suffix, a plural ending, a tense ending, or an *'s* are all considered morphemes because they are minimal sound-units that change the meaning of the utterance in which they appear.

Like the phoneme, the morpheme is a class of sounds or sound-groups that all perform an identical function. All the members of a given morpheme are called *allomorphs,* and, when separated entirely from the utterance in which they occur, simply *morphs.*

MORPHOLOGY

The "form" changes of a given word. For example, most English verbs have four forms (for example, *change, changes, changed,* and *changing*); in the Romance languages every verb has dozens of different forms.

PAROLE

Parole is the active, individual, and innovational side of language, in contrast with *langue,* which is institutional and communal. *Parole* is what each speaker does with language as he talks. Its essential characteristic is a freedom of combination; its typical unit is the sentence. The speaker takes *langue* as he finds it, and uses it in the practice of *parole.* The student needs training in listening comprehension, which involves *langue,* and in speaking, which involves *parole.*

PATTERN PRACTICE

The term *pattern practice* refers to the learning of language structure through the repetition of utterances in which the patterns (of sound, order, form, and choice) either are identical or have only small and consistent differences. It makes the explanation of grammar largely unnecessary and encourages the function of analogy.

PHONE

Any sound produced by the human vocal apparatus and audible to the ear.

PHONEME

The phoneme lends itself only reluctantly to definition, not so much because the concept is especially difficult but because a number of varying factors work together to compose this concept, and all must be accounted for in a satisfactory definition.

A phoneme is not a sound but a class of sounds. Each member of this class is called an allophone. When a person talks, he produces not phonemes but allophones. Again the *langue-parole* concept is useful, for phonemes pertain to *langue* while allophones pertain to *parole.*

One phoneme is distinguished from another by the fact that all the differing allophones of a phoneme are sufficiently alike to be accepted—given the neighboring sounds with which they occur—as identical. At the same time, all the allophones of one phoneme are recognized—again given the sequence of sounds in which it occurs—as being distinctly different from the allophones of any other phoneme. Thus *keep* and *cool* begin with the same phoneme, *map* and *cap* have the same phoneme after the initial consonant, and the final sound of *cup* is the same phoneme whether we end the word with the lips closed or with a puff of air. In all these pairs, the sounds are actually different, but since in English these differences are not used to contrast one meaning with another, they are considered to be the same.

Every language, every dialect operates with a fixed number of phonemes. This number varies from one language or dialect to another. There are seldom fewer than twenty or more than fifty phonemes in a language. Standard American English has thirty-two phonemes: nine vowels and twenty-three consonants.

Phonemes cannot be represented by the regular letters of the alphabet because the same letters sometimes represent different phonemes (the *th* of *this* is not the same as the *th* of *thing*) while the same phoneme may be represented by different letters (*cat* and *kite* both begin with the same phoneme).

A word is made up of a sequence of phonemes. In the word *big* there are three phonemes, an initial consonant, a vowel, and a final consonant. The phonemic transcription is /big/. In the word *by* there are three phonemes, an initial consonant and two vowels. The transcription is /bay/. In the word *daughter* there are six phonemes. The transcription: /dɔhtər/.

Sounds are grouped into phonemes primarily in terms of their distribution (that is, the sequence of sounds in which they occur) rather than in terms of their physical similarities and differences.

Phonemes contrast with each other and indicate differences in meaning; allophones of the same phoneme are unlike phonetically but do not contrast with each other phonemically because they do not indicate a change in meaning.

A phoneme by itself does not carry meaning.

A phoneme cannot be identified apart from the system in which it occurs.

If we hear *cab, cap, cad, cat,* we hear words that differ both in sound and in meaning. The difference cannot be in the first two-thirds of these words, for here they are identical; the difference must lie in the final third. Each of these areas of minimal contrast is called a phoneme; in this instance we are dealing with four of the phonemes in English: /b, p, d, t/.

What advantages has this analysis over the simple differences in spelling, *b, p, d,* and *t?* It has many, but perhaps the easiest to grasp is the fact that the same speaker often pronounces these sounds in different ways, even in the same word. For example, a person may say *cap* and end the word with the lips tightly closed; in the next utterance he may use the same word and after pronouncing the *p* he may open his lips a little and allow a slight puff of air to escape. Clearly he has uttered different sounds, but since there is no change in what is meant, we say that the words are phonetically different but phonemically the same. The two pronunciations of *p* are allophones of the same phoneme. In *phonetic* transcription the two pronunciations would differ, one showing the puff of air and the other not. In *phonemic* transcription the two pronunciations would be the same, for there is no change in meaning.

The concept of the phoneme makes it possible to analyze and represent sounds more accurately than with ordinary spelling (consider the sounds represented by the letter *s* in the first word of the two expressions "Close the door" and "close friends"). On the other hand, it is far more economical than phonetic analysis, which takes us into minute sound-differences of which only a relatively small number make a difference in meaning. Phonemes classify these many differences in sound into a certain number of groups or classes that make a difference in meaning.

All the foregoing statements refer to the category of phonemes called segmental, that is, those speech sounds or phones (usually called vowels and consonants) that strung together one after another make up the words of a language.

Another category of phonemes is recognized in the over-all sound-features of utterances, called *suprasegmental* phonemes; they have such characteristics as pitch (intonation), loudness, and juncture. These are sometimes referred to as the *melody* of the language.

The briefest utterance in English will then have at least two segmental phonemes and in addition three suprasegmental phonemes.

In an attempt to give a rough definition of a phoneme we may say this: An allophone is a sound I make that you take to be the sound I intended to make; a phoneme is a range or spectrum or class of allophones that are all a little different but still enough alike to perform identically in communication. A phoneme is not a physical occurrence but a concept.

PHONETICS

A branch of physics that studies the nature of speech sounds and the way in which they are produced by the vocal apparatus and received by the ear. The respelling of a language in phonetic transcription is but a minor detail in a subject area of vast proportions.

PHONOLOGY

The system of sounds employed in the utterances of a given language, or the study or organization of those sounds. For details, see *phoneme* above. The learner should first work with simple utterances as entities, paying particular attention to the "melody" of what he is saying. His attention should be drawn to individual sounds only when those first learnings are well established.

PREAMBLE

By beginning every class with a monologue in the target language on a subject that is familiar or unfamiliar to the students, the teacher provides not only the best possible aid in the psychological shift that reduces English to a recessive role, but also constant practice in listening comprehension. He should speak at normal colloquial speed, without repetition, and using a vocabulary that invites the full attention of the listener without discouraging him. The ability to listen accurately and with comprehension is a skill in which nearly all students can hope to attain a satisfactory competence.

REJOINDER

A rejoinder is, strictly speaking, a reply to a reply, but is often used to mean just a reply. The term in the second sense is useful in the language classroom because it implies much more than an answer to a question. When two people are talking, usually only a limited part of the interchange is in the form of question and answer; by far the greater part is in the form of statement and rejoinder. It is important for the learner to know how to answer a question, but much more important to make appropriate rejoinders and statements.

In training students to make rejoinders, the words *yes* and *no* are ruled out. Typical rejoinders in English are:

Of course.	I hope so.
Not at all.	Really?
Neither do I.	That's all right.
I thought so.	Don't mention it.
Everybody does.	I never knew that.
I agree.	Imagine!

REPETITION EXERCISE

A kind of exercise that can be made easy enough for the beginner to engage in or difficult enough to challenge advanced learners is a simple repetition of what has just been said. By varying the length, the choice of sounds and forms, the content, and the speed of speech, the teacher can make this a valuable exercise from the first weeks of Level I to literary studies in Level IV or V. It is, incidentally, an excellent means of checking orally on familiarity with a text that has been assigned for reading. It is a challenge for abler students to be asked to repeat in sequence a number of statements that have just been repeated aloud by several different students.

Repetition provides a means of extracting sounds from the most reticent learners and a way of getting students to produce whole utterances and to say quite as much as the teacher—an objective not easily achieved.

RESTATEMENT EXERCISE

This refers to the "tell me" "ask me," "tell him" "ask him" type of directive which requires the student to make shifts in point of view that are reflected in structural changes of many kinds. It provides an excellent workout in problems of number, person, auxiliaries, reflexive pronouns, possessives, and the like.

SITUATION

An indispensable third factor with speaker and hearer in the triad of talk. It involves the who, where, when, what, and how of language in action. In the preparation of materials it is important that dialogues be set within the framework of a situation that is clearly defined. The following points will help to make a suggested situation more plausible.

1. Locate the situation precisely in place and time.
2. Identify the speakers: number, sex, age, occupation.
3. Indicate the interpersonal relationship of the speakers and the emotional overtone of the talk. Express, for example:

Politeness
Companionship
Authority
Surprise
Disagreement
Information
Persuasion

Invitation
Impatience
Agreement
Cordiality
Regret
Astonishment
Excuse

4. Name the subject of discussion, for example:

Food: buying, eating, preparing
Money: buying, borrowing, earning
Boy meets girl
Health, sickness, accident
Work: school, home, business
Travel: to and from school, another city, abroad
Sports
Auto: driving, license
Radio and television
Directions: in street, in building

Careers
Holidays
Birthdays
Departure and arrival
Lateness
Clothing: winter, summer, sport, dress
Mail: getting, writing, sending
Telephone
Movies
Books
Music
Examinations
Prizes

SAMPLE SITUATION: Two neighbors, a boy and a girl, wait for the school bus on a street corner near their home on an icy morning in March. A third friend joins them. They talk about why the bus is late.

SPEED OF SPEECH

Speed of speech is a different matter for the speaker and for the hearer. As a hearer, one must be prepared to follow the stream of talk at a speed determined by the person to whom one is listening. As a speaker, one can choose his own rate of speed. This fact is of great importance in second-language learning. One must learn to listen as fast as the native speaker is accustomed to talk. As a speaker the learner may choose his own speed, and is well advised not to try to equal that of the native speaker. He has nothing to lose by being deliberate, though of course this has a lower limit.

SUPPLEMENT

In addition to the basic dialogues, there are many items of linguistic, cultural, and literary value that may be introduced in Level I. The *supplement* section of each unit may contain material such as formulas of politeness, calendar terms, comments on health and the weather, numbers, rhymes and proverbs, and brief selections of poetry, all of which may be memorized.

SYNTAX

This has to do with the order of words and the relation of changes in order to meaning. For example, in English we may say, "He has closed his door," "He has his door closed," or "Has he closed his door?" These are all common syntax patterns, each with its special meaning. However, as every five-year-old speaker of English knows, we cannot say, "He door his closed has"; this syntax pattern is not permitted in English, though its counterpart may be in other languages.

TALK

Language in all its forms rises from a broad base of high-frequency small talk. If the student participates early in a wise and generous sampling of such talk, he learns what is immediately rewarding and perennially useful.

TARGET LANGUAGE

The word *target* is a useful term that may supplant *new, foreign, second,* and other more complicated terms in distinguishing between the learner's native language and the one he is studying. Though it is relatively new in this use and perhaps at first distasteful, *target* is unequivocal and fits the facts of the language classroom.

UTTERANCE

A word or series of words functioning as a unit in the give-and-take of communication. It is comparable to a sentence in its use, but does not need to have the completeness usually required of a sentence. Typical utterances are "Hi!" "Never!" "What for?" "Who knows?" and "Now it's time to begin."

BIBLIOGRAPHY

Agard, Frederick B., and Harold B. Dunkel. *An Investigation of Second-Language Learning.* Boston: Ginn, 1948.

Andersson, Theodore. "The Teacher of Modern Foreign Languages," in Ernest Stabler, ed., *The Education of the Secondary School Teacher.* Middletown, Conn.: Wesleyan University Press, 1962.

———. *The Teaching of Foreign Languages in the Elementary School.* Boston: Heath, 1953.

Angiolillo, Paul F. *Armed Forces' Foreign Language Teaching.* New York: Vanni, 1947.

Arsenian, Seth. "Bilingualism in the Postwar World." *Psychological Bulletin,* XLII, 2 (February 1945), 65–86.

Benedict, Ruth. *Patterns of Culture.* Boston: Houghton Mifflin, 1934.

Birkmaier, Emma M. "Modern Languages." *Encyclopedia of Educational Research.* 3rd ed. New York: Macmillan, 1960, pp. 861–88.

———. "Modern Languages: Vehicle for the Humanities." *Educational Leadership,* January 1963, pp. 238–42.

Bloch, Bernard, and George L. Trager. *Outline of Linguistic Analysis.* Baltimore: Linguistic Society of America, 1942.

Bloomfield, Leonard. *Introduction to the Study of Language.* New York: Holt, 1914.

———. *Language.* New York: Holt, 1933.

Brooks, Nelson. "Preservice Training for Language Teachers." In Marjorie C. Johnston, ed., *Modern Foreign Languages in the High School.* Washington, D.C.: United States Office of Education, 1958.

———. "Using Tape to Test the Language Skills." *International Journal of American Linguistics,* XXIX, 2, Part 3 (April 1963), 121–28.

Brown, Rollo W. *How the French Boy Learns to Write.* Cambridge, Mass.: Harvard University Press, 1915.

Buros, Oscar K. *Mental Measurements Yearbook.* Highland Park, N.J.: Gryphon Press, 1938, 1941, 1949, 1953, 1959.

Carmichael, Leonard. *Manual of Child Psychology.* 2nd ed. New York: Wiley, 1954.

Carroll, John B. *The Study of Language.* Cambridge, Mass.: Harvard University Press, 1953.

Cassirer, Ernst. *Language and Myth.* Tr. by Susanne K. Langer. New York: Harper, 1946.

Chomsky, Noam. *Syntactic Structures.* 's Gravenhage: Mouton, 1962.

College Entrance Examination Board. *Curriculan Changes in the Foreign Languages.* Princeton, N.J.: College Entrance Examination Board, 1963.

Comenius, John A. *The Great Didactic* (1628–32). Tr. by M. W. Keatinge. London: Black, 1907.

Committee on the Objectives of a General Education in a Free Society. *General Education in a Free Society.* Cambridge, Mass.: Harvard University Press, 1945.

Delattre, Pierre. "A Technique of Aural-Oral Approach: Report on a University of Oklahoma Experiment in Teaching French." *French Review,* XX (January and February 1947), 238–50, 311–24.

Donovan, J. "The Festal Origin of Human Speech." *Mind,* XVI (1891), 498–506.

Dunkel, Harold. *Second-Language Learning.* Boston: Ginn, 1948.

Eddy, Frederick D. "1959 Revisited." *Audiovisual Instruction,* VII, 9 (November 1962), 602–23.

Eisenson, Jon. *The Psychology of Speech.* Ed. A. T. Weaver. New York: Crofts, 1938.

Foerster, Norman, and others. *Literary Scholarship.* Chapel Hill, N.C.: University of North Carolina Press, 1941.

Fries, Charles C. *American English Grammar.* New York: Appleton-Century, 1940.

———. *Teaching and Learning English as a Foreign Language.* Ann Arbor, Mich.: University of Michigan Press, 1945.

Gardiner, Sir Alan H. *Theory of Speech and Language.* Oxford: Clarendon Press, 1932.

Georgetown University, School of Foreign Service. *Reports of the Round Table Meetings on Linguistics and Language Teaching.* Washington, D.C.: Georgetown University Press, 1951 to date.

Gesell, Arnold, and Frances L. Ilg. *The Child from Five to Ten.* New York: Harper, 1946.

Sturtevant, Edgar H. *An Introduction to Linguistic Science.* New Haven, Conn.: Yale University Press, 1947.

Sweet, Waldo E. *Latin, A Structural Approach.* Ann Arbor, Mich.: University of Michigan Press, 1958.

Thomas, Elizabeth M. *The Harmless People.* New York: Knopf, 1959.

Thorpe, Louis P., and Allen M. Schmuller. *Contemporary Theories of Learning.* New York: Ronald, 1954.

Tocqueville, Alexis de. *Democracy in America.* Tr. by Henry Reeve. New York: Adlard and Saunders, 1838.

Tomkins, Calvin. "The Last Skill Acquired." *New Yorker,* September 14, 1963, pp. 127–57.

Twaddell, W. Freeman. "Does the Foreign-Language Teacher Have to Teach English Grammar?" *PMLA,* LXXVII, 2, Part 2 (May 1962), 18–22.

UNESCO. *The Teaching of Modern Languages.* Paris: UNESCO, 1955.

United States Office of Education. *The Language Development Program.* Washington, D.C.: United States Government Printing Office, 1963. Brochure on Title VI.

Weinreich, Uriel. *Languages in Contact.* New York: Publications of the Linguistic Circle of New York, No. 1, 1953.

Wellek, René, and Austin Warren. *Theory of Literature.* New York: Harcourt, Brace & World, 1949.

Wells, Rulon S. "De Saussure's System of Linguistics." *Word,* III, 1–2 (August 1947), 1–31.

Whitehead, Alfred N. *The Aims of Education.* New York: Macmillan, 1949.

Williams, Robin. *American Society.* New York: Knopf, 1951.

Wylie, Laurence. *Village in the Vaucluse.* Cambridge, Mass.: Harvard University Press, 1958.

Yerkes, R. M., and A. W. Yerkes. *The Great Apes.* New Haven, Conn.: Yale University Press, 1929.

INDEX

Page numbers in italics refer to illustrations.

A

ABCD test, 130, 254
   definition of, 261–62
accent marks, 167, 169
achievement tests, 205, 206
adjectives, 54
adolescent, 116 (*see also* child; secondary school)
Advanced Placement Program, 125, 245
advanced requirement, 122, 124–25
Agard, Frederick B., 59, 283
allomorph, 274
allophone, 27, 277
   definition of, 262, 275
alphabetic writing, 232
analogy
   definition of, 262–63
   learning by, 154–55
   in pattern practice, 51, 143, 146–47, 152–53
analysis, 146–47, 263
Andersson, Theodore, 139, 239, 283
Angiolillo, Paul F., 283
animals, response of, to signs, 7–9
anthropology, cultural, 11–12, 86, 233
Arsenian, Seth, 283
art, definition of, 98
assignments, 257–58
   sequence of, 241–42
attitude changes in FLES class, 118–19
audial aids in FLES class, 118 (*see also* audio-visual techniques; language laboratory; recording mechanisms; tape recorder)
audio-lingual aspect of language, 16, 17, 20, 24–25, 75, 228, 263
   in coordinate system, 50–52
   grading of, 245
   literature and, 99
   scholarship and, 230
   testing of, 215–16, 261–62
   (*see also* listening comprehension; speaking; speech; talk)
audio-visual techniques, 263–64
   (*see also* language laboratory; tape recorder; visual aids)
audition, 4 (*see also* listening comprehension)

B

basic course, 122–23
behaviorist learning theory, 4
Benedict, Ruth, 96, 283
bilingualism, 41–43, 107–08
   definition of, 265
Birkmaier, Emma M., 80, 239, 283
Bloch, Bernard, 33, 283
Bloomfield, Leonard, 24, 34, 283
body-motion test, 216, 254
book, use of, 265–66 (*see also* literature; reading selections; textbooks)
booth, laboratory, 192
bound morpheme, 29, 54
Broca's area, 36
Brooks, Nelson, 126*n*, 283
Brown, Rollo W., 179, 283
Buros, Oscar K., 225, 283

291

C

Carmichael, Leonard, 284
Carroll, John B., 112, 229, 284
Carroll, Lewis, 181
Cassirer, Ernst, 284
change in language, 15, 20, 32–33
Chaucer, Geoffrey, 199
child
    language learning by, 35–41
    second-language learning by, 57–58, 115–19, 137
    (*see also* infant)
Chomsky, Noam, 34, 284
choral response, 131, 143, 146
    how to conduct, 242–43
class program, 130–32
    in learning level I, 130–31
    in learning level II, 131
    in learning level III, 131–32
    in learning level IV, 132
classical conditioning, 46
classroom, 74–76
    language laboratory and, 194–97, 246–47
    language study in, 48, 55–58
    rules of, 133, 149
    (*see also* schools)
clusters, sound, 5
cognates, 266
college, language study in, 61, 115, 119, 120, 136 (*see also* classroom; levels of learning; schools)
College Entrance Examination Board, 77, 114, 125, 239, 245, 284
college entrance tests, 77–78
Comenius, John Amos, 138, 139, 140, 154, 284
Committee on the Objectives of a General Education in a Free Society, 230, 239, 284
communication
    language as, 82, 142, 149, 227, 264
    pattern practice and, 146
completion exercises, 132, 267
    in pattern practice, 156, 158
completion test, 216, 267

composition (*see* writing)
compound system, 49–50
    definition of, 267
    (*see also* decoding)
concept, 82
    definition of, 14
conception, definition of, 14
consonants, 168
conditioned learning, 46
conformity in speech, 12–13
content, 127–29
    in learning level I, 127
    in learning level II, 127
    in learning level III, 127–28
    in learning level IV, 128–29
    testing for, 215
    (*see also* levels of learning)
"content" words, 55, 182
continuity in language learning, 70–71, 113–39
contraction in pattern practice, 156, 159
coordinate system, 49–52
    definition of, 267
    (*see also* bilingualism)
correction of error, 58, 148, 267–68
cultural anthropology, 11–12, 86, 233
cultural insight as learning objective, 111–12
cultural island, 96, 131, 149
culture
    definition of, 83, 268
    language and, 85–96
    literature and, 149
    in learning levels, 130
    as refinement, 83–84
    teaching of, 88–96 (*see also* cultural island)
    tests and, 201
    as way of life, 83–88, 232
curriculum, 70–71, 115
    content and, 127–29
    tests and, 77
    (*see also* levels of learning)

D

dead language, 20–21
decoding, 107–08 (*see also* compound system)

Delattre, Pierre, 59, 284
descriptive linguistics, 3, 5, 25–30, 155, 232
dialect, 32
dialogue, 145–46, 149, 150, 253, 279
   levels of learning and, 127, 130
   preparation of, 241–42, 243–44, 247
   tape recording of, 195–96
   (*see also* language event; situations)
dialogue adaptation, 145–46
dictation, 268–69
direct method of language teaching, 269–70
discursive form, 10
Donovan, J., 19, 284
drill, 143 (*see also* pattern practice; repetition)
drop-out, 136–37
   definition of, 270
Dunkel, Harold B., 59, 283
duration, 28
dyadic behavior, 143
   definition of, 271

E

ear training (*see* listening comprehension)
earphones, 189, 192
Eddy, Frederick D., 198, 284
education (*see* college; elementary school; learning; schools; secondary school)
Eisenson, Jon, 284
elementary school, language study in, 115–21 (*see also* child; levels of learning)
English, use of
   in classroom, 117, 129, 133–34, 142, 143, 144–45, 244–45, 252, 257, 258
   with glossary, 251
   in tests, 217–24
environment, individual and, 11–13
error (*see* correction of error)
etymology, 15
Everett, Edward, 64

examination, college entrance, 77–78 (*see also* tests)
exercise book, 72
exercises, 150
   completion, 132, 156, 158, 267
   fill-in, 132
   Gouin Series, 271–72
   integration, 272
   repetition, 279
   restatement, 279
   (*see also* drill; pattern practice; quiz; tests)
expansion in pattern practice, 156, 159
exposition, use of, 271
extensive reading, 173

F

Fant, C. G., 285
figurative meaning, 15
fill-in exercises, 132, 267
fixed-response test, 200, 210
FLES (*see* Foreign Languages in the Elementary Schools)
Foerster, Norman, 106, 284
foreign language (*see* second language)
Foreign Languages in the Elementary Schools (FLES), 114, 116–19
Foreign Language (FL) Program, 236
free morpheme, 29
French, John W., 77*n*
frequency word lists, 147, 259, 271
Fries, Charles C., 59, 188, 227*n*, 284
function words, 54

G

Gardiner, Sir Alan H., 22, 284
Gesell, Arnold, 36, 38, 40, 44, 284–85
Gestalt psychology, 47
gestural-visual aspect of language, 16–17, 24, 50, 144, 228, 263–64
gesture (*see* body-motion test; gestural-visual aspect of language)

INDEX / 293

Gleason, H. A., Jr., 34, 285
Gouin, François, 59, 163, 271, 285
Gouin Series, 152, 271-72
grades, 245
grammar, 134-35
  changes in, 33
  in coordinate learning, 51, 56-57, 141
  traditional, 29-30
  (*see also* structure)
grammar circle, *162*
grammar-translation-completion exercise, 200
graphic-material aspect of language, 16-18, 20, 24, 144, 263-64
  grading of, 245
  (*see also* reading; writing)
Gravit, Francis W., 163, 285

H

habit-forming and language learning, 51
Halle, Morris, 183, 285
Haugen, Einar, 42, 285
Hayes, Alfred S., 198, 285
hearing (*see* listening comprehension)
Heisenberg, Werner, 239, 285
Hill, Archibald A., 285
Hockett, Charles F., 34, 126*n*, 285
homemade test, 212-14
homework, 245-46
humanism and language, 235
Hunt, Maurice P., 61
Hutchinson, Joseph C., 198, 285

I

idioms, 182
Ilg, Frances L., 44, 284
imitation in speech learning, 37-38
individual and environment, 11-13
  (*see also* parole)
infant
  language learning by, 21-22
  speech in, 36-37
  (*see also* child)
inflection in pattern practice, 156, 157
instrumental learning, 46

integration exercise, 272
  in pattern practice, 156, 159
intensive reading, 172-73
intonation pattern (*see* suprasegmental phoneme)
Iodice, Don, 198, 285
Italian Grammar, 152
Item types, 214-24

J

Jakobson, Roman, 183, 183*n*, 285
Jespersen, Otto, 19, 80, 285
Johnston, Marjorie C., 114, 139, 238*n*, 285
juncture, 28
junior high school, 70 (*see also* schools)

K

Keller, Helen, 39
Kellogg, L. A., 9, 19, 285
Kellogg, W. N., 9, 19, 285
Kluckhohn, Clyde, 96, 286
Köhler, Wolfgang, 59, 286
Kroeber, A. L., 96, 286

L

laboratory (*see* language laboratory)
Lado, Robert, 225, 286
Lambert, Wallace E., 42, 44, 286
langage, 13
Langer, Susanne K., 6*n*, 19, 23, 40, 229, 262, 286
language, 232-39
  aspects of, 232-35
  teaching of, 235-37
  (*see also* linguistics; learning)
language bands, 17, *17*
language event, 2-5, *4*, 12 (*see also* dialogue; molecule of speech; situations)
language laboratory, 148, 150, 189-98
  integration of, with classroom, 194-97, 245-46
  indispensability of, 190
  other uses of, 198
  (*see also* recording mechanisms; tape recorder; tape recording)

language requirement, 122, 123–24
langue, 13, 21, 33, 144, 148
 definition of, 272–73
 reading and, 167
 testing and, 215
 vocabulary and, 183
languistics, 232–39
 characteristics of languists, 237–38
 foreign-language teaching and, 238–39
Laski, Harold J., 64, 80, 286
Latin, 21, 137
learner, 55–58
 activities of, 252
 continuity for, 70–71, 113–39
 (*see also* learning; student)
learning
 by analogy, 154–55
 bilingual, 41–43, 107–08
 continuity of, 113–39
 culture and, 88–96
 definition of, 273
 levels of (*see* levels of learning)
 literature and, 101–06, 234
 of mother tongue, 21–22, 35–41
 of second language, 21–22, 43–44, 45–59, 107–12
 theories of, 45–48, 148
 (*see also* teaching)
Leopold, Werner F., 36, 38, 44, 286
letters
 appearance of, 167
 sounds and, 168–69
levels of learning, 119–38
 I, 130–31
 II, 131
 III, 131–32
 IV, 132
 assignments and, 242
 standards for, 123–36
 tests for, 224–25
 (*see also* content)
Lewis, M. M., 36, 38, 286
Lindquist, Everet F., 225, 286
linguistics
 descriptive, 3, 5, 25–30, 232
 language and, 229, 232

listening comprehension, 110–11
 skill in, 134, 144, 278
 testing of, 200, 212, 214, 215
 (*see also* audio-lingual aspect of language)
literacy, 24–25
literal meaning, 15
literal translation, 184–85
literary scholarship, 230–31
literature, 143, 148
 appreciation of, 111–12
 comprehension of, 102–04
 culture and, 149
 definition of, 97–99
 language and, 97–106, 234
 selection of, 104–06
 (*see also* book; reading selections; textbooks)
living language, 20–21
loudness, 28

M

MacAllister, Archibald T., 81, 286
McCarthy, Dorothea, 37, 38, 44, 286
McGeoch, John A., 286
Madariaga, Salvador De, 286
Mallinson, Vernon, 59, 112, 179, 286
materials, choice of, 141–42, 149
 (*see also* book; literature; reading selections; tape recording; textbooks)
meaning, 13–15
 definition of, 273–74
 learning of, 111
 meaning of, 14
 phonemes and, 26–29, 276
 testing and, 215
 vocabulary and, 180–88
measurement (*see* examination; quiz; tests)
"melody" of language (*see* suprasegmental phoneme)
metaphor, 15–16
Metcalf, Lawrence E., 61
method, 71, 140–51
microphone, 189, 192
Mildenberger, Kenneth W., 239, 286

Miller, George A., 286
Mirrielees, Lucia B., 179, 287
Modern Language Association (MLA), 76–77, 114, 151, 236, 287
molecule of speech, 31, 54, 84
Montagu, Ashley, 287
Morize, André, 106
morph, 274
morpheme, definition of, 29–30, 274
morphology, 11
  definition of, 274
  progress in, 148
Morris, Charles W., 23, 188, 229, 287
mother tongue, 227
  learning of, 21–22, 35–41, 116
  (*see also* English)
Moulton, William G., 163, 287
mutual unintelligibility, 19
Myers, L. M., 163, 287

N

Najam, Edward W., 198, 287
National Defense Education Act, 114
Newmark, Maxim, 287
Nicholson, Harold, 179
Nostrand, Howard Lee, 287
nouns, 53–54

O

objectives of language course, 107–12
objective test, 206–07
O'Connor, Patricia, 151, 287
Ogden, C. K., 287
origin of language, 18–19
O'Rourke, Everett V., 126*n*
orthography, 17–18, 51
Osgood, Charles E., 16*n*, 23, 36, 37, 188, 288
overlearning (*see* pattern practice)

P

paradigms, 50
paragraph writing, 176–78
Parker, William R., 81, 114, 139, 236, 239, 288

parole, 13, 21, 33, 144
  definition of, 274–75
  reading and, 167
  testing and, 215
  vocabulary and, 183
pattern generalization, 153–54 (*see also* grammar; structure)
pattern practice, 51–52, 54, 142, 143, 146–47, 148, 152–63, 263, 275
  assignment of, 241
  in learning levels, 130–32
  preparation of, 251
  types of, 155–63
  (*see also* drill; repetition)
patterns of speech, 50–52, 53, 56–57
Pavlov, Ivan, 46
Peal, Elizabeth, 44, 286
Perrot, Jean, 288
personality, speech and, 32
philology, 25, 234
philosophy and language, 233
phonation, 2, 4
phone, 26–28
  definition of, 26, 275
phoneme, 2, 5
  definition of, 26–29, 275–77
  segmental, 28, 277
  suprasegmental, 28–29, 127, 145, 146, 277, 278
phonemic analysis, 28
phonemic transcription, 276
phonetics, 5, 26
  definition of, 278
phonology
  definition of, 278
  progress in, 148
physics and language, 3–5, 229
physiology of language, 2–3, 36–37
Piaget, Jean, 36, 44, 288
pictures, use of, in tests, 254
Pimsleur, Paul, 163, 225, 288
pitch, 28
Politzer, Robert L., 34, 87, 151, 288
preamble, use of, 89–96, 129–31, 133, 259, 278
presentational form, 10
Prewett, Clinton R., 67

296 / INDEX

profession, language teaching as, 228–40
professional activities of language teachers, 75–77
proficiency tests, 205–06
prognostic tests, 202–04
progress tests, 204–05
pronunciation, 32
proposition, 14–15
prosodic phoneme (*see* suprasegmental phoneme)
psychology, 3, 232
  of language learning, 21–22, 37–39, 229
punctuation marks, 167, 169

Q

quality words, 54
questionnaire, preparation of, 247–48 (*see also* quiz)
quiz, in learning levels, 130–32 (*see also* exercises; questionnaire; tests)

R

reading, 164–79
  development of, 170–73
  difference from writing, 166–68
  extensive reading, 173
  intensive reading, 172–73
  as learning objective, 110
  sequential steps in, 169–70
  skill in, 134, 144
  testing of, 215, 255
  vocabulary and, 183–84
  (*see also* graphic-material aspect of language)
reading selections as textbooks, 72–73
  (*see also* book; literature; short story)
ready-made test, 207
realia, 243
recording mechanisms, 145 (*see also* tape recorder)
recordings in teaching culture, 243 (*see also* language laboratory; tape recording)
re-entry, 146
reference books, 72, 133

reinforcement, 142, 143, 268
  in infant speech learning, 37–38
  secondary, 47
rejoinder
  definition of, 278–79
  in pattern practice, 156, 160–61
repetition exercise, 279
  in correction, 267–68
  in pattern practice, 156–57
  (*see also* drill; pattern practice)
replacement in pattern practice, 156, 157–58
reproduction of sounds, 110
restatement exercise, 132, 279
  in pattern practice, 156, 158
restoration in pattern practice, 156, 161
rhythm, 28
Richards, I. A., 287
Roberts, Paul, 163, 288
Ronjat, Jules, 36
Russell, Bertrand, 288

S

Santayana, George, 98, 106, 184, 288
Sapir, Edward, 32, 34, 86, 96, 227, 288
Saporta, Sol, 23, 112, 288
Saussure, Ferdinand de, 13, 272, 289
Scherer, George A. C., 288
Scherman, Katharine, 96
Schmuller, Allen M., 289
schools, 63–68
  development of, 63–64
  language study and, 61–62
  orientation of, 65–68
  (*see also* classroom; college; elementary school; secondary school)
Schrödinger, Erwin, 229, 288
science and language, 228–30, 234–35
Sebeok, Thomas A., 16n, 23, 36, 37, 288
second language
  learning of, 21–22, 42–44, 45–59, 107–12, 267
  teaching of, 60–81, 238–39

INDEX / 297

secondary school, language study in, 115, 119, 121 (*see also* classroom; levels of learning; schools)
secondary reinforcement, 47
segmental phoneme, 277 (*see also* phoneme)
selected readings (*see* reading selections)
sentence writing, 175–76
Shaw, George Bernard, 32
short story
 questionnaire on, 247–48
 teaching of, 249–52
 (*see also* literature; reading selections)
signs
 meaning and, 13
 words as, 6–10, *10*
 (*see also* symbols)
situations, 2–3, 54, 142, 242, 279–80
 cultural, 85
 levels of learning and, 130
 (*see also* dialogue; language event; molecule of speech)
skills, 109–12, 134, 143, **144–45**
 measurement of, by tests, 200–01
 productive and receptive, 134, 183
 (*see also* listening comprehension; reading; speaking; writing)
Skinner, B. F., 188, 288
small talk, 281
sound clusters, 5
sound waves, 4
sounds
 and letters, 168–70
 recording of, 191 (*see also* phone; phoneme; phonetics)
speaking
 evaluation of, 252–53
 skill in, 134, 143, 144
 testing of, 200, 215, 244–45
 (*see also* audio-lingual aspect of language; speech; talk)
speech, 3, 32, 54, 84, 280–81
 conformity and, 12–13
 "fit" to writing, 164–65

 in language learning, 50–52
 physiology of, 36
 (*see also* audio-lingual aspect of language; speaking; talk)
speech event (*see* language event)
speech systems, 53
speed of speech, 280–81
spelling, 168
standardized test, 207–12
standards, educational, 66
 for language courses, 113-14
Starr, Wilmarth H., 225, 288
streams of learning, 119–39, *121*
 (*see also* levels of learning)
structural modes, 274
structure, 142, 143
 in learning levels, 130–32
 testing and, 215
 (*see also* grammar; pattern generalization)
structure drill (*see* pattern practice)
student, 68–70 (*see also* learner)
Sturtevant, Edgar H., 289
style of speech, 32
subsentence writing, **175**
Suci, G., 188, 288
supplement, 281
suprasegmental phoneme, 28–29, 127, 145, 146, 277, 278
Sweet, Waldo E., 163, 289
symbolization, 18–19, 227
symbols
 meaning and, 13–14
 words as, 6–10, *10*
 (*see also* signs)
syntax, 11
 definition of, 281
 development of, 19
 progress in, 148

T

take-home disc, 146
talk, 24–34
 changes in, 32–33
 definition of, 29–30, 281
 by student, 253–54
 (*see also* audio-lingual aspect of language; speaking; speech)
Tannenbaum, P., 188, 288

298 / INDEX

tape recorder, 75, 191–94 (*see also* recording mechanisms; tape recording)
tape recording, 150
　making of, 195–96
　preparation of script for, 248–49 (*see also* language laboratory)
target language, 281–82 (*see also* second language)
teacher, 62–63, 66–81
　classroom activities of, 251–52
　culture and, 83–84, 89
　of FLES class, 118
　problems of, 68–80
　training of, 63, 66, 229–32 (*see also* teaching)
teaching, 45, 60–81
　of culture, 88–96
　of foreign language, 238–39
　methods of, 140–51
　new orientation of, 235–37 (*see also* language; learning; second language; teacher)
television, teaching by, 118
tests, 110, 141, 199–225
　ABCD, 254, 261–62
　achievement, 205, 206
　body-motion, 216, 254
　completion, 216, 267
　development of, 199–202
　dictation, 268–69
　examples of, 217–24
　fixed-response, 200, 210
　goals of, 201–02
　homemade, 212–14
　item, 214–24
　in language laboratory, 197
　level of learning and, 130–32, 224–25
　listening - comprehension, 214, 215
　objective, 206–07
　preparation of, 254–55
　proficiency, 205–06
　prognostic, 202–04
　progress, 204–05
　standardized, 207–12
　vocabulary, 147
　(*see also* examination; exercises; questionnaire; quiz)

textbooks, 71–73 (*see also* book; literature; reading selections)
thing words, 54
third language, study of, 120, 137
Thomas, Elizabeth M., 96, 289
Thorpe, Louis P., 289
Tocqueville, Alexis de, 35, 289
Tomkins, Calvin, 179, 289
Trager, George L., 33, 283
transfer of learning, 262
transformation in pattern practice, 156, 159
translation, 52, 79, 130, 136, 141, 143, 251
　correct use of, 255–57
　literal, 184–85
　as objective of learning, 110
transposition in pattern practice, 156, 159
trial-and-error learning, 46
Twaddell, W. Freeman, 163, 289

U

units (*see* levels of learning)
utterance
　definition of, 282
　types of, *162–63*

V

Valdman, Albert, 163, 285
verbal form, 10–11
verbal image, 10–11
verbs, 54
Vigneron, Robert, 106
visual aids, 265
　in elementary teaching, 118
visual forms, 10–11
visual image, 10–11
vocabulary, 134–35, 180–88, 258
　active and passive, 183
　aids to, 185–86
　assignments and, 241
　in coordinate learning, 50, 53–55, 142, 143
　development of, 19, 135
　emphasis of, 181–82
　in language laboratory, 197
　literal translation and, 184–85
　measurement of, 147–48
　as objective of learning, 109, 111

personality and, 32
reading and, 183–84
receptive and productive, 183
standards for, 128, 130, 132
types of, 182–83
(*see also* words)
vocabulary drill, preparation of, 259–60
voice dynamics, 32 (*see also* speaking; speech)
vowels, 168

W

Warren, Austin, 104, 106, 227, 289
Weinreich, Uriel, 44, 289
Wellek, René, 104, 106, 227, 289
Wells, Rulon S., 13, 23, 289
Whitehead, Alfred N., 289
Williams, Robin, 289
Wilson, Woodrow, 87
word lists, 50, 130, 186–87
  frequency, 147, 259
word order (*see* syntax)
words
  appearance of written, 167–68
  classification of, 53–55
  meaning of, 13–15
  as signs, 6–10
  as symbols, 6–10, 18–19
  types of, 182–83
  (*see also* vocabulary)
word study, 128, 187–88
writing, 164–79
  assignments for, 178–79
  audio-lingual preparation for, 128
  difference from reading, 166–68
  as learning objective, 110
  paragraph, 176–78
  phases of, 173–78
  sentence, 175–76
  sequential steps in, 170
  skill in, 125–26, 129, 132–34, 143, 144
  subsentence, 175
  testing of, 215
  (*see also* graphic-material aspect of language)
Wylie, Laurence, 96, 289

Y

Yerkes, A. W., 19, 289
Yerkes, R. M., 19, 289